Celebrating Vermont:
    Myths and Realities

Celebrating Vermont: Myths and Realities

Richard H. Saunders and Virginia M. Westbrook, exhibition curators

Edited by Nancy Price Graff

With essays by Nancy Price Graff & William N. Hosley, Jr.,
J. Kevin Graffagnino, and William C. Lipke

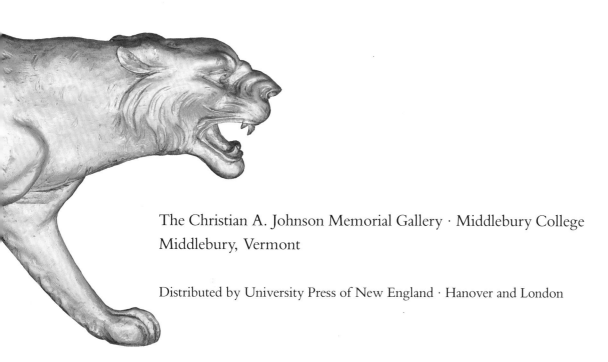

The Christian A. Johnson Memorial Gallery · Middlebury College
Middlebury, Vermont

Distributed by University Press of New England · Hanover and London

Exhibition tour:

Vermont Historical Society
Montpelier, Vermont
July 9 – September 1, 1991

The Bennington Museum
Bennington, Vermont
September 19 – November 24, 1991

The Christian A. Johnson Memorial Gallery
Middlebury College
Middlebury, Vermont
February 9 – April 5, 1992

23178560

LIBRARY OF CONGRESS CATALOGING-IN-PUBLICATION DATA
Celebrating Vermont: myths and realities / Richard H. Saunders and Virginia M.
    Westbrook, exhibition curators; edited by Nancy Price Graff; with essays by
    Nancy Price Graff, William N. Hosley, Jr., J. Kevin Graffagnino, and
    William C. Lipke.
        p.   cm.
        Exhibition tour: Vermont Historical Society, Montpelier, Vt.,
    July 9 – Sept. 1, 1991; Bennington Museum, Bennington, Vt., Sept. 19 –
    Nov. 24, 1991; Christian A. Johnson Memorial Gallery, Feb. 9 – Apr. 5, 1992.
        Includes bibliographical references
        ISBN 0–9625262–2–3
        1. Material culture—Vermont—Exhibitions.   2. Arts,
    American—Vermont—Exhibitions.   3. Vermont—Industries— Exhi-
    bitions.   I. Saunders, Richard H., 1949–   .   II. Westbrook, Virginia M.,
    1948–   .   III. Graff, Nancy Price, 1953–   .   IV. Hosley, William N.
    V. Graffagnino, J. Kevin.   VI. Lipke, William C.   VII. Vermont Historical
    Society.   VIII. Bennington Museum.   IX. Christian A. Johnson Memorial
    Gallery.
    F49.5.C43 1991   974.3—dc20   91–9299
                                                            CIP

COVER ILLUSTRATION: *Village of Stowe, Vermont* (detail) by Luigi Lucioni.
Courtesy of The Minneapolis Institute of Arts. (cat. no. 50).

TITLE PAGE ILLUSTRATION: *Catamount* (wood, gilded), *c.* 1891. Courtesy of the
Collection of Ken Arthur. (cat. no. 40).

Contents

Lenders to the Exhibition

Abenaki Cultural Center, Swanton, Vermont
American Museum of Fly Fishing, Manchester, Vermont
Ken Arthur
Beeken and Parsons, Shelburne, Vermont
Ben & Jerry's Homemade, Inc., Waterbury, Vermont
The Bennington Museum, Bennington, Vermont
Bennington Potters, Bennington, Vermont
Bread and Puppet Theatre, Glover, Vermont
Cabot Farmers Cooperative Creamery Company, Inc., Cabot, Vermont
Calais Historical Society, Calais, Vermont
Catamount Brewing Company, White River Junction, Vermont
Champlain Chocolate Company, Burlington, Vermont
The Fairbanks Museum and Planetarium, St. Johnsbury, Vermont
Farrar-Mansur Museum, Weston, Vermont
Sabra Field
Robert Hull Fleming Museum, University of Vermont
Grafton Goodjam Company, Grafton, Vermont
Holy Cow, Inc., Middlebury, Vermont
The Howard Bank, N.A., Burlington, Vermont
Jericho Historical Society, Jericho, Vermont
Mr. and Mrs. Frederick W. Lapham, III
Leader Evaporator Company, St. Albans, Vermont
J. Robert Maguire
Manoogian Collection
Maple Supplies, Barre, Vermont
The Minneapolis Institute of Arts, Minneapolis, Minnesota
Museum of American Folk Art, New York, New York
Museum of Fine Arts, Boston, Massachusetts
Museum of Fine Arts, Springfield, Massachusetts
The Old Constitution House, Windsor. Vermont Division for Historic Preservation
The Old Stone House Museum, Brownington, Vermont
Ransomvale Farm, Castleton, Vermont
The Norman Rockwell Museum at Stockbridge, Massachusetts
Rokeby Museum, Ferrisburgh, Vermont
Shelburne Museum, Shelburne, Vermont
Sheldon Museum, Middlebury, Vermont
Gerard Rancourt Tsonakwa
Wall/Goldfinger, Inc., Northfield, Vermont
The Henry Francis du Pont Winterthur Museum, Winterthur, Delaware
The Woodstock Historical Society, Woodstock, Vermont
Private Collections

Foreword

Those who have wandered along the banks of the Otter Creek, in search of the beautiful and picturesque, may have extended their rambles, perhaps, to lake Dunmore, which lies embosomed among the hills a few miles to the eastward of that quiet stream. If so, their taste for natural scenery has doubtless been amply gratified; for there is no spot in the whole range of the Green Mountains that combines more of the requisites for a perfect landscape than this romantic sheet of water and its surrounding shores.

So BEGINS Daniel P. Thompson's *The Green Mountain Boys*, the most famous novel to extoll the virtues of Vermont and its colonial settlers. Although many authors since have written eloquently about Vermont in both verse and prose, the romance of this environment has conditioned much of the commentary. In fact, in many instances the myths of this place have overshadowed more objective interpretations, a circumstance which may provide some insight into our own psyche.

This exhibition, timed to coincide with the two hundredth anniversary of our admission to the Union, is an appropriate moment to take stock of the truths and fictions of our past. It is fitting that such an exhibition should be organized by Middlebury College, near Otter Creek and only a few miles from Lake Dunmore. Many of those responsible for the development and direction of Vermont over much of the past two centuries, or the interpretations of its history, have had some association with this small college, which like the state itself, has had influence far disproportionate to its size. Vermont writers and artists with a Middlebury College connection have included Thompson (Class of 1820), James Hope (Honorary Degree 1853), Dorothy Canfield Fisher (Honorary Degree 1921), Robert Frost (Honorary Degree 1924), Sabra Field (Class of 1957), and William ("Woody") Jackson (Class of 1970), among others. It is gratifying, as well, to see that the contributors to this exhibition include Middlebury College graduates: Nancy Price Graff (Class of 1975), William N. Hosley (Class of 1977), and Erik W. Borg (Class of 1967).

It is also appropriate that Middlebury College shares this exhibition with two of Vermont's most distinguished cultural institutions: The Vermont Historical Society and The Bennington Museum. The Vermont Historical Society, one of the oldest historical societies in the country, was founded in 1838 to properly preserve and interpret Vermont's cultural and literary history. Over the past one hundred and fifty years, through such publications as *Vermont History*, it has been both a catalyst and a forum for exploration of our culture. Similarly, The Bennington Museum, founded in 1927, has grown to become a major repository for collections of Vermont's historical objects, which range from materials related to the Battle of Bennington to extensive collections of pottery, glass, furniture, and silver. Sited as it is in the southwest corner of the state, The Bennington Museum has acted as a literal gateway to many thousands of visitors and residents alike into the richness of Vermont history.

Celebrating Vermont: Myths and Realities is a major contribution to the literature about our state. Many of the objects assembled here are being seen in public for the first time. This event should remind us of some basic truths about ourselves: that although we may seem homogeneous, Vermont has a rich ethnic heritage essential to its growth of character; that although our historical memory may selectively recall the good times, we have had our bad times as well; and, finally, that although we think the present Vermont landscape is affected by rapid change, in fact the landscape has seen continual change for most of the past two hundred years. Whatever our individual perspective, this exhibition and the accompanying catalogue should enable all Vermonters to better understand where we have been and where we are going, as the state embarks on its third century of existence.

Timothy Light
PRESIDENT
MIDDLEBURY COLLEGE

Advisory Committee

Glenn M. Andres
Professor of Art
Middlebury College

Eloise Beil
Director of Collections
Shelburne Museum

Jane C. Beck
Director
Vermont Folklife Center

Virginia H. Brown
Director
The Sheldon Art Museum

Charles Browne
Co-Director
Fairbanks Museum and Planetarium

Frank M. Bryan
Associate Professor of
    Political Science
University of Vermont

Reed Cherington
Director
The Old Stone House Museum

Alison Devine
Independent Curator
Brattleboro

David A. Donath
Director
Billings Farm & Museum

Roz Driscoll
President, Board of Trustees
Brattleboro Museum & Art Center

John Duffy
Professor of Humanities and
    Writing/Literature
Johnson State College

Christine Hadsel
Director
Vermont Museum
    & Gallery Alliance

William A. Haviland
Professor of Anthropology
University of Vermont

Frederick W. Lapham
Lapham & Dibble Gallery

Laura C. Luckey
Director
The Bennington Museum

J. Robert Maguire
Shoreham

Mary Ellen Martin
Essex Junction

Meg Ostrum
Assistant Director
Vermont Folklife Center

Linda D. Paradee
President
Wood Art Gallery

Ann Porter
Interim Director
Robert Hull Fleming Museum

Louise Roomet
Hinesburg

Gregory C. Schwarz
Director
Woodstock Historical Society

Michael Sherman
Director
Vermont Historical Society

Tom Slayton
Editor
Vermont Life Magazine

Frederick M. Wiseman
Ambassador for Scientific
    and Cultural Affairs
Abenaki Nation at Missisquoi
    AND
Associate Professor
Department of Humanities
Johnson State College

Acknowledgements

THIS EXHIBITION, *Celebrating Vermont: Myths and Realities*, grew out of several conversations I had in the summer of 1988 with Laura Luckey, Director, The Bennington Museum. We agreed then that time was quickly running out to organize an exhibition of substance in time to coincide with the bicentennial. In January 1989 a number of scholars knowledgeable about Vermont and its history were invited to two meetings in Middlebury to discuss possible directions that such an exhibition might take. As a result the Christian A. Johnson Memorial Gallery and The Bennington Museum agreed to cooperate on the development of this exhibition. At virtually the same time Michael Sherman, Director, the Vermont Historical Society, agreed to participate in the exhibition tour and enable it to be seen at a third venue in the state. Simultaneously, an Advisory Committee was formed to help guide this project and provide both a network to gather information and a sounding board for ideas under consideration. Without the support and participation of this committee, the exhibition in its present form would not have been possible.

The administration of Middlebury College quickly embraced the idea of such an exhibition, which by fortunate coincidence would occur at a time when our new fine arts center was to open, and provided the financial support to make the exhibition a reality. Our provost, Bruce B. Peterson, and his successor, John M. McCardell, gave their complete support to the development of this exhibition.

In the spring of 1989 a trio of scholars, William N. Hosley, Jr., Curator of Decorative Arts, Wadsworth Atheneum; J. Kevin Graffagnino, Curator of the Wilbur Collection, Bailey/Howe Library, University of Vermont; and William C. Lipke, Associate Professor of Art, University of Vermont, were invited to contribute essays to the exhibition catalogue. At the same time, meetings were planned to begin to assemble a potential object list for the exhibition. In subsequent months, Virginia M. Westbrook, an independent scholar based in Crown Point, New York, and Nancy Price Graff, a writer and historian, in Montpelier, joined the project as co-curator and editor, respectively. The contributions of these five people have been fundamental to its success. Rowland E. Robinson, the nineteenth-century Vermont writer, would undoubtedly be proud of this group, which like the mythical Danvis pioneer of his stories, battled difficult odds to make a "real" contribution to the Vermont way of life.

Once the object list for the exhibition was complete, individual scholars across the state were invited to contribute catalogue entries. In addition to Virginia M. Westbrook, William N. Hosley, Jr., and William C. Lipke, this group included Lauren J. Barth, Assistant Curator of Decorative Arts, and Celia Y. Oliver, Curator, the Shelburne Museum; David A. Donath, Director, Billings Farm and Museum; John M. Hunisak, Professor of Art, Middlebury College; J. Robert Maguire; Karen E. Peterson, Director, Rokeby; Frederick M. Wiseman, Ambassador for Scientific and Cultural Affairs, Abenaki Nation at Missisquoi; and Catherine M. Zusy, Curator of Decorative Arts, The Bennington Museum. It is their ability to capture a sense of the importance of the individual object that has helped to give life and substance to this exhibition.

To give the readers of this catalogue and the visitors to the exhibition a thumbnail chronology of the state's history, albeit brief and highly subjective, a time line is included at the end of the catalogue. I am extremely grateful to Tom Slayton, Editor, *Vermont Life*, and the staff of his magazine for permitting us to use an expanded version of a time line developed by them.

Part of the joy of working on an exhibition such as this is the opportunity to discover material that is unknown to the public at large or that has been out of the limelight for many years. In our search for both objects and photographs many people within and outside the state gave assistance. Others provided access to aspects of Vermont's history without which this exhibition would have been considerably diminished. We owe a debt of gratitude to the following individuals: Ed Broadway; John Carnahan; Colin Calloway; Paula Glick; Dawn Hance; Suzanne Harrell, University of Oklahoma Press; Charles Kellogg; Steve and Robin Kipp; David Plowden; Bill Souci; and Glen Russell. Special thanks to the Eva Gebhard-Gourgaud Foundation whose generous contribution made possible, in part, the restoration of the Titus Hutchinson family portrait.

Additional assistance was ably provided by Eloise Beil, Director of Collections, Shelburne Museum; Mary B. Bradshaw, President, Weston Historical Society, Curator of the Farrar-Mansur Museum; Alanna Fisher, Curator, American Museum of Fly Fishing, Manchester; David Gil, Bennington Potters; Maureen Hennessey, Curator, The Norman Rockwell Museum at Stockbridge; Judi Hurd, Interim Registrar, Robert Hull Fleming Museum; George Keyes, Curator of Paintings, Minneapolis Institute of Arts; William W. Jenney, Regional Historic Site Administrator, Division For Historic Preservation, Plymouth Notch Historical District; Pauline Mitchell, Registrar, Shelburne Museum; Verbena Pastor, Curator, Barre Museum; Carrie Rebora, Assistant Curator, American Paintings and Sculpture, Metropolitan Museum of Art; Peter Schumann, Bread and Puppet Theatre, Glover; Gregory C. Schwarz, Executive Director, Woodstock Historical Society; Marc A. Simpson, Edna Root Curator of American Art, Fine Arts Museums of San Francisco; Jean K. Smith, President, Jericho Historical Society; and Linda Wells, Librarian, Craftsbury Common Library.

One of the difficulties of a project such as this is that many of the objects required photography. Everyone involved with this project owes a great debt of thanks to the exhibition's photographers: Erik Borg, Middlebury; Ken Burris, Shelburne; and Sherman Howe, Woodstock. Erik traversed the state probably more times than he cares to remember, but he did so with considerable aplomb and dramatic results. The work of each of these photographers is ample evidence of their integral contribution to this exhibition.

The cooperation of the staffs of all three institutions who supervised the exhibition's tour was crucial. In Montpelier, special thanks are owed to Jacqueline Calder and Mary Labate Rogstad, while in Bennington appreciation is extended to Catherine M. Zusy and Ruth Levin.

The enthusiasm of my colleagues at the Johnson Gallery—Emmie Donadio, Assistant Director; Christine Taylor, Registrar; Maureen Rutherford, Secretary; and Jennifer M. Miller '91, gallery intern—has also been an essential ingredient in bringing this exhibition together. In particular I wish to thank Ken Pohlman, Gallery Technician, whose imagination and dexterity have left a profound impact on the installation of the exhibition at all three venues. Further, David Dexter, Director, Academic Computing, and Sheldon Sax, Assistant Director–User Services, Academic Computing, Middlebury College, helped to ease the transition of the catalogue from typed manuscript to computer disk.

The production of this catalogue is among the best evidence of the enduring graphic skills to be found in Vermont. It is entirely fitting that on an anniversary of such significance this publication should be produced by The Stinehour Press, acknowledged as one of the finest printers in the country. Christopher Kuntze has given lasting definition to the thoughts and images of this entire experience.

Finally, a special debt of gratitude is owed to all the lenders to this exhibition. It is their participation, above all, that has enabled these ideas about myth to become a reality.

Richard H. Saunders
DIRECTOR
CHRISTIAN A. JOHNSON MEMORIAL GALLERY
MIDDLEBURY COLLEGE

Introduction

People talk about the meaning of life; there is no meaning of life—there are lots of meanings of different lives, and you must decide what you want your own to be.[1]

JOSEPH CAMPBELL

Before he died, Joseph Campbell did us the enormous service of restoring myth to respectability. Until he and journalist Bill Moyers demonstrated the power of myth at work in our culture, most Americans thought of mythology as a force at work only in "other" cultures. Myth was equated with fantasy and tall tales, with cultural fabrications that were lives and worlds apart from the pragmatism which we Americans perceive to be so fundamentally a hallmark of our own culture and our concept of ourselves as a people. In our culture, history has reigned supreme. In the United States, as in Vermont, historical events have formed the foundation of our sense of identity.

Celebrating Vermont: Myths and Realities, an exhibition organized in observance of the bicentennial of Vermont's statehood, proves that myth and history are not mutually exclusive. Indeed, the "myths" around which this investigation are focused are the stories, traditions, and beliefs, many of them based in fact, which have contributed to the collective sensibility that is Vermont's cultural legacy. In text and images, the exhibition explores the interplay between myth and reality, both in our past and in our present. It establishes and elaborates on those aspects of our cultural history which have created and sustained the state's myths and explores the reasons why myths have diverted us, in some instances, from knowing and understanding the truth about ourselves and our past.

We hope it becomes clear from reading these essays and the accompanying catalogue that some myths about Vermont have remained largely unchanged over long periods of time. Such are the myths surrounding our state's first hero, Ethan Allen. Other myths have disappeared or emerged over time. Consider, for a moment, the perspective promoted so successfully in the nineteenth century to the emerging middle class, that Vermont was a beckoning playground. Some myths have their roots in the particular circumstances of our history. The myth of Yankee ingenuity, for example, confirms truths about the state's culture and Vermonters' uncanny creativity. Other myths, such as the myth that Vermont in the 1700s was a vast wilderness inhabited tenuously by a very small number of peripatetic Abenaki, are fabricated from circumstances and ideas that had their origins both within and outside of the state.

What becomes apparent is that our myths predominately reflect ideas that we have about ourselves. It is also clear that our myths are surprisingly rich and varied; and they have been an integral part of the Vermont experience for virtually the state's entire history.

The first essay, for example, co-authored by Nancy Graff and William Hosley, examines the reasons why settlers were willing to pioneer life in a new land and the true circumstances and economy of the Vermont frontier, thereby establishing how we derived the image of the state's first settlers as independent, ambitious, frugal, and inventive. It also provides insight into the pragmatic means local and state boosters used to promote their state, their communities, and themselves, and why we made heroes of those who were most successful at it.

J. Kevin Graffagnino, in the second essay, discusses how and why dynamos of progress, which propelled the rest of the country onward and upward throughout the nineteenth century, by-passed Vermont. To many living here in the 1800s, the Green Mountain State was economically stagnant, and the lure of the states and territories to the west was strong. During the second half of the century, however, those who stayed transmogrified the pain of depressed agriculture into the myth of pastoral arcadia, proving that Vermonters have a long tradition of capitalizing on the virtues of their environment.

In the third essay, with the difficult task of interpreting a history not yet cold, William Lipke explores the myths and realities of our own generation and the one that preceded it. He examines particularly the idea that Vermont in this century has qualities both mythic (pastoral) and progressive (real), by tracing the evolution of those qualities through pieces of our past as seemingly unconnected as the paintings of Norman Rockwell and the politics of Bernie Sanders.

The objects selected for this exhibition illuminate these investigations. Their selection was the culmination of a lengthy process. We realized at the outset that the assembled objects would have to represent far larger groups than could be adequately addressed in the exhibition or the accompanying text. While members of our advisory committee cautioned that the ambitious nature of the theme would invariably lead to omissions, our hope is that the result, even if flawed, outweighs the merits of a more modest venture.

Several criteria conditioned the selection of objects. Those we chose had to help explain the juxtaposition of myth and reality, be visually engaging, and/or contribute significantly to the better understanding of our cultural history. In most cases, little-known objects were given preference over examples well known in the existing literature. Unfortunately, a few objects we wished to include were simply unavailable.

Joseph Campbell has shown us that myths help to define our underlying spiritual goals. We depend upon them because they provide the very images which shape our collective lives.[2] He has helped us to see how much poorer our lives would be without them. It is, after all, the romanticism we associate with farming, making maple sugar, and a nineteenth-century rural Vermont, simple and uncorrupted, that lifts our spirits through difficult times. We may know in our hearts that life in Vermont over the past 200 years has been far more difficult, far more poverty stricken, and far more complex than we want to imagine, but the myth of what we believe Vermont is sustains us and gives us a sense of direction.

To those who ask, "Why celebrate another bicentennial?" we must answer: Commemorative observations give us the opportunity to re-examine the past from new vantage points. The real goal, then, of a project such as this is not to undermine the myths which have become part of our cultural heritage but rather to remind ourselves how they came into being and why we are so acutely dependent upon them. If we can achieve that understanding, perhaps we will truly be in a position to let the past transform the present.

Richard H. Saunders
Virginia M. Westbrook

Notes

1. Joseph Campbell, *An Open Life* (1988; reprint ed., New York: Harper & Row, 1989), p. 110.

2. Campbell, *An Open Life*, pp. 35, 110.

Celebrating Vermont:
Myths and Realities of the First Sixty Years of Statehood

Twenty years ago, when a young historian was being interviewed for a faculty position in the history department of the University of Vermont, he was asked whether he thought he could put together a course for undergraduates in Vermont history. As eager as any of us would be in that kind of situation, he said, "yes." Only later, when he had the job and the challenge of compiling a respectable bibliography for a course in the state's history, did he discover that Vermont lacked a single-volume, comprehensive state history.

The shelves of Vermont's historical societies and libraries are filled with innumerable catalogues of information about the state's past—tomes as slight as Samuel Hall's *Geography and History of Vermont* (published in 1871) and as weighty as Abby Marie Hemenway's five-volume *Vermont Historical Gazetteer* (published between 1868 and 1891)—but most of these amount to little more than inventories and narratives. Almost none of it is analytical in the way that modern history expects and demands. Very little of it "explains" anything to us unless we have context and understanding of our own to illuminate the data. Moreover, to a great extent the volumes suggest, as historian Charles Morrissey remarked ruefully in *Vermont: A Bicentennial History*, that "Vermont's history itself has been rolling downhill since early in the nineteenth century and isn't worth retrieving."[1]

This lack of a readable, comprehensive history of Vermont is unfortunate. It has made Vermont a difficult place to know accurately. The lack is all the more disturbing because the days have probably passed when anyone would even attempt to write such a thing. Very simply, history is no longer what it once was. Largely gone are the days of epic histories, stories painted with broad brushes across vast canvases of time and space. Historians today, like so many professionals in the modern world, are specialists. They are seeking the details that have been lost and overlooked. Their interests are most often the hitherto untold stories of the underrepresented and dispossessed. The most recent and best offerings of Vermont history, with the exception of Charles Morrissey's *Vermont*, are collected works, collaborative products of many historians speaking to us in many voices.

The result of this state of the state's affairs is that Vermont's myths are as well or better known than its history. Who among us has not heard that the state was always a thoroughfare, never a home, for Indians? Whose pulse does not quicken when he hears again that Vermont refused all federal aid after the tragic Flood of 1927 and pledged to rebuild itself using only the state's resources of strong backs and hard cash? Who has not boasted that Vermont has more cows than people? The fact is, Native Americans have lived and made their homes in Vermont for 11,000 years, Vermont did eventually accept federal aid to help it recover from the devastations of the flood, and the last claim is patently false. What's more, it was never true.

Probably no single character in history better evidences the enduring conflict between truth and myth in Vermont than the state's original hero, Ethan Allen (*Fig. 1.1*). The stirring speech he delivered upon capturing Fort Ticonderoga from the British in 1775—"Surrender in the name of the Great Jehovah and the Continental Congress"—is as fixed in our memory as the unmistakable profile of Camel's Hump, no matter that we have only Allen's own bombastic *Narrative* to document the quotation (and another witness's word that Allen said something quite different

Fig. 1.1 Larkin G. Mead. *Ethan Allen.* 1876. Marble. Statuary Hall, Capitol, Washington, D.C. Courtesy, Office of the Architect of the Capitol.

and earthier). Vermonters have always felt a special kinship with Allen. We admire his love of liberty and his defiance in the face of injustice, his shrewdness as well as his uncommon courage and determination (cat. 1). But the qualities that give Allen his mythic dimensions in our history do him an injustice as a person if we look no further. He was a complex person. The same analytical and detached intelligence that made the account of his imprisonment by the British during the American Revolution "a masterpiece [that] took the country by storm and gave a much-needed boost to American morale,"[2] cost him the affection of much of the country when he applied it to religion. One Connecticut minister went so far as to call Allen after his death "An awful Infidel, one of ye wickedest men that eer walked this guilty globe."[3] The same degree of passion that made him capable of inflicting brutal, frontier-style justice (cat. 2) on the Reverend Benjamin Hough infused his happy marriage to his second wife, Fanny. When it comes to Ethan Allen—or for that matter to much of the state's history in general—we have, in short, remembered only that which we admire, ignored the parts that shame us by association, and in the instance of Allen's likeness, invented the parts that don't exist.

Vermont's Deputy Secretary of State Paul Gillies has said that "Myth is a strong elixir, especially in Vermont."[4] This truth makes the occasion of the bicentennial of Vermont's statehood an opportunity to ask ourselves how it has come to pass that myths have overwhelmed our history. And what has made them so supremely durable across the generations? According to historian Bruce Catton, people fall victim to myths about their past for universal and compelling reasons. "Realizing that things can never again be as once they were," he writes,

> we are all too likely to conclude that the golden age lies somewhere behind us. The people who lived in it may not have known that it was a golden age, but we discover it for them and string out long tales, sad and beautiful in sunset red and gold, about the ease and peace that once lay upon the earth.[5]

In his recently published *Roadside History of Vermont*, however, Peter Jennison suggests that Vermonters may have a right to make a special claim to their myths. The reasons, he claims, are multiple, complex, and unique to Vermont, combining "geography, original patterns of settlement, an aggressive defense of territorial integrity, vigorous self-government, ingenuity, and a high degree of tolerance for the right of other people to be eccentric or misguided."[6]

The Europeans Arrive

When European settlers began pushing in the eighteenth century into the region that would become Vermont, they discovered a country that would shape their destiny as surely as they tried to shape it themselves. Products of pre-industrial cultures both here and abroad, they were land-centered people trying to put down roots in a place as intractable and unyielding as any they could imagine. What they found and what became Vermont was a dominating rock-ribbed spine of mountains covered with dense forests and thin soil. On the west, the land fell away into the fertile lowlands of Lake Champlain in the north and into the lesser hills and valleys of the Taconic in the south. On the eastern side of the spiny ridge the land fell away again, but not as dramatically, into the piedmont, a familiar pattern of rolling hills and valleys which stopped abruptly along the silt-rich banks and in the intervales of the Connecticut River. Here was a landscape that recalled the homes many of the settlers had left behind in southern and eastern New England. Encompassing nearly the whole southern border of the state and inviting their entry from Connecticut and Massachusetts was the Vermont Valley, a funnel-shaped depression narrowing to a mouth near Brandon. More than any other single factor, this geography explains Vermont's early settlement patterns and economy.[7]

The area was not virgin. Historians now estimate that as many as 10,000 Native Americans were living in the region of Vermont when Columbus stumbled upon San Salvador in 1492 (cat. 4). As contemporary researchers and surviving petroglyphs in the upper Connecticut Valley tell us, these native inhabitants were not newcomers (*Fig. 1.2*). Indeed, they had been present in

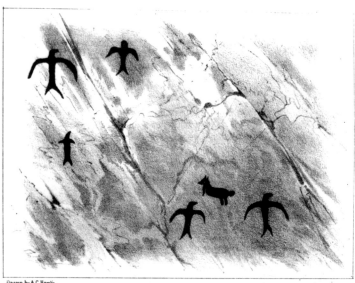

Fig. 1.2 Petroglyphs at Bellows Falls and inscriptions at West River. Reproduced from Henry R. Schoolcraft, *Information Respecting the History, Conditions and Prospects of the Indians of the United States* [1854–60]. Courtesy, Newberry Library.

Drawn by A.C. Hamlin

TOTEMIC DEVICES, WEST RIVER, (Vermont).

Drawn by A.C. Hamlin

PICTOGRAPHIC INSCRIPTION AT BELLOWS' FALLS, (Vermont).

the region for more than 10,000 years. Over time and generations, they had cut extensive trails, hunted, trapped, fished, farmed, burned over forests to make cropland, and created perhaps as many as twenty settlements, principally along major waterways, with primary sites around the present-day locations of Newbury and Swanton. If the strength of their numbers was not immediately apparent to the Europeans who initially explored their territory, it was because the Europeans were generally unfamiliar with the densely wooded interior landscape into which the threatened Abenakis melted (cat. 3).[8]

The French arrived in Vermont first. They came as explorers and Jesuit missionaries in the mid-1600s, followed a half century later by Dutch traders and settlers from New York who penetrated Vermont's southwest and northwest borders. These first Europeans intruded upon the Abenakis (a branch of the Algonquin tribe), negotiated land claims in the southern part of the state, and traded extensively, exchanging their steel for native-made baskets, brooms, and tool handles.[9] It was particularly these early joint claims of the French and resident Abenakis on Vermont lands that discouraged English settlers until after the end of the Seven Years War and the British conquest of New France in 1759 (cat. 5).

The inability of the Abenakis to hold their land claims, first south of a line drawn from the present site of Springfield across the state and later north of the line as well, was a tragic development for them in the face of an irreversible tide of European immigration. Very quickly, these early Europeans forced the Native Americans into a position which doomed their viability as a tribe and reduced them to paid soldiers in the European battle for conquest of the North American continent. All in a desperate effort to preserve the integrity and abundance of their ancient homelands, Vermont's native people now acquired European goods (such as guns and steel fish hooks and axe blades) and adjusted their ally relationships accordingly among the English, the French, and the Americans in the coming disputes. When all of their efforts eventually failed (with the defeat of the French by the British in 1759 and with the defeat of the British by the Americans in the American Revolution and the War of 1812), they earned only the scorn of the white settlers, who had decided, without understanding their own role, that the Indians were disloyal and untrustworthy. In the course of the conflicts, they also earned for themselves an equally undeserved reputation as warriors. These myths, perpetuated in the years to come by land speculators such as Ira Allen, made it all the easier, when the time came, to deny the native inhabitants rights to the land they had held for a hundred centuries.[10]

It has been postulated that if the Erie Canal had been opened in 1774 rather than in 1824, Vermont would never have been settled.[11] The state's rugged terrain was no one's idea of Eden; it would have looked even worse in comparison had the state's first settlers had the opportunity to take the canal westward for a peek at the endless, fertile prairies of the Midwest. However, when at last Vermont was available for English settlement in the years after 1760, the over-crowded settlements of western Connecticut and Massachusetts began to vent themselves by releasing the landless, the unlucky, and the ambitious to emigrate.

What began as a trickle of immigration in the late 1760s swelled to a flood in the succeeding half century. The newcomers moved in the only directions easily open to them, northward and westward. They pushed first up the Connecticut River Valley as far as Ryegate and up the western boundary of the state as far as Tinmouth. Others followed these pioneers and, finding those first choice stretches taken, pushed up into the Vermont Valley as far as the foot of the Green Mountain Range in Plymouth and Shrewsbury, where they diverged, like lava flowing around a rock, scattering themselves as far north as Hardwick on the east and up the Champlain Valley to the Canadian border on the west. By 1791, the year of Vermont's statehood, only pockets of highlands remained to be settled: the mountains of Ripton and Goshen; of Underhill, Stowe, and Jay; and of the Northeast Kingdom.[12]

Settlements took root and flourished, despite poor roads and cultural isolation. Chartered as early as 1749 under the New Hampshire Grants, Bennington is a case in point. By 1789, when the Reverend Nathan Perkins left West Hartford, Connecticut, to witness firsthand the Christian temperament of this new region, he found Bennington to be a crowded village of houses, a meetinghouse, "some elegant building," a courthouse, a grammar school, and a jail (*Fig. 1.3*). He also found local manners that he described as "proud, scornful, conceited & somewhat polished."[13]

The increases in population were staggering to a young state, newly formed and trying to

Fig. 1.3 Ralph Earl. *View of Bennington.* 1798. Oil on canvas. Courtesy, The Bennington Museum.

provide essential services. Between 1790 and 1810, the population of Vermont increased 150 percent. In the decade between 1800 and 1810 alone, population boomed from 154,475 to almost 218,000, not counting the changes in the Native American population.

Throughout the state, towns filled rapidly with restless go-getters eager to shape communities in the mold of the new republic. They had little use for any legacy of radicalism that may have lingered from Vermont's days as a republic. Indeed, Vermont's flirtation with independence during the tumultuous years between 1777 and its entry into the union in 1791 was neither long enough nor sincere enough to generate a culture markedly different from that which the hordes of new immigrants were bringing with them from states lying to Vermont's south, east, and west. Indeed, Vermont's independence, to the extent it existed, was more a factor of the continuing dispute with New York state over land grants than an aversion to union. As the overwhelming vote to approve statehood makes clear, the leaders of Vermont had no intention of creating a republic that would outlast the resolution of the grants dispute. Once title to lands occupied under the New Hampshire Grants was accepted and a negotiated settlement was reached with claims under New York Grants, Vermont was only too glad to join the union.

Nonetheless, Vermont's flirtation with independence, the feuding and raiding that marked the dispute over grants, and the pluck and color of characters like Ethan Allen, Seth Warner, and the Green Mountain Boys had the elemental qualities of myths. This, then, is where our memories begin to cloud. Historian Richard Carlson has pinpointed Ethan Allen's grandstanding and the formation of the Green Mountain Boys at the conclusion of the grants trial in New York as the hour in time when Vermont's history begins to become indistinct. "If every society needs to possess a mythical moment of creation," he wrote, "this was Vermont's."[14]

Life on the Frontier

For the English colonists who established farms and occupations in Vermont during the 1780s and later, issues of politics were subordinated to the concerns of everyday life. Even Ethan Allen, despite his reputation as a military leader, author, and real estate speculator, devoted the years following the Revolution to making a living clearing and cultivating lands on the Onion (now Winooski) River east of Burlington. This was the frontier experience at the most basic level, and Allen's exploits did not immunize him from the struggle every pioneer faced to confront the elements, to wrest tillable land from the forest, to work the soil adequately to provide food and the raw resources for clothing, to manage livestock, and to build a home.

In Vermont, the early years of statehood until Jefferson's embargo on the eve of the War of 1812 were booming years despite the regular ravages of illness, drought, and unseasonable frosts. In 1800, two-thirds of the state's citizens were less than 26 years old. With youthful energy and ambition to spur them on, they wasted no time in building roads (91 turnpikes were chartered in Vermont between 1791 and 1810, although only a third of these were finally built), erecting grist and saw mills, and generally creating profitable avenues of commerce both within the state and, thanks to the waterways of the Connecticut River and Lake Champlain, with the world beyond. In short order, newspapers were being published in all the major population centers of the state to keep citizens informed of state and national affairs, and a university and a college were chartered in Burlington and Middlebury, respectively, to ensure that native sons were properly educated. By 1808, a steamboat was plying the waters of Champlain, making it possible and profitable for the first time to consider southerly trade routes that ran counter to the natural flow of the lake.[15]

During these years dreams and propaganda were virtually indistinguishable from one another. In 1797, John A. Graham, a Rutland attorney, traveled through Vermont observing the progress of the state's settlement, recording the price of land, and taking notes for a book that would shortly be published in England entitled, *A descriptive sketch of the present state of Vermont*. Everywhere he went, he was impressed by the signs of civilization and the bounty of the new land. In his hometown, he praised the town's "excessive crops of hay & Indian corn." Sandgate's soil was so fertile, he assured potential emigrants, that farmers would make back their investment two times over with their first harvest. He saved his highest praise for Chittenden County: "Finer land there cannot be in any part of the universe."[16]

The second stage of frontier town building, usually commencing within 20 years of first settlement, was one of the signs of this boom. During this period, networks of civic leaders coalesced, and through their efforts civic institutions and the engines of free enterprise were set in motion. The study of Vermont's early civic boosters is a study of the urban frontier, a peculiarly American phenomenon born out of the commingling of patriotic and enlightenment ideology and the frenetic excitement engendered by the availability of new land and opportunity.

Vermont's early leaders embody the qualities historians have assigned to the town boosters who shaped community life across the American west during the nineteenth century. Historian Daniel Boorstin described them as a select brand of individuals whose "starting belief was in the interfusing of public and private prosperity." They were, he says, the kind of people who take an interest in public affairs, join organizations, are open to new experiences, operate on the basis of time-thrift and planning, and believe completely in man's ability to improve the natural and social environment.[17]

In Vermont, these leaders were distributed across a network of prominent commercial centers: Bennington, Rutland, Middlebury, Windsor, and Burlington. Intensely competitive and devoted totally to the self-interested and enlightened notion of improving themselves by advancing their towns, men like Jedediah Dewey and Moses Robinson in Bennington, Cephas Smith in Rutland, Ira Allen in Burlington, Ebenezer and Samuel Crafts in Craftsbury, and Jonathan Hubbard and Jesse Lull of Windsor played critical roles in developing their communities.

Middlebury's Gamaliel Painter is a good example (*Fig. 1.4*). Arriving in Middlebury from Salisbury, Connecticut, around 1773, Painter and his brother-in-law John Chipman built log houses for themselves south of the falls along Otter Creek and began surveying lands and laying out public roads. With the outbreak of war three years later, Middlebury was abandoned, and Painter, who was acquainted with Ethan Allen from their common background in Salisbury, eventually became a commissioned officer in the colonial forces during the Revolution. After the war, Painter resettled in Middlebury and began maneuvering to consolidate a host of civic institutions around an enormous village green north of the falls. Anticipating the town's develop-

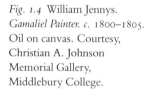

Fig. 1.4 William Jennys. *Gamaliel Painter. c.* 1800–1805. Oil on canvas. Courtesy, Christian A. Johnson Memorial Gallery, Middlebury College.

ment, he built for himself an end-chimney, saltbox house nearby in 1787 that reflected his high hopes for the town. He also built mills, promoted settlement, and sold and probably leased building lots to immigrant families. By one account, "as early as 1791, when the village was little else than a wilderness, standing on the lot he had deeded to the County, he said to the bystanders, 'This is the place for the court house.'"[18]

It was a prophecy he helped to fulfill in the coming years as he served successive terms in the state legislature and later as county judge and sheriff. Moderator at town meetings and head of the building committee for the Congregational Church, Painter was also both a trustee and incorporator of the nearby college, which he helped to found in 1800. In every respect, Painter was the prototypical town booster of Vermont's urban frontier.

To celebrate and manifest his success, Painter in 1802 built and occupied a third house, a large and stylish mansion encrusted with ornament and capped by a parapet from which his family and guests could view a prospect of the growing town below. The view soon included thriving marble works and textile mills at the falls and a host of civic institutions that Painter gathered together around the town green. In little more than a decade, Middlebury emerged as one of the fastest growing and most prosperous towns in New England. Painter's crowning achievement was in marshalling the resources needed to design and build between 1806 and 1809 what is today regarded as one of the most ostentatious and sophisticated meetinghouses of its period in the United States, architect Lavius Fillmore's soaring masterpiece, Middlebury's Congregational Church.

The same story might as easily be told across the state in Windsor, where Asher Benjamin, New England's most accomplished country builder-cum-architect was lured in 1798 to design Vermont's first country Palladian-style meetinghouse. At the same time he was asked to design a series of mansions for the town's proud and ambitious frontier elite (*Fig. 1.5*). During the next four years, Benjamin helped transform what was already Vermont's largest and richest town into a model of urbanity and cosmopolitanism.

Even towns and villages that eventually failed to thrive had their boosters and their benefactors, men who believed passionately if futilely in their town's golden future. In Craftsbury, for example, Ebenezer and Samuel C. Crafts invested their hearts and their purses, and for as long as their presence held the town in their grasp, Craftsbury achieved an eminence unequaled in the region (*Fig. 1.6*). Indomitable and entrepreneurial, Ebenezer cleared the road north of Cabot shortly after his arrival in Craftsbury in 1780, built mills, and essentially opened the town for business. At the first town meeting, Crafts was chosen moderator and subsequently the town's representative in the state legislature. His son Samuel was made town clerk, an office he held for thirty-five years, serving alternately as Vermont's governor and as a member of the United States Senate.

In that remote and culturally isolated place, Samuel Crafts was a Renaissance man, a graduate of Harvard, class of '90, whose presence and interests illuminated everything they touched. As chairman of the building committee for Vermont's statehouse in 1834, he toured New England in the company of Boston architect Ammi B. Young, studying statehouse architecture. He wrote essays on history, astronomy, mathematics, and architecture, and was appointed a member of the congressional committee on public buildings while he was serving in Congress.

Even in death, the Crafts were beneficent and self-interested, fusing the distinction between private prosperity and public good. Ebenezer's will made provision for furnishing the Congregational Church with a communion table and two silver tankards carved with his name, plus it

Fig. 1.5 Asher Benjamin. *The Fullerton House, Windsor. c.* 1799–1800. Courtesy, the Society for the Preservation of New England Antiquities.

provided funds to purchase a bell and clock for the new meetinghouse and a steeple to house them.[19] The result was that long after the momentum of the Crafts's influence had ceased propelling the town, their family name remained literally on the lips of the local communicants, while their clock kept the town on notice of minutes spent and wasted (cat. 19).

In the private sphere of their lives, Vermont's early leaders measured up to the grandeur and enterprise of their public acts. In astonishingly short order, men such as Titus Hutchinson of Woodstock (cat. 21) and Cephas Smith of Rutland adopted genteel rituals and expensive luxuries that today seem regal and incongruous in the settings of the times. In 1806, for example, when Rutland's population barely numbered above 2000, Smith commissioned companion portraits of himself, his wife, and daughter from the artist William Jennys (*Fig. 1.7*). The portraits are among the earliest three-quarter-length likenesses painted in Vermont, a fact which alone speaks to the sitter's lofty sense of self. Situated at a table-desk, pen in hand, Smith is depicted with stylish bangs and a ruffled collar in the act of commencing correspondence from Rutland, a task emblematic of his profession as an attorney and his role as one of the architects of that town's prosperity and its link to the commercial and professional cultures beyond.

The startling speed with which the leading men on Vermont's frontier adopted the elegance and gentility of such long-settled places as New Haven, Connecticut, and even Boston, belied the relative poverty of the average Vermonter at the turn of the nineteenth century. In contrast

Fig. 1.6 Winthrop Chandler. *Ebenezer and Samuel Crafts. c.* 1781. Oil on canvas. Courtesy, Craftsbury Public Library, Craftsbury Common.

to Smith's estate in 1815, valued at $14,877 at a time when a dollar a day was good wages, were the estates of the average Vermonters of the era. Most were fortunate to own a modest amount of land and a house, usually a sparsely furnished story-and-a-half dwelling of post and beam construction (*Fig. 1.8*). Silver, the great delineator of wealth and status in colonial America's cosmopolitan cities, was practically non-existent on Vermont's frontier. Conversely, almost everyone owned some pewter, most of it produced in England; half the families owned a glass bottle or two, perhaps produced by the state's fledgling glass manufactories (cat. 14, 15, 16); but few homes had more than a single candlestick and almost none contained a clock. Fine cabinetry was uncommon (cat. 6, 20); more often than not, a simple bedstead was a luxury. Bedding itself was inevitably valued higher than the furniture it served (cat. 8). Fewer than half of the homes contained a single book (usually a Bible), and in an era often characterized today by images of gun-toting frontiersmen, only a third of the households contained a firearm.[20]

The presence of any luxury in the lives of the typical Vermont pioneer was a rarity. Instead, he invested his meager resources in livestock, storage containers, agricultural tools, and vehicles. A recent survey of 110 Vermont estate inventories from the turn of the nineteenth century revealed that agricultural tools represented the single largest category of family possessions. Each of the major functions associated with frontier agriculture—land clearing and fencing, soil cultivation, grain harvesting and processing, textile processing, dairying, stock raising, and

Fig 1.7 William Jennys.
Cephas Smith. c. 1806. Oil on
canvas. Courtesy, Museum of
Fine Arts, Boston.

transportation—required specialized equipment, a burden made all the more onerous by the widespread practice of extensive rather than intensive agriculture. In other words, farms needed a wide variety of equipment that was not easily shared. It is not surprising, then, to discover that when men like wealthy Lemuel Bush of Arlington died in 1789, his estate included a list of debts he was owed by 200 individuals in Arlington and the neighboring towns as well as titles to two dozen farmsteads that were worked by tenant farmers.[21]

Myths of Early Vermont

The frontier in America was a fertile ground for myths. Indeed, myths and heroes became an integral part of the frontier experience. They filled voids in places where as yet there was no history and they provided food for dreams in places where the future seemed limitless.

On the Vermont frontier in the late eighteenth and early nineteenth century, myths had a critical part to play. What, after all, could have lured tens of thousands of pioneers to strike out from the crowded but civilized towns they knew in southern New England for the Vermont wilderness if not the naive belief—perpetuated by propagandists such as John Graham—that they would be able to make a life that had hitherto been denied them? They emigrated on hearsay

Fig. 1.8 Herbert W. Congdon. *Hulett House, Pawlet. c.* 1793. Courtesy, Special Collections, University of Vermont.

and hope, as often as not becoming victims of Vermont's first great myth: that this startlingly beautiful beckoning country was theirs for the taking and making.

Unfortunately, they were but the first generation of Vermont immigrants to have their hopes dashed by what Charles Morrissey has described as "hard living in a hard place."[22] Consider Seth Hubbell, one of Wolcott's first settlers. Hubbell and his family left Norwalk, Connecticut, in the spring of 1789 "on my journey for Wolcott, to commence a settlement and make that my residence." In a brief memoir published in 1824, he described his journey with his wife and five daughters on which he was forced to take his place in the yoke when one of his oxen failed, to travel the last eight miles on snowshoe with his wife and two children, and to ferry his remaining children on his back through the spring snows. Hardships beset them immediately:

> I had now got to the end of my journey, and I may say almost to the end of my property, for I had not a mouthful of meat or kernel of grain to buy with, or property that I could apply to that purpose. I however had the good luck to catch a saple [sable]. The skin I carried fifty miles, and exchanged for half a bushel of wheat and backed it home.[23]

Although Hubbell survived those brutal first years—more than once walking 60 miles to

New Hampshire and back for provisions—his wife and a daughter and a whole series of cows did not. The expenses associated with those illnesses eventually cost him the farm, which he was permitted to stay on only through the charity of relatives. The entire family spent years living on the edge of starvation and indeed, on the edge of life itself. After more than thirty years of struggle, and still not a landowner, Hubbell published his story in a pamphlet aptly titled, *A Narrative of the Sufferings of Seth Hubbell & Family.*

Equally compelling was the myth that resettlement to Vermont offered a guarantee of easy land ownership, which is to say in the terms of those times—financial security. Unfortunately, this often proved false or at least a considerably more complex and expensive process than many settlers expected. Although the territory of Vermont was not completely unknown, it was enough unknown that settlement of it often preceded accurate surveying. Pioneers arrived on their grants after walking hundreds of miles along dark roads and narrow trails and discovered that their right of ownership was under dispute. Early surveyors, for example, mistakenly calculated the amount of land in Johnson and laid out two towns to occupy the same plot. The first settlers, arriving there in the 1780s, expected to find sufficient land for both the towns of Johnson and Brownington. Instead, they were dismayed to be dragged into legal wrangles that stretched on for almost a decade and eventually cost an entire township of grantees their claims.

Other settlers mortgaged their futures only to be met with broken promises. Once again, Seth Hubbell was a victim:

> I moved from Connecticut with the expectation of having fifty acres of land given me when I came on, but this I was disappointed of, and was under the necessity soon after I came on of selling a yoke of oxen and a horse to buy the land I now live on, which reduced my stock to but one cow; and this I had the misfortune to loose [lose] the next winter. This left me wholly destitute of a single hough [hoof] of a creature.[24]

Frequently, the fledgling towns and villages physically embodied the myths that sustained the frontier. The medium was often architecture, the most conspicuous and in some ways the most portable of the fine arts. At the intersections of dirt roads that disappeared into the backwoods of Vermont's hills, country carpenters working with the new genre of builder's guides, such as those by Asher Benjamin, were able to create palatial homes in current architectural styles with accurately rendered Corinthian columns or stylistic subtleties such as splayed lintels and elliptical fanlights. Each of the designs arrived with cultural baggage, an allusion to a history or a tradition that the young town was too new to have acquired legitimately but one that it was content, even proud, to appropriate under the circumstances.

In terms of the message they were meant to convey, hotels, taverns, and inns have had a special place in the American experience (cat. 25). Unlike Europeans, who traditionally designed their courthouses and churches to convey a sense of a community's moral and civic worth, Americans on the frontier in Vermont and elsewhere consistently lavished their resources on pretentious public hotels that spoke to passing travelers not of the town's high-mindedness but of its ambition and energy. As early as 1797 in Vermont, itinerant Rutland attorney John Graham could observe the difference and its implications for the social status of the community's inhabitants:

> however odd it may sound to a European ear, [it] is the custom nearly all over New England, where the most respectable part of the Community are the innkeepers, and where it not infrequently happens that the landlords are men of erudition, independent fortunes, and magistrates.[25]

The architectural hyperbole had its roots in competition. In Vermont in the decades surrounding 1800, fledgling towns and villages fought fiercely among themselves to determine which would flourish and which would stagnate after an initial burst of activity. In the six decades between 1790 and 1850, the four towns of Guilford, Windsor, Middlebury, and Burlington vied for the title of most populous, and an additional nine towns were growing vigorously enough to be considered serious contenders.[26] In an era when communities on the frontier measured themselves by how quickly they grew, their prestige depended on their ability to sell themselves.[27] The stakes in Vermont were high: a new state needed a capital, county seats, major roads, and eventually, railroad connections. Accordingly, scores of sophisticated public buildings and elegant taverns were erected as lures in the hope of attracting visitors passing through to settle there and invest. The point of all such architectural splendor, especially that of the hotels, was to convey the message that here was not a destination resort, but indeed, a life's destination.

In retrospect, the mythic dimensions of Vermont's early architectural monuments are obvious. Consider Windsor, whose population was approximately 2500 in 1805. Its main street was lined with houses on the cutting edge of architectural fashion, brick commercial buildings and factories, a three-story co-op for local artisans known as the Tontine Building, and of course, a meetinghouse which was second to none in Vermont until Middlebury's was completed four years later. Prominent even amid such grandeur was Pettes Coffee House, a three- or four-story hotel described by contemporary visitors as "the best public house in Vermont." Pettes was a much-glorified tavern, featuring an elegantly furnished dining room, rooms for guests, and a large assembly room used as a meeting place for the town fire company and militia, the Royal Arch Chapter of the Free Masons, and as a place of business for itinerant portrait painters, silhouette artists, theatrical troupes, and dancing instructors.[28] What purpose was served by such a sublime collection of architecture? It distracted the eye, and perhaps the heart and mind, from the hardships of life on the frontier.

Life After the War of 1812

The War of 1812 disrupted life in Vermont and derailed its developing economy. It pitted the state's residents who depended on trade with Canada—which included most residents of the Champlain Valley and anyone who lived on a trade route that flowed into the lake—against President Jefferson's embargo of British trade. As a result, smuggling flourished during the war years. However, when trade routes were reestablished in the years afterward, British goods, particularly cotton cloth, flooded the American market, and the state's industry suffered dramatically. In the decade between 1810 and 1820, the value of Vermont's manufacturing wealth declined to less than a quarter of its pre-war value. Historians today date the zenith of Vermont's early economic development no later than the conclusion of the war.[29]

Immigration slowed abruptly and the demographics became complex. Large numbers of Vermonters, having come to an appreciation of the hardships of their new home, began to emigrate. In the coming decades, the rate of their departure nearly equalled the rate of immigration.

As if these were not problems enough, Vermont's bounty of natural resources had been seriously compromised by the state's rapid settlement. Game and timber had noticeably declined. Soil fertility had fallen alarmingly in places where the land had been relentlessly farmed. In other places, where timber had been clear-cut, soil had simply washed away, leaving behind nothing but bedrock and despair.[30]

Most Vermonters who found cause for celebration in the years after the war were invested in sheep. The craze began in 1811 when William Jarvis imported several hundred Spanish Merino sheep to his farm in Weathersfield. The long-haired Merinos quickly proved to be remarkably well adapted to Vermont's difficult climate and marginal grazing lands, and thereafter the numbers of sheep in Vermont increased exponentially. During the war prices for wool soared, and though they fell after the war, they rebounded in the mid 1820s thanks to a high protective tariff that limited competition from abroad. According to Vermont historian Lewis Stillwell, "Not even the lower South in the heyday of 'King Cotton' was more thoroughly committed to a single crop than was Vermont of the '30's." By 1840, when the state's population of sheep had already begun to decline, sheep outnumbered Vermonters six to one.[31]

As the number of sheep increased, so did the number of industries to service wool. In the decade between 1810 and 1820, the number of fulling and carding mills in Vermont tripled. Factories, where the spun wool was woven into finished products, multiplied accordingly until, by 1840, the state could boast of 80 textile factories, at least one with a work force of more than a hundred.[32] The factories were concentrated in Addison, Chittenden, and Caledonia counties, but the impact of sheep and wool on the state's economy as a whole in the decades immediately after the War of 1812 cannot be overestimated. Unfortunately, neither can its vulnerability.

Fortunately, Vermont had other fledgling industries developing during the first half of the nineteenth century. Three industries in particular merit mention, not only for the artistic quality of what they produced but for their distinctive niche in the economic life of the young state.

No other state in the union claims so distinguished a history in the stonecutting industry as Vermont, dating from the opening of Reuben Bloomer's marble quarry in Dorset in 1785. The quarry tapped the rich vein of marble and limestone that stretches from the Canadian line south into Connecticut and opened the way for the development of a marble district along the state's western border. The first products from the Dorset quarry were fire-jambs, chimney backs, hearthstones, and lintels, which although utilitarian, were such a novelty that their market rapidly expanded beyond Vermont's borders. Shortly thereafter, a stonecutter named Jonas Stewart of Dorset is reputed to have made the first marble gravestone (cat. 22). By 1808, Elijah Sykes, a gifted stonecutter from central Massachusetts, had relocated to Dorset, where he opened a quarry and began manufacturing highly decorated marble gravestones. The advent of neoclassicism at the turn of the nineteenth century, with its allusions to Greek and Roman architecture, greatly enhanced the appeal of white, highly polished stone, and a network of quarries and stonecutters, based primarily in Dorset, Pittsford, and Middlebury, developed rapidly (cat. 10). By 1810, Vermont's marble industry had already earned a national reputation.

Accounts of the Middlebury Marble Manufacturing Company, functioning as early as 1802 and incorporated in 1808, document the output from its large, two-story factory set on a marble ledge at the falls in the center of town. Carved, turned, and polished fireplace jambs, mantels, gravestones, sinks, door and window caps, columns, and custom architectural details were marketed in Boston, Albany, New York, Montreal, and even London, England, before 1810 (*Fig. 1.9*). The discovery and opening of a black marble quarry in Shoreham in 1826 advanced Vermont's marble interests to a unique position in American architecture and produced artistic gravestones unmatched in quality and quantity anywhere in the nation.[33] In the decades to come, the marble operations in Vermont reached their stride and became a national industry.

Endowed with rich iron ore deposits, Vermont also developed in the first decades of the nineteenth century an early lead in the iron casting industry. Decorative parlor stoves were manufactured in the state as early as the 1810s, and over the next 20 years stovemaking developed

Fig. 1.9 Turned marble columns. 1829. *Eben Judd House* (now the Sheldon Museum), Middlebury.

into a flourishing industry with more than a dozen manufacturers located in towns as widely scattered as Bennington, Poultney, Woodstock, Brandon, and Montpelier (cat. 11). The most prolific manufacturer of cast iron stoves was Isaac Tyson, whose Windsor and Plymouth Ascutney Iron Company commenced production at Tyson's Plymouth furnace in 1837. At its peak during the early 1840s, Tyson's company employed 175 men in the smelting of pig iron, cast iron stoves, holloware, machinery parts, and water pipes, all of which were marketed throughout New England.[34] Isaac Tyson was not without his competitors, however, and after 1826 the Wainwright brothers of Middlebury began manufacturing decorative parlor stoves of remarkable sophistication.[35]

Like its architecture and perhaps more than any other field of the decorative and fine arts, Vermont's furniture in the early nineteenth century reflected a surprisingly rich cultural life in the young state. But as was the case with architecture, natural resources and cultural values helped shape the way Vermont furniture looked and how it functioned in the state's new homes. Abundant timber resources (which became seriously depleted as the century progressed) and the availability of woods like basswood and exotic cuts of maple imparted a special quality to Vermont furniture that distinguished it from the work of other states and regions.

Vermont's earliest cabinetmakers were generalists. They built houses, repaired and maintained barns and out-buildings, and produced the chests, chairs, and tables used in Vermont homes. Before 1800, Vermont furniture makers were invariably farmers as well, liberally dispersed throughout the state's towns and districts. As resources and manufacturing became increasingly concentrated in major trading centers like Rutland and Windsor, cabinetmaking became established as a specialty, and families who craved and could afford stylish cabinetwork no longer had to bring it with them or import it from cities such as Hartford, Connecticut.[36]

The economy of furniture making in Vermont changed dramatically between 1800 and 1810, as city-trained cabinet- and chairmakers flooded into Vermont to take advantage of the building boom then underway. Small towns like Norwich could support single, talented cabinetmakers such as George Stedman, who was capable of producing work as pretentious in frontier Vermont as bombé chests of drawers (cat. 20), but nearby Windsor emerged as a leading cabinetmaking center, supporting a cluster of competing cabinetmakers and clockmakers capable of work equal to the best available outside Boston or New York. Julius Barnard, one of the most prominent of Windsor's early cabinetmakers, served as a journeyman cabinetmaker in New York before opening a shop in his native Northampton, Massachusetts. By 1805, Barnard was operating out of a brick workshop in Windsor's commercial district, employing "workmen at each of the different branches" of the trade, including carriage and wagon making (cat. 13). He advertised twenty-five types of high-end cabinetwork including sideboards, secretaries and bookcases, ladies' writing desks, card tables, sofas, lolling chairs, Windsor chairs, and high-post bedsteads.[37] Specialists and entrepreneurs like Barnard serviced clientele from throughout the county, on both sides of the Connecticut River, and beyond, including Montreal.

For every cabinetmaker who advertised in the newspapers and operated a shop in the commercial district of one of Vermont's large towns, dozens—perhaps hundreds—of others worked out of their homes, supplying goods and services to neighbors and families and never advertising at all. Furniture makers such as Asa C. Loomis of Shaftsbury (cat. 7), George Stedman of Norwich, Norman Jones of East Hubbardton, and Dexter Durby of Bridport were far more numerous than their urban counterparts and, for the most part, their work better reflects the qualities that distinguished Vermont furniture and gave it its regional character: an extravagant use of local woods, caricatured decorative motifs, and a tendency toward practical economy in determining the function and use of furniture forms.[38]

All in all, Vermont's prospects in 1840, while perhaps not as bright as Vermonters would have hoped, invited optimism. Nothing excited them more than the railroads being planned and built in southern New England. Here at last was an opportunity for the state to be linked to the great commercial centers of the Atlantic seaboard and the emerging markets of the westward-moving frontier. Indeed, Vermonters believed they were poised on the threshold of a great new era.

The Myths of Progress

The myth that Vermont was somehow a promised land for the young, the ambitious, and the restless died in the years between the depression of 1837 and 1850. At mid-century, Vermont's population stood at 314,120, barely 22,000 higher than it had been a decade earlier. While the nation's rate of growth per decade topped 35 percent, Vermont's was a mere 7.6 percent.[39] For complex reasons, an entire century would pass before Vermont regained its allure and began attracting immigrants in any numbers, and by then the state's image and the world's circumstances would be sufficiently changed that the backwaters in which Vermont drifted were appealing.

The reasons for the decline are numerous and intertwined with other myths, but it is critical to remember that the myths of promised lands belong to frontiers, and by the 1840s, Vermont was no longer a frontier. It was even by then suffering from a shortage of available choice lands, and it was competing with a new frontier in the west. Very simply, in a nation where wealth still depended largely on land ownership, Vermont had little to offer immigrants after 1820. The towns in northern Vermont that were settled between 1820 and 1850 were generally settled by Vermonters moving off marginal lands elsewhere in the state.[40] The landless, the unlucky, and the ambitious of southern New England now looked elsewhere, and what they saw were the vast rippling plains of the Midwest and the Erie Canal to take them there.

Vermonters struggling on hill farms looked hard, too, and often followed their gaze. "I can never be happy there in among so many mountains," eighteen-year-old Sally Rice wrote home to her parents in southern Vermont in 1839.[41] Like Sally, tens of thousands of Vermont sons and daughters fled Vermont and its hard living in the second quarter of the nineteenth century. They streamed not only west to new farms and upstart towns but south, as Sally Rice had, to the developing industrial cities of Massachusetts and Connecticut. They left in such numbers that by 1850, half again as many Vermonters were living beyond the state's borders as there were Vermonters at home.

The railroad was a disappointment from the start, although most of a century passed before most Vermont cities and towns could admit that. For decades, they clung hopefully to the myth that prosperity followed inevitably wherever the rail lines went. Most Vermont towns learned the painful falseness of that myth only through experience. However, from the moment the railroad arrived in 1848, it was a double-edged sword. Without question, Vermonters in the coming decades gained access to the major transcontinental routes and to all the markets that lay along them, but in the end the only truly successful lines in Vermont ran north and south, not east and west. Vermont became a state criss-crossed by spur lines, lines that ended abruptly on the eastern shores of Lake Champlain, and bankrupt lines that foundered for lack of sufficient local traffic.[42] Moreover, emigrating Vermonters quickly discovered the ease with which the railroad would take them to new places, and they took advantage of that ease in alarming numbers, while those Vermonters who stayed behind soon found the products of their local industry competing in their hometown stores with goods inexpensively brought by rail from distant places.

Vermonters clung tenaciously to the myth that sheep would be the saving grace of the state's economy until the railroads opened the west for settlement and development. Then that dream, too, went up like so much smoke. The western territories were much better suited to grazing than were Vermont's over-grazed hill farms. Moreover, the canals in Pennsylvania and Ohio and the railroad could inexpensively transport the wool from the west to the growing numbers of textile factories in southern New England, thus minimizing any economic advantage Vermont had envisioned because of its physical position within the union. By 1840, the sheep population was already on the decline in Vermont (cat. 28). By the time the nation's protective tariff on wool was lowered later that decade, destroying the state's last remaining advantage in the woolen market, all realistic hope was gone that sheep farming would be a primary part of Vermont's economy.

One bright spot was that the drastic economic readjustment necessitated by the shrinking numbers of sheep farms in Vermont did not completely destroy the industries that had been created in the state to service them. However, the growing number of factories consolidating wool processing—from carding and fulling to weaving—under one roof meant a corresponding decrease in the number of small carding and fulling mills scattered around the state in backhill towns like Guildhall, Berkshire and Lunenburg. Instead, manufacturing capital tended to concentrate in places where it already existed, in places such as Bennington, Colchester (Winooski), Middlebury, and Springfield, thus widening the abyss between the economies of the state's "poor" towns and its "rich" ones.[43]

Vermont in 1850

As Vermont stood poised in 1850 on the brink of the second half of the nineteenth century, its life was so unstable as to prevent Vermonters from seeing into the future with any accuracy. Sheep farming was dead, even if the last breaths remained to be drawn. Dairy farming was on the increase. In some counties, such as Franklin and Washington, dairy farming was already more important than sheep farming, but this was a difficult portent to interpret. Vermonters struggling on hill farms had little notion of how the population of the cities of the northeast would explode in the coming decades or of how the developing technologies of refrigeration and the railroad would make it possible for them to supply butter, cheese, and eventually milk to these distant, teeming urban masses.

Neither did Vermonters see themselves in 1850 as industrialists. Although the state had hundreds of small mills and dozens if not hundreds of inventors—some as talented as Bradford farmer James Wilson (inventor of the first commercial geographic globe in America) and Asahel Hubbard (inventor of the rotary water pump)—more than half the adult men in Vermont still worked in agriculture; a mere 14 percent in manufacturing (cat. 17,18). By 1900, the gap between the percentages would close to 15 percent, and by 1920, equal numbers of Vermonters would be employed in agriculture and manufacturing. But again, these trends were not clearly discernible in 1850.[44] The possibility that Vermont's economy would eventually become service-dominated never entered anyone's dreams.

Equally unimaginable to any Vermonter of 1850 was the idea that the state might become a center of higher education or white collar industry. The University of Vermont and Middlebury College were both struggling a full half century after admitting their first students. Norwich University, just thirty years old, had not yet found its final home. The Troy Conference Academy, one day to become Green Mountain College, was too young to evaluate. The state's best-known medical school, founded in 1827, would be closing its doors in a few years, a victim of factionalization within the faculty. The National Life Insurance Company of the United States, later the National Life Insurance Company of Vermont, had just opened for business.

In 1850, the largest cities in Vermont, in order, were Burlington, Bennington, Brattleboro, Rutland, and St. Albans, but the populations of all five cities taken together accounted for a mere six percent of the state's population. The concept of urban areas in Vermont was too far-fetched in a state where Burlington, the largest city, had a population of 6,110, and where of the next four cities in rank, all were half the size that Middlebury is today.[45]

Vermonters in 1850 were just awakening to an interpretation of their pastoral landscape that contemporary theories of romanticism made popular and therefore marketable. After all, it was still within older Vermonters' lifetimes that the Rev. Nathan Perkins had come north to

Vermont from Hartford, Connecticut, and observed " . . . ye Wilderness, ye people with nothing to eat, — to drink, — or to wear, . . . I think how strange! . . . Sleep quietly amid flees — bedbugs — dirt and raggs."[46] Within the next decade, as railroad lines facilitated the travel of the new urban tourists, large resort hotels would be constructed in Manchester, Clarendon Springs, Middletown Springs, Panton, Brunswick, and Alburg Springs (all sites of mineral springs and earlier, small hotels), but it was too early in 1850 to envision what role either railroads or tourism would one day play in Vermont.[47]

Romanticism also played a part in the continuing myths about Vermont's first inhabitants. As European settlement continued apace in Vermont through the last decades of the eighteenth and first half of the nineteenth century, the land was increasingly unable to provide the Abenakis with their traditional way of life. Their tribal communities splintered into small units, sometimes no larger than a single extended family, and became nomadic or lived on the periphery of white communities in places as widely scattered as Salisbury, Vergennes, Milton, Swanton, Newbury, and Braintree.[48] Unable to hunt or trap or otherwise practice the self-sufficient way of life that had sustained them for thousands of years, they were unavoidably drawn into the culture of the people who had taken over their homeland. Although many of them privately preserved the customs and oral traditions of their tribe, they outwardly became laborers, farmers, hired hands, guides, and tradesmen. They also developed an extensive trade in utility baskets with the settlers that opened the way for them to begin marketing native baskets to the growing numbers of tourists in the decades to come. Each step they took to make themselves less visible to their white neighbors fitted the sentiment of the times that "the disappearance of the Indians [was] a tragic, romantic, but ultimately desirable thing."[49] In time, even such an astute and distinguished observer of the state as Dorothy Canfield Fisher would declare confidently that resident Native Americans in Vermont had never existed.

In short, Vermont in 1850 existed in a twilight state, neither sheep nor cow country, neither cow nor manufacturing country, neither frontier nor wholly domesticated. In the gray light of uncertainty of these years, many Vermonters departed for places, both urban and westward, where the future was brighter and more clearly visible. The highly respected Vermont writer Dorothy Canfield Fisher says that this is when her own godfather, then a young boy, left Vermont with his family for Kansas. He grew into adulthood there and became a prosperous attorney in Kansas, where he "earned every year of his life an income seven or eight times the salary of the Governor of Vermont . . . ," she wrote. "But he never got over the feeling that he was in essence a Vermonter." In his old age, according to Fisher, her godfather still dreamed of Vermont. He would frequently remark that, "What ought to be done with the Old State is to turn it into a National Park of a new kind — keep it just as it is, with Vermonters managing just as they do — so the rest of the country could come in to see how their grandparents lived."[50]

In 1850, that remark would have struck Vermonters as absurd. Hard living in a hard place left no room for nostalgia. And yet great numbers of those who left in the nineteenth century carried away something of Vermont with them, some qualities of character that were perhaps distinctive of the state and the people who had settled it. If they took nothing else, they took the names of Brandon, Castleton, Crown Point, Montpelier, Vergennes, Winooski, and even Green Mountain and Vermont, and scattered them throughout the upper Midwest in states like Ohio, Illinois, Michigan, and Wisconsin, and even as far away as North and South Dakota.[51]

But those who stayed behind may have lived more interesting and varied lives than we tend to imagine for them if we consider only Vermont's economy. Certainly, today's typically over-crowded house museums imply that Vermonters of the early nineteenth century had more abundant material possessions than estate inventories indicate they did. However, Vermont in the first half of the nineteenth century was a richer place ethnically than its often whitewashed history suggests. In 1850, the number of Native Americans in the state was quietly on the increase as refugees from Plains tribes, displaced by the relentless advance of western settlements, emigrated east. In addition, nearly 10 percent of the state's residents were Irish or French Canadian. These new immigrants were arriving in increasing numbers, refugees from over-crowding and famine abroad and open rebellion to the north, to work in Vermont's emerging industries. They arrived with new languages and new customs and without the cultural condi-tioning that homogenizes the origins of most modern Vermont immigrants. Soon to be followed by Scots and Italians, they settled in Vermont's small cities and lived apart from but under the careful scrutiny of the state's established Anglo residents, and they constituted a sizable enough part of the population to be alarming to the old settlers.

Moreover, the state enjoyed a lively political life. Although the fervent Anti-Masonry of the 1830s had abated, temperance debate had reached such a fever pitch in Vermont by 1850 that the state was on the verge of enacting a prohibition law which would drop the bottom out of the lively liquor business in the state. The Anti-Slavery Society was also unusually active in Vermont, where families such as Rowland Robinson's and Middlebury College President Ezra Brainerd's risked their lives and security by working on the Underground Railroad. It is true the state could claim only 674 free blacks among its population in 1850, but it is also true that the number fell over the next 120 years.

Vermont proved to be a particularly fertile place for religion, perhaps because the land seemed to resist so stubbornly all other forms of cultivation. Congregationalists, Free Will Baptists, Methodists, Universalists, Quakers, even Jews and Roman Catholics and little-known sects such as the Dorrilites, engaged the minds and hearts of Vermonters in competitive soul-saving throughout these early decades. Brigham Young and Joseph Smith, founders of the Mormon Church, were born in Vermont during these years. Even Utopians, such as John Humphrey Noyes, took advantage of Vermonters' traditional tolerance toward free-thinkers to build a community in Putney in 1838, until his preaching on the acceptability of polygamy motivated his neighbors to relocate him to New York.[52]

The legacy of these intense religious rivalries is a powerful and moving architectural heritage in Vermont. Consider East Poultney, where the Baptists in 1805 commissioned one of the most extravagant meetinghouses in the state as a last and spiteful step in a feud with the local Congre-gational Society. The differences stretched back a full decade to 1795, when the Con-gregationalists of East Poultney decided they could no longer share a meetinghouse with the Baptists of East Poultney and went off to worship with the neighboring Baptists in Middletown Springs. An attempt at reconciliation was made following the departure of the "town's" Congre-gational minister, but a surprise electoral victory placed the Baptists in a position to appoint one of their own as the new town minister. In 1802, the Congregationalists, presumably weary of the commute, erected in East Poultney a meetinghouse (demolished in 1958) far larger and more impressive than that from which they had withdrawn. The Baptists were not to be outdone. The local society budgeted the godly sum of $6000 before contracting with Elisha Scott, a young Connecticut-trained architect, to build one of Vermont's most noteworthy architectural trea-sures.[53] Within the next 25 years, East Poultney had a settlement of Jews and a society of Episcopalians who were themselves planning a new meetinghouse. By 1840, in a community that contained only 60 houses, stylish meetinghouses in three denominations faced each other across a village common (*Fig. 1.10*).[54]

Fig. 1.10 Anonymous. *View of East Poultney. c. 1860.* Contemporary print from original glass negative. Private Collection.

Ironically, Vermont's village greens today convey a serenity and timeless pastoralism that is often in contradiction to the competitive and politically charged processes by which they evolved as church societies, town leaders, and even towns themselves struggled for local dominance. If we could speak to the Vermonters of 1850 and tell them of this modern image, they would probably laugh at our naiveté. Nevertheless, the myth that the whitewashed Vermont townscape bespeaks a quieter, less tumultuous time, draws tourists by the millions each year. If we mentioned that to those early Vermonters and waited for the numbers to sink in, they would probably fall down laughing. But then—unless it's just another myth—Vermonters have always enjoyed a good joke.

Nancy Price Graff
William Hosley

Notes

1. Charles T. Morrissey, *Vermont: A Bicentennial History* (New York: W. W. Norton & Co., Inc.; Nashville: American Association for State and Local History, 1981), p. 61.

2. Ethan Allen, *A Narrative of Colonel Ethan Allen's Captivity, Containing His Voyages & Travels* (1930; reprint ed., "Introduction" by John W. Krueger, Rutland, Vt.: Vermont Heritage Press for the Vermont Statehood Bicentennial Commission, 1988), pp. v–vi.

3. Quoted in Jack McKnight, "Ethan Allen, Philosopher," *Vermont Life*, 45, No. 2 (Winter 1990), p. 26.

4. Paul Gillies. Letter to Vermont newspapers. 13 Dec. 1990.

5. Bruce Catton, *Waiting for the Morning Train: An American Boyhood* (Garden City, N.Y.: Doubleday & Co., 1972), p. 229.

6. Peter S. Jennison, *Roadside History of Vermont* (Missoula, Montana: Mountain Press Publishing Company, 1989), p. 2.

7. Harold Meeks, *Time and Change in Vermont: A Human Geography* (Chester, Ct.: The Globe Pequot Press, 1986), pp. 1–6.

8. Gordon Day, "Western Abenaki," *The Handbook of North American Indians*. ed., Bruce Trigger (Washington, D.C.: Smithsonian Institution, 1978), p. 78.

9. John Moody, "The Native American Legacy," in *Always in Season: Folk Art and Traditional Culture in Vermont*. ed. Jane C. Beck (Montpelier, Vt.: Vermont Council on the Arts, 1982), pp. 54–59.

10. Colin Calloway, "Surviving the Dark Ages: Abenakis During the Contact Period," *Vermont History*, 58, No. 2 (Spring 1990), p. 76.

11. Meeks, *Time and Change*, p. 15.

12. Meeks, *Time and Change*, p. 16.

13. Jennison, *Roadside History*, p. 11.

14. Richard Carlson quoted in Morrissey, *Bicentennial History*, p. 81.

15. Morrissey, *Bicentennial History*, pp. 107–108.

16. John A. Graham, *A descriptive sketch of the present state of Vermont* (1797; reprint ed., Bennington, Vt.: Vermont Heritage Press, 1987) p. 52.

17. Daniel J. Boorstin, *The Americans: The National Experience* (New York: Random House, 1965), pp. 115–123.

18. Samuel Swift, *History of the Town of Middlebury* (Middlebury, Vt.: A. H. Copeland, 1859), pp. 167, 190, 283–285.

19. Will, Ebenezer Crafts, June 4, 1810, Newport District Probate Court Records, Vol. 1, pp. 200–204.

20. Christine Ermenc and William Hosley, Jr., "Household Furnishings and Domestic Economy on the Vermont Frontier," (Unpublished ms., Ethan Allen Homestead Trust, 1985). The estates inventoried from the Manchester district ranged in date from 1774–1789; in Marlboro, 1781–1789; and in Chittenden, 1796–1803. A few estates from the Westminster and Bennington districts were also sampled between 1778–1786. This manuscript cites each of the inventories sampled and provides almost forty pages of analysis.

21. Ermenc and Hosley, "Household Furnishings."

22. Morrissey, *Bicentennial History*, p. 14.

23. Seth Hubbell, *A Narrative of the Sufferings of Seth Hubbell & Family, in His Begginning a Settlement in the Town of Wolcott, in the State of Vermont* (1824; reprint ed., Bennington, Vt.: Vermont Heritage Press; Hyde Park, Vt.: Vermont Council on the Humanities and Public Issues, 1986), p. 3.

24. Hubbell, *A Narrative of the Sufferings*, p. 5.

25. Graham, *A descriptive sketch of Vermont*, p. 52.

26. H. Nicholas Muller, III, and Samuel Hand, eds. *In A State of Nature: Readings in Vermont History* (Montpelier, Vt.: Vermont Historical Society, 1982), p. 403.

27. Boorstin, *The National Experience*, p. 114.

28. William N. Hosley, Jr., "Architecture and Society of the Urban Frontier: Windsor, Vermont, in 1800," *The Bay and the River: 1600–1900* (Boston: The Dublin Seminar for New England Folklife and Boston University, 1982), pp. 75–76.

29. Morrissey, *Bicentennial History*, p. 110.

30. Morrissey, *Bicentennial History*, pp. 110–111.

31. Lewis Stillwell quoted in Morrissey, *Bicentennial History*, p. 112. Lewis Stillwell's study of the exodus of Vermonters, published as *Migration From Vermont* (Montpelier, Vt.: Vermont Historical Society, 1948), is one of the state's most important historical works.

32. Meeks, *Time and Change*, pp. 97–98.

33. Glenn M. Andres, "Middlebury's Marble Fireplaces," *Vermont History*, 55, No. 4 (Fall 1987), pp. 197–211. Middlebury specialized in the production of elaborate marble chimneypieces, priced as high as $150 for examples in black marble with turned and carved pillars. Prominent architects like Charles Bulfinch, Ammi B. Young, and Town and Davis included Middlebury marble fireplaces in their designs, and examples attributed to Middlebury have been found as far away as Milledgeville, Georgia (Winterthur Museum's "Empire Dining Room"). Black marble columns from Vermont were installed on expensive Empire-style pier tables by city cabinetmakers.

34. Sylvia Bugbee, "The Tyson Iron Company Papers, 1783–(1835–1868)–1916, *Vermont History*, 58, No. 3 (Summer 1990), pp. 199–201.

35. Swift, *History of Middlebury*, p. 338. Although the Wainwrights opened their furnace about 1814, it was destroyed by fire in 1826 and subsequently rebuilt and enlarged. Wainwright stoves in the collections of the Sheldon Museum, Middlebury, and the Chimney Point Historic Site, testify to the artistic merits of Wainwright's products, while suggesting, on stylistic grounds, a date after the furnace was rebuilt in 1826.

36. *Spooner's Vermont Journal* (Windsor), March 10, 1794, contains an advertisement by the cabinetmaking partnership of Kneeland and Adams, addressed to "the Gentlemen & Ladies of Windsor . . . that they can furnish them with every kind of Cabinet Work, made in the newest and most approved fashions from Europe . . . cased and delivered at the water side Hartford."

37. William N. Hosley, Jr., "Vermont Furniture, 1790–1830," in *New England Furniture, Old-Time New England*, 72, No. 259 (Boston: Society for the Preservation

of New England Antiquities, 1987), pp. 247–248. In addition to Barnard, the cabinetmaking partnership of Pomeroy and Hedge, Rufus Norton, and the chairmaker John Wilder, each advertised as Windsor furniture makers before 1810. Many other furniture makers, too small to advertise, also worked in the local industry.

38. Although hundreds of furniture makers worked in Vermont prior to 1840, very few of those operating outside the major centers can be associated with documented work. Notable exceptions include a bureau by Dexter Durby of Bridport, dated 1836 (Sheldon Museum, Middlebury); chairs and cabinetwork made by Prosper Millington of Shaftsbury (Shaftsbury Historical Society); a card table made and signed about 1820, by Royal H. Gould of Chester (Art Institute of Chicago); and a remarkable tambour desk signed by Jonathan Tilson of Pittsford in 1811 (Private collection). See Hosley, "Vermont Furniture," pp. 258, 264, and 274–275.

39. Meeks, *Time and Change*, p. 104.

40. Meeks, *Time and Change*, pp. 89– 91.

41. Sally Rice quoted in Morrissey, *Bicentennial History*, p. 122.

42. Meeks, *Time and Change*, pp. 107–108.

43. Meeks, *Time and Change*, pp. 100–103.

44. Meeks, *Time and Change*, p. 300.

45. Muller and Hand, *In a State of Nature*, p. 403.

46. Reverend Nathan Perkins, *A Narrative of a Tour through the State of Vermont from April 27 to June 12, 1789* (1789; reprint ed., Woodstock, Vt.: The Elm Tree Press, 1930), pp. 20–21.

47. Meeks, *Time and Change*, pp. 147–148.

48. Moody, "Native American Legacy," pp. 54–64.

49. Calloway, "Dark Ages," p. 76.

50. Workers of the Federal Writers' Project of the Works Progress Administration for the State of Vermont, *Vermont: A Guide to the Green Mountain State* (Boston: Houghton Mifflin Company, 1937), p. 3.

51. Meeks, *Time and Change*, p. 90.

52. Morrissey, *Bicentennial History*, pp. 112–113.

53. Reverend John Goadby, *Remembrances of Past Years: A Discourse Delivered at the Baptist Meeting House, Poultney, Vermont, on the Fiftieth Anniversary of the organization of the Church, April 8, 1852* (Rutland, Vt.: Tuttle's Book & Job Office, 1852), p. 35.

54. Zadock Thompson, *History of Vermont, Natural, Civil and Statistical* (Burlington, Vt.: Chauncey Goodrich, 1842), p. 35. A Jewish burying ground in Poultney contains stones dating from the 1830s.

Arcadia in New England:
Divergent Visions of a Changing Vermont, 1850–1920

THE MODERN POPULAR IMAGE of Vermont is familiar to all who know the state. Residents and outsiders alike can recite the slogans, bumper stickers, and promotional phrases — "Vermont is a special world;" "Vermont is what America was;" "Vermont is a state of mind" — that proclaim the virtues of the beauty, heritage, and lifestyle of the Green Mountain State. In logical terms the inadequacies of such a uniformly idyllic vision of any place are readily apparent; yet the widespread perception remains that Vermont really is an unspoiled oasis free of most of the problems of an urbanized, industrialized, polluted twentieth-century America. Perhaps it is the cumulative effect of the unceasing promotional efforts of the state's tourist industry; perhaps it is some fluid combination of idealization and the undeniable reality of Vermont's many positive features; or perhaps it is simply that many people find comfort in the romantic belief that there is some place, somewhere, that offers a haven from the problems of modern society. For whatever reason, most individuals who think of Vermont at all agree with the notion that the state is indeed "a special world."

A surprising number of people, however, are unaware that the roots of Vermont's positive image go back well over 100 years. The drive to promote the state as a land that has avoided the nation's rapid population growth, industrial development, and hectic "modernization" started long before the arrival of *Vermont Life*, ski weekends, time-sharing condominiums, and interstate highways. It took nearly three-quarters of a century—from the beginning of Vermont's railroad era in the 1850s to the advent of automobiles in the 1920s as a comfortable, practical way for urbanites to reach the Green Mountains—to lay the foundation of today's vision of Vermont. The great waves of tourists and new residents who have flocked to Vermont since World War II had their predecessors in the large numbers of outsiders who came in the Victorian and Edwardian eras; and although the details have changed, many of the attractions and reasons behind this long-running "flatlander invasion" have remained the same over the passing decades. The "selling" of Vermont's attractions, which in this bicentennial year occupies the talents of innumerable advertising agencies, state government bureaucrats, freelance writers, and "destination resort" employees, was already a burgeoning statewide industry when the state celebrated its one-hundredth anniversary in 1891. In short, the "Vermont dream," complete with hard-working promoters and outsiders eager to experience "Arcadia in New England," has been a part of the Green Mountain scene for a long, long time.

Yet although today's Vermonters and their forebears might well agree on the accuracy of the state's pastoral, unhurried image, reactions to the implications of that image and to the conditions it describes have changed dramatically. In the late twentieth century, most Vermonters, whether natives or newcomers, are delighted that the state remains relatively rural, uncrowded, undeveloped, and out of step with the pace of the modern American technocracy. Conditioned as we are today to regard those as positive characteristics, it is hard to imagine that they were a source of considerable anxiety and worry for the majority of Vermonters between 1850 and 1920. If outsiders saw the state as a near-mythic Arcadia in those decades, most insiders perceived it as a place of economic stagnation, where the best young people were leaving to pursue better opportunities and brighter prospects elsewhere and where the nation's abundant prosperity and growth were little in evidence.

Today we have lost touch with the perspective that Vermont's lack of change, widely regarded as a plus now, equalled lack of progress and hope then, but in looking back at the middle period of Vermont's 200 years of statehood, we must keep in mind that for nearly a century that same lack of change was a major factor in Vermonters' attitudes toward their state's present and their hopes for its future. Depending on the individual, "Arcadia in New England" could have meant two very different things in Vermont between 1850 and 1920.

Vermont and the New Middle Class

The "selling of Vermont" in the modern sense of promoting the state as a destination for urban vacationers and seasonal visitors began in earnest just before the Civil War. The extension of southern New England railroad systems north to the Green Mountains in the 1850s coincided with the emergence of a large new American middle class that had the money and the time to go on holidays and pleasure trips. Tourism, which had little economic effect on early nineteenth-century Vermont, now had the potential to bring new vitality to the state. The nation's social and financial elite would summer at Saratoga and Newport rather than in Vermont, but the recreational patronage of the northern middle class was available to the rural states and regions that could best publicize their attractions. While Green Mountain promoters and entrepreneurs found keen competition in the promotional campaigns of their counterparts in the Adirondacks, the Berkshires, the Catskills, and the White Mountains, they held their own. By the end of the nineteenth century, Vermont's status as a popular tourist and vacation area was secure.[1]

Given the intensity of the struggle for tourist dollars, imagination, ingenuity, and an ability to capitalize on changes in public taste were required to lure outsiders to Vermont between 1850 and 1920. During the early decades of the railroad era, when mineral-springs hotels and hydropathic spas were quite popular, establishments at Clarendon, Brattleboro, Woodstock, Brunswick, and a dozen other communities touted the medicinal value of water from Vermont mountain springs. According to the publicity, drinking sufficient amounts of "highly efficacious" Vermont water would cure rheumatism, diabetes, syphilis, cancer, and virtually any other human ailment. For a time Victorian Americans responded favorably, filling hotels like the Montvert at Middletown Springs and the Missisquoi House at Alburg to enjoy the benefits of large daily doses of what were often bad-tasting and foul-smelling local mineral waters. Only a few of the Victorian Vermont spas, most notably the Clarendon Springs Hotel (*Fig. 2.1*), flourished for more than a decade or two, but even the temporary success of the state's mineral-springs towns was an encouraging and instructive sign: By reacting to the fads and moods of the American middle class, Vermonters could attract significant numbers of cash-paying visitors to their communities.[2]

Many of Vermont's late-nineteenth and early twentieth-century hotel and resort owners demonstrated a flair for this game of giving the public what it wanted. The socially conscious could enjoy concerts, dances, and the company of both cosmopolitan fellow guests and quaintly entertaining locals; there were train excursions, steamboat cruises, well-groomed paths for horseback riding, and trails for hikers, as well as broad piazzas, billiards rooms, "modern conveniences," recent issues of big-city newspapers and magazines, and good cigars for guests who preferred more sedentary pursuits. Moreover, convenient travel connections made getting to and from any Vermont hotel a veritable breeze; menus offered the best home-cooked country

Fig. 2.1 James Hope. *View of Clarendon Springs, Vermont.* 1853. Oil on canvas. Courtesy, The Currier Gallery of Art, Manchester, New Hampshire.

foods and the latest *haute cuisine*; and accommodations at a single establishment could be either invigoratingly rustic or up to the standards of the most luxurious urban hotels. Even the Vermont landscape was adaptable: If a prospective tourist wanted grand and sublime vistas, the Green Mountains were rugged peaks; if the goal was a quiet sojourn in the country rather than an adventure in the untamed wilderness, then God had smoothed over Vermont's landscape to make it more pastoral and inviting than that of northern New York or New Hampshire. There was more fiction than fact in such promises as "visitors to Lake St. Catherine invariably carry back with them blood that pulsates with renewed vigor, a store of health that defies insidious illness, and a joy of mere living hitherto unknown;" nonetheless, Vermont's genuine natural attractions helped the owners of Newport's Memphremagog House, Stowe's Mount Mansfield Hotel (*Fig. 2.2*), Manchester's Equinox Hotel, and dozens of other Green Mountain tourist establishments meet the expectations of the vacationers who came to Vermont after 1850.[3]

Keeping up with the latest national trends in recreation was equally crucial to Vermont's relative success in the competition for tourist dollars in the Victorian and Edwardian decades. In the 1860s, Vermont hotel owners turned their grounds into croquet lawns; in the 1880s local

Fig. 2.2 Mount Mansfield Hotel. Stowe, Vt. c. 1865. Lithograph. Courtesy, Robert Hull Fleming Museum, University of Vermont.

Green Mountain bicycle clubs held well-attended summer meets and tournaments; and by the turn of the century guests at the more successful Vermont resorts could while away the hours playing golf and tennis. The Lake Champlain Yacht Club, founded in 1887, offered well-to-do vacationers the opportunity to enjoy the lake in the company of "gentlemen of intelligence, public spirit and standing."[4] As America's interest in sports and recreation increased, so did the variety of Vermont's offerings. Beginning in the 1880s, such Vermont towns as Burlington, Rutland, St. Johnsbury, and Montpelier even succeeded in drawing visitors to winter carnivals that featured snowshoeing, toboggan rides, skating, ice boating, and hockey games (*Fig. 2.3*).[5] By 1910, when a state Bureau of Publicity pamphlet declared Vermont "the Playground of the Continent," the drive to promote the state as a year-round recreation paradise was well under way.[6]

Hunting and fishing, almost unknown as tourist activities in Vermont prior to the Civil War but increasingly popular in the United States after 1865, became important factors in the outdoor life that brought outsiders to the Green Mountains. As the potential economic benefits of luring sportsmen to Vermont became clear, the state Legislature authorized the restocking of Vermont's badly depleted waterways and forests. Establishment of the position of a full-time

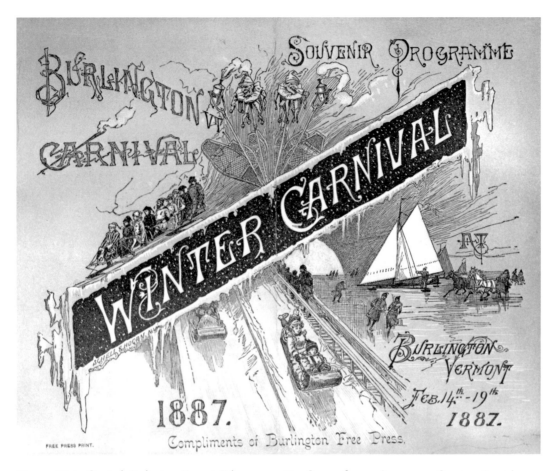

Fig. 2.3 *Winter Carnival, Burlington, Vermont*. Feb. 14–19, 1887. Cover of souvenir program. Courtesy, Special Collections, University of Vermont.

Fish and Game Commissioner in 1904 gave additional direction to the state's programs. In the private sector, local clubs, many of them consisting largely of out-of-state summer residents, established their own wildlife preserves, while the Vermont Fish and Game League and other statewide organizations worked energetically to promote hunting and fishing and to publicize the need for sound wildlife management policies. Such widely read authors as William H. H. "Adirondack" Murray and Rowland E. Robinson popularized Vermont as a destination for outdoorsmen. Charles F. Orvis of Manchester (cat. 43) and Thomas H. Chubb of Post Mills led the contingent of entrepreneurs ready to supply equipment or lodging to the growing numbers who came to the Green Mountains to enjoy the use of rod and gun.[7] The results were impressive, and when Charles R. Cummings surveyed "Our Fish and Game Asset" in 1916, he could accurately report that Vermont had laid a solid foundation for the state's twentieth-century efforts to develop "profitable sources of income from flesh and fowl."[8]

As the railroad era progressed and most of Vermont remained rural in an increasingly urban and industrialized nation, nostalgia also became a significant element in the state's attempts to draw seasonal visitors. Unable to secure the technology, factories, growth, and change evident elsewhere, many small Vermont towns gradually began out of necessity to capitalize on the marketability of appearing old-fashioned, backward, and quaint. Some communities were quite successful, especially at inducing nostalgic natives who had moved away to return to their home towns for a week or two, spend some money, and perhaps put up the funds for a new town hall, library, Civil War monument, or other local improvement. Emigrant Vermonters in distant cities were sometimes sufficiently moved by the promotions and their own rosy reminiscences to organize "Vermont Clubs" (*Fig. 2.4*). In 1901 the state stepped in to help expand this early version of the "Come Home to Vermont" theme by creating an official Old Home Week and promoting it as a statewide celebration. An impressive success in its debut that year, Old Home

Fig. 2.4 Flag. Sons of Vermont, Boston chapter. c. 1900. Courtesy, Vermont Historical Society, Montpelier.

Week and its many local variations became regular features of the Green Mountain summer scene in the years that followed.[9] Not until after World War II would most Vermonters come to view their state's relative absence of change and "progress" as a blessing; in the meantime they would make the best of what the majority regarded as a bad situation.

The Selling of Vermont

Vermonters developed an impressive variety of ways to let outsiders know about the state's many attractions between 1850 and 1920. Eager to increase passenger traffic and business at the hotels they owned, Vermont's railroads turned out dozens of promotional brochures, pamphlets, and broadsides aimed at the tourist market. Illustrated booklets describing the charms of particular resorts also became quite common, as did publicity pieces on individual lakes, towns, and counties. In the 1890s the State Board of Agriculture began to issue pamphlets such as *A List of Desirable Farms and Summer Homes in Vermont* and *Resources and Attractions of Vermont*.[10] In 1911 the legislature established the state's first Bureau of Publicity in response to the perceived need to increase the quality and quantity of information that reached prospective visitors. *The Vermonter*, a popular monthly magazine that Charles S. Forbes of St. Albans founded in 1895, published a steady stream of unremittingly enthusiastic articles about the state and its charms.[11] Combined with occasional Vermont stories in metropolitan magazines and newspapers, the work of these Green Mountain writers and unabashed boosters deluged American readers with tourist-oriented publicity and the myth of the state's laconic, plain-spoken inhabitants (*Fig. 2.5*).

Fig. 2.5 Rowland E. Robinson. *"Kid Glove Farm Assistant."* c. 1875. Illustration from unidentified journal. Courtesy, Rokeby, Ferrisburgh.

KID-GLOVE FARM ASSISTANT.

"I AM informed, Sir, that you desire to obtain the assistance of an experienced person in your agricultural labors : if so, I am willing to engage for that purpose for a term of months."

Farmer.—"Law no ! I only want to hire a man to work on the farm !''

In addition to the printed word, pictures played a major role in creating the proper image for Vermont during these decades. Vermont artists such as Charles L. Heyde of Burlington (cat. 26), James Hope of Castleton, Thomas Waterman Wood of Montpelier (cat. 34.1), Frank Childs of Clarendon, and H. Custer Ingham of Vergennes, as well as some of their leading American counterparts—Frederick E. Church, Asher B. Durand, Martin J. Heade, Thomas Moran, Jerome Thompson (cat. 27)—turned out paintings of a pastoral, idealized rural Vermont free of dilapidated hill farms or impoverished villages. Chromolithographed reproductions of the Vermont work of these and other painters made artistic representations of the Green Mountains widely available at low prices. Also popular during this period were birds-eye views, elevated-perspective prints which depicted more than forty pristine, prosperous, and inviting Vermont cities and towns between 1850 and 1900 (cat. 34).[12] Photography, the emerging pictorial technology of the age, came into play in the form of Vermont stereopticon views, postcards, snapshots, and magazine illustrations. The net effect of these and the other pictures of this period—lithographs of prize-winning Vermont sheep and horses (cat. 28); illustrated broadsides advertising Vermont railroad and steamship lines; promotional chromolithographed pictures of Green Mountain factories, marble quarries, and hotels—was to fix the image of a beckoning Vermont in the mind of the American public.[13]

Challenges to Yankee Hegemony

While the state successfully aimed most of its publicity at prospective tourists and seasonal visitors, large numbers of more permanent newcomers also came to Vermont after 1850. The railroads, factories, and industries developing in Vermont's larger communities created non-agricultural employment, and successive waves of Irish, French-Canadian, European, and other immigrants arrived in search of jobs. Fairbanks Scale of St. Johnsbury (cat. 36), Estey Organ of Brattleboro (cat. 37), the Vermont Farm Machine Company of Bellows Falls (cat. 30), the textile mills of Winooski and Bennington, Lane Manufacturing of Montpelier, the Central Vermont and Vermont & Canada railroad yards at St. Albans, and dozens of other Vermont industrial employers attracted workers from the state's hill towns as well, but it was the influx of foreigners that changed the social structure of what had previously been a largely native-born, Yankee, Protestant state (cat. 39). The introduction of new perceptions of what Vermont should be, languages, religions, values, and traditions made the state considerably less homogeneous in 1920 than it had been in the 1850s. The Yankees managed to maintain political and social control for most of the period, but by its end such descendants of the newcomers as James Burke, an Irish-American blacksmith who became mayor of Burlington in 1903, had begun to assert themselves in both local and state government.[14]

Foreign immigrants made up an important part of the work force in Vermont's rapidly growing extractive industries during the railroad era as well. Crucial to the success of Vermont's urban manufacturers, the sweat of immigrant laborers also proved essential to the expansion of the state's stone and lumber production after the Civil War. Irish millhands ran Burlington's huge lakeside lumber yards, while French-Canadian loggers cut trees, burned charcoal, and made fortunes for Silas L. Griffith of Danby, the Beatty brothers of Essex County, and the state's other Victorian timber kings. Italian and Scottish stoneworkers (cat. 33) risked early deaths from silicosis to create beautiful works of art from Barre granite (*Fig. 2.6*). Welsh miners and quarrymen arrived to work in Orange County's copper mines and Rutland County's slate quarries (cat. 32). Marble baron Redfield Proctor imported carefully selected Swedes, Finns, and Italians

Fig. 2.6 Milne, Clarihew and Gray Quarry [Barre]. *c.* 1899. Courtesy, Aldrich Public Library, Barre.

for his Vermont Marble Company operations at Proctor and West Rutland (cat. 31). By 1900 more than 13 percent of Vermont's residents were foreign-born, adding considerable fresh energy, fluidity, and diversity to Green Mountain society as the nineteenth century gave way to the twentieth.[15]

A less obtrusive but still noteworthy element of social diversity in Vermont during these years came from the ongoing presence of the state's Native Americans. Forced off much of their ancestral land in northern Vermont, the Abenakis maintained strong ties to the Champlain Valley. Opting for a nonconfrontational style of interaction with their white neighbors, they quietly followed their traditional lifestyle (cat. 44, 45, 46) around loosely structured villages in Swanton and elsewhere in Franklin County (*Fig. 2.7*). In the eyes of most Victorian and Edwardian Vermonters, the Abenakis disappeared from the state; in reality, however, they remained and kept their own culture alive and vital. Their numbers in Vermont were relatively low—perhaps 1,000 to 2,000, depending on seasonal migration up and down the Champlain-Richelieu corridor—but throughout the late nineteenth and early twentieth centuries the Abenakis held onto both a strong sense of tribal identity and a tenacious belief that much of northern Vermont was Abenaki territory.[16]

Fig. 2.7 Abenaki camp, Highgate Springs. c. 1890–1900. Courtesy, Vermont Historical Society, Montpelier.

The Decline of Rural Vermont

For the newcomers, whether American middle-class tourists who came for seasonal visits or foreign-born workers who settled in the state as permanent immigrants, and for most of the non-Abenaki natives as well, the image Vermont projected between 1850 and 1920 was undeniably positive. Throughout the railroad era, as tourism, manufacturing, and the extractive industries brought economic growth and vitality to Burlington, St. Albans, Bennington, St. Johnsbury, Rutland, Brattleboro, Newport, Barre, Montpelier, and Proctor, they prospered.[17] During those decades, it was the enthusiastic, optimistic attitude of the towns fortunate enough to secure a share of this elusive success that dominated the publicity of the campaigns to "sell" Vermont. For some communities, the cheerful boosterism and promotion that attracted vacationers from outside Vermont were accurate reflections of local conditions. In those areas, "the Vermont dream" was both good salesmanship and a reasonable approximation of actual conditions in the Green Mountain State.

Yet for most Vermonters in the late nineteenth and early twentieth centuries the gap between the popular myth and harsh reality in the state was far too wide to foster any sense of satisfaction or hope. The growth and economic opportunity that seemed so prevalent outside the state were hard to find in the majority of Green Mountain communities in the years between 1850 and

1920. While the population of the United States was nearly quintupling in those seventy years, Vermont's rose by a mere 12 percent.

Even when change and development came to Vermont in this period, they were often mixed blessings: The railroad, for example, so eagerly awaited as the savior of Vermont's economy, brought in urban goods to compete with the products of local firms and wound up providing quick, cheap transportation out of the state for natives heading west or to the eastern seaboard cities. Devoted boosters like the Reverend Silas McKeen of Bradford might declare that "we have abundant cause to be thankful to God for giving us our home among these Green Mountains," but such sentiments became increasingly hard for Victorian Vermonters to accept.[18] As the perception of relative stagnation grew, the majority of Vermonters, especially those living outside the state's larger railroad, industrial, and commercial centers, came to agree with Zuar E. Jameson of Irasburg, who observed in 1872 that "Stillness and dullness and almost a mouldiness" were Vermont's predominant characteristics.[19]

The focal point of this dismal attitude was the apparent decline of Vermont's small towns and hill-farm communities after 1850. While Burlington, Rutland, and a handful of other places were growing and prospering, in part from an influx of small-town Vermonters seeking industrial jobs, more than half of the state's towns were watching their populations drop with each new decennial census. Declining populations, abandoned hill farms, and steadily shrinking local tax bases became the norm throughout most of Vermont. That rural New Hampshire and Maine were experiencing the same problems did nothing to make the situation seem more palatable; being part of a regional northern New England decline brought no comfort to small-town Vermonters. By 1900, the popular perception of rural Vermont's present and future was filled with frustration, pessimism, and despair (*Fig. 2.8*).[20]

To contemporary observers, the woes of most small Vermont towns were the direct result of two problems: The towns could neither keep native residents from leaving nor develop any local economic base other than agriculture. Viewed against the other careers and opportunities easily available elsewhere, life on a Green Mountain hill farm was not a popular option. To make matters worse, it seemed to the Yankees who remained in Vermont that the best and brightest young natives were the ones who were leaving. "Our young men, *our men of ability and enterprise*, have been and are constantly leaving us," mill-owner and farmer Albert Dwinell of Calais complained in 1874. "We who are left, are left to suffer loss, and feel the paralyzing effect of a virtue, a strength, a motive power, gone out from us."[21] At the same time, the small percentage of Vermont's Irish, French-Canadian, and East European newcomers who did settle in rural communities were unacceptable replacements to many small-town Yankees. In a typical Yankee comment of the day, Rowland E. Robinson, Vermont's most popular Victorian author, wrote of the state's French-Canadian immigrants, "The character of these people is not such as to inspire the highest hope for the future of Vermont if they should become the most numerous of its population."[22] The state considered ways to repopulate the hill towns with what Vermonters deemed more "desirable" immigrants, as with a quixotic 1890 program to place Swedish farmers in Weston and Wilmington, but these ideas proved impractical at best.[23] There was no ready solution to the problem, and throughout the railroad era the outlook for rural, agricultural Vermont remained dark and uncertain.

Fig. 2.8 Poor Farm, Manchester, Vermont. c. 1890. Courtesy, Special Collections, University of Vermont.

Vermont Agriculture Evolves

However, the nature of farming in Vermont did change considerably between 1850 and 1920. In the first half of the nineteenth century, the foundation of Green Mountain agriculture had been the Merino sheep industry and the wool that the state's 1.6 million Merinos produced. But inconsistent wool prices, increasing competition from the western states, fluctuations in the national protective tariff duties, and the rise of the railroad as speedy transportation for perishable products led most Vermont farmers after 1840 to switch to dairy farming (cat. 29).

By 1870 Vermont ranked first in New England in dairy production. At the turn of the century Vermont was shipping forty million pounds of butter, more than five million pounds of cheese, and 140 million gallons of milk to metropolitan markets annually. A major factor in the state's bucolic popular image, agriculture remained until well into the twentieth century the backbone of Vermont's economy, providing employment for far more people than the state's stone quarries, factories, railroads, and other industries.[24]

Yet despite agriculture's ongoing significance, relatively few Vermonters prospered at sheep or dairy farming during the railroad era. After the Civil War, most Green Mountain farmers found it necessary to diversify into the production of maple sugar, apples, firewood, potatoes, corn, wheat, Morgan horses, and a variety of other crops and livestock just to make a living. Vermont's expanding state government, the Patrons of Husbandry (better known simply as the Grange), and several dozen state and county farmers' organizations tried to help farmers and improve the quality of Green Mountain agriculture, but the results seldom matched Vermonters' needs or expectations. Even in the best of years, Vermont farming often consisted of a great deal of hard work for very little return. Many owners of marginal hill farms gave up and left small-town Vermont for better prospects in the cities or out West; the majority of those who remained found isolation, stony soil, uncertain incomes, and grinding toil far more real than the popular myth of the yeoman farmer.[25]

The problems of Vermont's farmers, the ongoing emigration from the rural communities, the abandoned hill-country acreage, and the general malaise of the state's small towns combined to foster a powerful sense of loss and despair in Vermont. The pervasive anxiety that resulted manifested itself in a variety of ways during the post-Civil War decades. A stream of magazine articles, newspaper editorials, and bureaucratic reports presented dark assessments of conditions in rural Vermont.[26] Many small-town Yankees maintained a cool and distant watch on the foreign immigrants who helped the industrial and commercial centers grow, noting with outspoken disapproval the unfamiliar ways the newcomers brought to Vermont. Some Vermonters sought solutions to their state's problems in reform movements, pouring emotion and energy into the crusades of the Woman's Christian Temperance Union, educational organizations and programs, local social-welfare societies and charities, and other campaigns against injustice, immorality, and social decay.[27] Even when reform was not forthcoming, the emphasis that many of these groups put on the need for a return to traditional values, old-fashioned Protestant Christianity, and a rejection of the sins of modern, urban America fit in well with rural Vermont's growing nostalgia for its supposed antebellum heyday. With the national example of prosperity through progress apparently unattainable, memories of a happier bygone era became an important source of comfort in many Green Mountain hamlets and villages.

As the socioeconomic gaps between Vermont's thriving and declining towns widened after 1865, the level of tension and polarization in state politics and government increased accordingly. At each session of the legislature, the rural communities used their large majorities in the one-town, one-vote House of Representatives to hinder legislative and public policy that did not suit their needs. Although the larger towns complained frequently about the hill-country's control of the legislature, their many suggestions for reapportionment of the House fell on deaf rural ears in the House chamber. Burlington might have had a booming economy and 20,000 residents in 1920, but in the Vermont House the mighty Queen City had the same single vote as such sparsely settled towns as Stannard, Landgrove, Brunswick, and Brookline. Notwithstanding their disproportionate influence on state government, Vermont's small have-not communities were unable to translate their numerical advantage into tangible economic and demographic gains. The search for answers to their woes continued.[28]

A century and more later it is easy to see the gloomy perspective many Vermonters adopted between 1850 and 1920 as an exaggerated reaction to the natural process of change then occurring throughout agrarian New England. As revisionist studies have detailed, the "winter of Vermont" was never a state-wide phenomenon, and in all but the most depressed communities prosperity did eventually return.[29] At the time, however, such objectivity and detachment were impossible for Vermonters who valued the idealized tradition of a prosperous agricultural heritage. Instead, many of the state's inhabitants became increasingly anxious about the perceived decay and deterioration of rural Vermont.

Widely accepted by the 1870s, this belief that much of the state was locked into a bleak "winter" of decline and stagnation remained a significant part of the collective Vermont psyche for more than half a century. The national economic boom of the Roaring Twenties would bring a temporary infusion of life to some parts of the Green Mountains, but the problems that followed in the Depression only served to reinforce the pessimism that by then was a tradition in small-town Vermont. By the time Vermont's state-wide recovery and growth began after World War II, the idea was unchallenged that the late nineteenth and early twentieth centuries had brought little more than half-a-dozen successive decades of hard times to the state's rural areas. Hope would replace gloom after 1950, but nostalgia for the railroad era would emerge in the hill country only after the passing of the generations that remembered the despair of "a virtue, a strength, a motive power, gone out from us."

Different Versions of the Vermont Dream

Which of these two visions of Vermont between 1850 and 1920 survives in 1991? For today's Vermonters, more than half of whom are transplants rather than natives, the emphasis is clearly on a positive image of that period in the state's heritage. In an ironic combination of perceptions, we still accept the idea that not much happened in Victorian and Edwardian Vermont, but we've rejected the tradition that most of what did happen was bad. What Vermonters of 1891 saw as serious worries, their successors of 1991 look back on with ignorant approval. Quiet country villages, abandoned hill farms that have reverted to forest, rural calm instead of urban growth—these and the other legacies of 1850–1920 that distinguish Vermont today from much of the rest of America are all important elements in the "special world" of the Green Mountain State. The problems of a century ago have become some of the most significant assets of modern Vermont.

Virtually all of the collectibles, pictorial images, antiques, and other reminders of the railroad era that have come down to us in 1991 serve as reinforcements of this favorable historical assessment. Few Vermonters today bother to read the bleak commentaries of Albert Dwinell and the others who detailed the hill-country's woes; instead, we collect, enjoy, and believe the memorabilia that conveys the opposite message. Estey organs, Howe and Fairbanks scales, Norton stoneware (cat. 35), and Orvis fishing rods are symbols of Yankee ingenuity and economic prosperity; railroad passes, lanterns, timetables, and ephemera recall the heydays of St. Albans, Rutland, White River Junction, and Island Pond; and the advertising brochures, pamphlets, and booklets of the early tourist industry tell us of attractions that seem irresistibly appealing. The Vermont paintings of Jerome Thompson, James Hope, Charles L. Heyde, and their many contemporaries depict a pastoral wonderland of alluring scenery and rural charm. The old birds-eye views, chromolithographs, photographs, and stereopticon views all present an image of a world of happiness and hope rather than of decay and decline. With little evidence of hard times apparent in any of this, and less room for it in the popular vision of the state's past, it is not surprising that we recall the years between 1850 and 1920 as an idyllic prelude to what we value most in the Vermont of today.

Yet it is worthwhile to remember in commemorating the bicentennial of Vermont's statehood that there was another sense of reality for many of those who lived in the Victorian and Edwardian decades. Historical hindsight, modern values, and the belief that "it all turned out well in the end" do not negate the feelings and impressions of four Green Mountain generations. In the state's hill towns the human cost of keeping Vermont "unspoiled" between 1850 and 1920 was considerable, and our appreciation and approval of the results should not blind us to that fact. While the optimism captured in the tourist publicity was a significant part of the Vermont experience during those decades, so too was the despair that Albert Dwinell expressed. If the evidence of that dichotomy is now obscure and overlooked, perhaps the bicentennial is an appropriate time to begin reexamining it. Celebration of the positive aspects of "Arcadia in New England" tells part of the story, but an understanding of the railroad era's hill-country perspective is a valuable reminder that in 1891 and in 1991, alike, there can be more than one version of the Vermont dream.

J. Kevin Graffagnino

Notes

1. Andrea Rebek, "The Selling of Vermont: From Agriculture to Tourism, 1860–1910," *Vermont History*, 44, No. 1 (Winter 1976), pp. 14–27; Louise Roomet, "Vermont as a Resort Area in the Nineteenth Century," *Vermont History*, 44, No. 1 (Winter 1976), pp. 1–13.

2. Harold A. Meeks, "Stagnant, Smelly, and Successful: Vermont's Mineral Springs," *Vermont History*, 47, No. 1 (Winter 1979), pp. 5–20; J. Kevin Graffagnino, *Vermont in the Victorian Age: Continuity and Change in the Green Mountain State, 1850–1900* (Rutland, Vt.: Vermont Heritage Press and Shelburne Museum, 1985), Chapter 1.

3. Quote from H. D. Gates, *Lake St. Catherine* (Poultney: Poultney Journal Press, [1908]), p. 1; Rebek, "The Selling of Vermont"; Roomet, "Vermont as a Resort Area"; Graffagnino, *Vermont in the Victorian Age*, Chapter 11; Max L. Powell, "Selling Vermont Beauty," *The Vermont Review*, 1, No. 1 (May–June 1926), pp. 13–15.

4. William H. H. Murray, *Lake Champlain and Its Shores* (Boston: De Wolfe, Fiske & Co., [1890]), p. 158.

5. Betsy Beattie, "The Queen City Celebrates Winter: The Burlington Coasting Club and the Burlington Carnival of Winter Sports, 1886–1887, " *Vermont History*, 52, No. 1 (Winter 1984), pp. 5–16; Charles S. Forbes, "Vermont as a Winter Resort," *The Vermonter*, 4, No. 7 (February 1899), pp. 114–115; Fred H. Harris, "Skiing and Winter Sports in Vermont," *The Vermonter*, 17, No. 11 (November 1912), pp. 677–681.

6. *Vermont* (Montpelier: State of Vermont, 1910), an 80-page pamphlet issued by the Bureau of Publicity of the Department of State.

7. Graffagnino, *Vermont in the Victorian Age*, Chapter 21.

8. Charles R. Cummings, "Our Fish and Game Asset," *The Vermonter*, 21, Nos. 9–10 (November–December 1916), pp. 224–240.

9. On Old Home Week in 1901, see: [Charles S. Forbes], "Vermont Old Home Week," *The Vermonter*, 6, No. 10 (May 1901), pp. 165–177; [Forbes] "Vermont Old Home Week," *The Vermonter* 7, No. 2 (September 1901), pp. 298–312; and [Charles R. Cummings], "A Review of Old Home Week," *Inter-State Journal*, 3, No. 5 (August 1901), unpaginated.

10. (Montpelier: State of Vermont, 1895) and (Montpelier: State of Vermont, 1891).

11. Weston Cate, Jr., "The Vermonter: The State Magazine," "*Vermont History News*, 35, No. 1 (January–February 1984), pp. 3–8 and 35; No. 2 (March–April 1984), pp. 29–33.

12. On late nineteenth-century Vermont prints and views, see Graffagnino, *Vermont in the Victorian Age*, pp. ix-xxxii.

13. William C. Lipke & Philip N. Grime, eds., *Vermont Landscape Images, 1776–1976* (Burlington, Vt.: Robert Hull Fleming Museum, University of Vermont, 1976).

14. David J. Blow, "The Establishment and Erosion of French-Canadian Culture in Winooski, Vermont, 1867–1900," *Vermont History*, 43, No. 1 (Winter 1975), pp. 59–74; Elin L. Anderson, *We Americans: A Study of Cleavage in an American City* (1937; reprint ed., New York: AMS Press, 1967); Gene Sessions, "'Years of Struggle': The Irish in the Village of Northfield, 1845–1900," *Vermont History*, 55, No. 2 (Spring 1987), pp. 69–96; Betsy Beattie, "Community-Building in Uncertain Times: The French Canadians of Burlington and Colchester, 1850–1860," *Vermont History*, 57, No. 2 (Spring 1989), pp. 84–103.

15. In addition to the titles cited above, see: William Wolkovich-Valkavičius, "The Lithuanians of Arlington," *Vermont History*, 54, No. 3 (Summer 1986), pp. 164–174; Myron Samuelson, *The Story of the Jewish Community of Burlington, Vermont* (Burlington, Vt.: George E. Little Press, 1976); Mari Tomasi, "The Italian Story in Vermont," *Vermont History*, 28, No. 1 (January 1960), pp. 73–87.

16. William A. Haviland and Marjory W. Power, *The Original Vermonters: Native Inhabitants, Past and Present* (Hanover, N.H.: University Press of New England, 1981), Chapter 7; Colin G. Calloway, *The Western Abenakis of Vermont, 1600–1800: War, Migration, and the*

Survival of an Indian People (Norman, Okla.: University of Oklahoma Press, 1990), Epilogue.

17. Joseph Amrhein, "Burlington, Vermont: The Economic History of a Northern New England City," unpublished Ph.D. dissertation (Business Administration), New York University, 1958; T. D. Seymour Bassett, "Urban Penetration of Rural Vermont, 1840–1880," unpublished Ph.D. dissertation (History), Harvard University, 1952; Graffagnino, *Vermont in the Victorian Age*, Chapters 18–19, 24, and 28.

18. Silas McKeen, *The Claims of Vermont: A Sermon Delivered Before the Congregational Convention of Vermont, Bennington, June 18, 1857* (Windsor, Vt.: Vermont Chronicle Office, 1857), p. 4.

19. Zuar E. Jameson, "Vermont as a Home," in Vermont State Board of Agriculture, *First Annual Report . . . 1872* (Montpelier, Vt.: State of Vermont, 1872), p. 562.

20. Graffagnino, *Vermont in the Victorian Age*, Chapter 20.

21. Albert Dwinell, "What Can Be Done to Keep Our Young Men in Vermont?" in Vermont State Board of Agriculture, *Second Biennial Report . . . 1873–74* (Montpelier, Vt.: Freeman Steam Printing, 1874), pp. 681–682.

22. Robinson, *Vermont: A Study of Independence* (1892; reprinted, Rutland, Vt.: Charles E. Tuttle Co., 1975), pp. 330–331.

23. On the attempt to settle Swedes on abandoned Vermont hill farms, see: Alonzo B. Valentine, "Swedish Immigration," *The Quill*, 1, No. 1 (September 1890), pp. 27–32; Dorothy M. Harvey, "The Swedes in Vermont," *Vermont History*, 28, No. 1 (January 1960), pp. 39–58; Graffagnino, *Vermont in the Victorian Age*, Chapter 30.

24. Harold F. Wilson, *The Hill Country of Northern New England: Its Social and Economic History 1790–1930* (1936; reprint ed., New York: AMS Press, 1967); Edwin C. Rozwenc, *Agricultural Policies in Vermont, 1860–1945* (Montpelier, Vt.: Vermont Historical Society, 1981).

25. Scott E. Hastings, Jr. and Geraldine S. Ames, *The Vermont Farm Year in 1890* (Woodstock, Vt.: Billings Farm & Museum, 1983); [Joseph L. Hills], *The Vermont Dairymen's Association: A History 1869–1947* (No place or publisher listed, [1947]; Guy B. Horton, *The Grange in Vermont* (1926; rev. ed., St. Johnsbury, Vt.: The Cowles Press, 1968); Graffagnino, *Vermont in the Victorian Age*, Chapters 2, 10, 14.

26. Lewis Stilwell, *Migration from Vermont* (1948; reprint ed., Montpelier and Rutland, Vt.: Vermont Historical Society and Academy Books, 1983); J. S. Adams, "The Extent and Effect of Emigration from Vermont and Its Relation to Our Schools," *Fifth Annual Report of the Vermont Board of Education* (Burlington: Times Book and Job Printing Establishment, 1861), pp. 79–104; Guy W. Bailey, "Keeping Young Vermonters in Vermont, " *The Vermont Review*, 1, No. 1 (May–June 1926), pp. 5–6; the published biennial reports of the State Board of Agriculture from the 1870s and 1880s contain a number of brief articles on the problems of Vermont's rural districts.

27. T. D. Seymour Bassett, "The 1870 Campaign for Woman Suffrage in Vermont," *Vermont Quarterly*, 14, No. 2 (April 1946); Deborah P. Clifford, "An Invasion of Strong-Minded Women: The Newspapers and the Woman Suffrage Campaign in Vermont in 1870," *Vermont History*, 43, No. 1 (Winter 1975), pp. 1–19; *idem*, "The Drive for Women's Municipal Suffrage in Vermont, 1883–1917," *Vermont History*, 47, No. 3 (summer 1979), pp. 173–190; *idem*, "The Women's War Against Rum," *Vermont History*, 52, No. 3 (Summer 1984), pp. 141–160; Steven R. Hoffbeck, "'Remember the Poor' (Galatians 2:10) : Poor Farms in Vermont," *Vermont History*, 57, No. 4 (Fall 1989), pp. 226–240; Marshall M. True, "Middle-Class Women and Civic Improvement in Burlington, 1865–1890," *Vermont History*, 56, No. 2 (Spring 1988), pp. 112–127.

28. Samuel B. Hand, Jeffrey D. Marshall, and D. Gregory Sanford, "'Little Republics' : The Structure of State Politics in Vermont, 1854–1920," *Vermont History*, 53, No. 3 (Summer 1986), pp. 141–166.

29. The most influential expression of the "winter of Vermont" interpretation is Wilson, *The Hill Country of Northern New England*; an important revisionist study is H. N. Muller, III, "From Ferment to Fatigue? 1870–1900: A New Look at the Neglected Winter of Vermont," Center for Research on Vermont, University of Vermont, Occasional Paper no. 5 (1984); Graffagnino, *Vermont in the Victorian Age*, synthesizes the recent revisionist work on the railroad era.

From Pastoralism to Progressivism:
Myth and Reality in Twentieth-Century Vermont

I<small>N</small> 1976 the bicentennial celebration of the creation of the United States took many forms, including new published histories of each state commissioned by the American Association for State and Local History. Vermont's contribution to this aspect of the celebration was *Vermont: A Bicentennial History*, written by noted historian Charles T. Morrissey and published in 1981. It is a witty and personal account of the Green Mountain State wherein Morrissey claims, as do many residents of and visitors to the state, that Vermont is " . . . a bucolic and sparsely settled oasis in an urbanized and industrial nation. . . ."[1]

Photographs by David Plowden accompanied Morrissey's text, representing what general editor James Morton Smith saw as a visual essay reflecting "the state's contemporary flavor."[2] Plowden's photographs bear witness to Morrissey's claims of Vermont's uniqueness (*Fig. 3.1*). Collectively, the sixteen black and white photographs give the impression that neither time nor change has touched Vermont in the last one hundred years. Covered bridges, horse-drawn farm machinery and maple sap gathering, images of sheltered small towns, cemeteries, and details of wooden structures provide visual evidence that in a largely urban world, Vermont remains a pastoral Arcadia. If we are drawn to the images, we are to be forgiven: Pastoral Arcadia is one of the most central and compelling myths in the history of Western culture.

On the two-hundredth anniversary of Vermont's statehood, however, it seems fitting to ask if Plowden's photographs truly give an accurate rendering of twentieth century life in Vermont. Cannot the same bucolic images be found today in the Amish communities of Pennsylvania, the small towns in eastern North Carolina, or the fishing villages of Down East Maine? Is not Vermont as guilty as the rest of the country of suburban strip development and environmental pollution? Do not Vermont's contributions to the cultural, environmental, and political life of the nation challenge the once-popular view of the state as conservative?

If all this is true, why and how do the myths persist? How and in what ways do individuals and forces both inside and outside of Vermont consciously or unconsciously assert the myth or the reality of life in what Robert Frost once called this "state in a natural state"? How clearly can we determine from looking at selected examples of contemporary material culture which embodies fact, which fiction?

In a large sense, we want to understand the peculiar power invested in a place name, a slogan, or an object that determines identity and cultural expression. What emerges in this essay and in the accompanying exhibition is a more balanced picture of the diversity of Vermont's cultural life in the twentieth century; one that asserts both the pastoral (mythic) and progressive (real) qualities that indeed make Vermont "a special place."

It is important first to understand that these dichotomous constructs of myth (bucolic) and reality (industrial and technological change) are not new. They have co-existed in Vermont since early in the twentieth century. Coincidentally, they have been clearly expressed by photographers who preceded Plowden. Jericho native Wilson "Snowflake" Bentley, whose microphotographs (c. 1890–1925) made visible for the first time to a popular audience the inherent crystalline structure of snowflakes (cat. 49), clearly alluded metaphorically to the pristine nature of Ver-

Fig. 3.1 David Plowden.
*Hectorville Bridge, town of
Montgomery.* 1967. Copyright,
David Plowden.

mont. As a later Vermont writer noted, the startling symmetry and beauty of the microphotographs were "revelations of the Divinity as convincing as any in the Bible or the Koran."[3]

In stark contrast are Lewis Hine's photographs of young Vermont boys and girls from
Bennington to Burlington taken in 1909–1910 (cat. 48). These photographs are representative
of the five thousand images that Hine gathered from across the country for the National Child
Labor Committee to document the abuses of children in the workplace.[4] Hine's subjects,
photographed between 1906 and 1918, were not confined to Vermont nor to textile mills, but
they gave a poignant face to the children whom Vermont poet Sarah Cleghorn immortalized in
her quatrain:

> The golf links lie so near the mill
> That almost every day
> The laboring children can look out
> And see the men at play.[5]

As Hine portrayed so graphically, the lives of these children were not determined by the
cycles of nature associated with rural life, but by concepts of labor tied to industrial production
and urban living. In a larger sense, Hine showed us that industry and its resultant disturbance
of the pastoral, agricultural landscape emphasize the mechanical and the anonymous, while
Bentley's microphotographs of snowflakes reveal nature and its endless expressions of individu-
ality. As contrasting images, then, the photographs of Bentley and Hine symbolize in their own
ways the myths and the reality of Vermont in the first quarter of the twentieth century.

In the ensuing decades two contrary and sometimes controversial concepts figure prominently in the discussions of Vermont's future: How can the state keep young people from emigrating? and How can Vermont preserve its pure stock, now threatened by the immigration of outsiders? Both themes were addressed by Wallace Nutting in his 1922 publication, *Vermont Beautiful*. Written and illustrated for the newly emerging and growing numbers of out-of-state motor tourists, Nutting's book with its 304 photographs repetitiously presented the state in picturesque, bucolic formulas as an idealized landscape. Yet, on close examination of the text, particularly of the final chapter, Nutting's readers will discover his warning that Vermont's Anglo hegemony was threatened by the immigration of French Canadians. Specifically, Nutting expressed the fear that Vermont would become a "new French Canadian province" as descendents of the original English settlers continued to abandon their family homesteads.

In a final observation, Nutting concluded that "of course it is conceivable that Vermont may become predominantly foreign," but "we believe that as soon as the unrest left by the great war [World War I] has been calmed, the return to the land on the part of a select class of old Americans may be hoped for."[6] Somewhat prophetically, even inadvertently, Nutting's blatant call for the rescue of Vermont from what he viewed as "tainted stock" was heard nationally and locally. Eventually, a select material culture was rediscovered, around which a mythic, agrarian (and racially pure) past was reconstructed.

Calvin Coolidge and the Commission on Country Life

Many of the mythic qualities that characterized Vermont and Vermonters in the twentieth century are traceable to Calvin Coolidge's term in the White House and to Coolidge himself. A native son of Vermont born in Plymouth on the fourth of July 1872, Calvin Coolidge was suddenly thrust from the invisibility of the vice presidency to the visibility of the presidency by the death of Warren G. Harding on August 2, 1923. In the early hours of the following morning, the oath of office was administered by kerosene lamp at the Coolidge homestead in Plymouth, where the vice-president had been vacationing. The image quickly became as poignant to the twenties as was the image of Vice President Lyndon B. Johnson being sworn in on Air Force One forty years later.

Although Coolidge had practiced law in Massachusetts and was drafted into the vice presidency because of his forthright handling of the police riots in Boston while serving as governor of Massachusetts, his continued association with Vermont was seized on by the press to explain what it perceived and described as unique virtues of the Coolidge presidency (1923–1928). In a feature entitled "The Green Mountain State" which appeared in *National Geographic* in 1927, author Herbert Corey used even the name of Coolidge's hometown to conjure up images of the political virtues of the original seventeenth-century settlement in Massachusetts.[7]

Two images of Coolidge "the Vermonter" became associated particularly with his presidency. The first was Coolidge in his grandfather's woolen smock and straw hat plowing, haying, or performing other farm tasks. This image was enormously popular nationally, and even within the state, Coolidge's donning of his grandfather's smock was viewed "in the nature of a religious exercise, a tribute to the sterling virtues of his rugged ancestors."[8] The second image derived from a historic photograph taken in August 1924 on the front porch of the Coolidge homestead (*Fig. 3.2*). The president is shown with the captains of industry—Thomas Edison, Harvey Firestone, and Henry Ford—inscribing an old family sap bucket for Ford's newly created Greenfield Village. These symbolic shards of an agrarian, now mythic, American past had tremendous appeal to a decade characterized by unimagined economic prosperity and a fast-paced jazz age.

Fig. 3.2 C. E. Chalmers. *Calvin Coolidge Autographing Family Sap Bucket for Henry Ford's Greenfield Village Museum, August 1924.* Postcard. Courtesy, Special Collections, University of Vermont.

The images were reinforced in a biography of Coolidge written by the noted journalist William Allen White and published in 1925. White observed that Calvin Coolidge was the product of a state where what he called "the fundamentals of American life" persisted in spite of and isolated from major technological and social changes elsewhere in the country. He went on to call Calvin Coolidge the "man of the hour," but he warned that the moment was not likely to last:

> the sands run swiftly in the hourglass. Thrift, frugality, punctuality, precision—the business virtues—may not always suffice . . . Vermont—staunch as she is, often is alone in her simplicity.[9]

And White was not the only one to question whether the image of Vermont projected by President Coolidge was misleading and one-dimensional. As early as 1924, Waldo Glover, writing in *The Vermonter*, observed that Coolidge's farmer's smock was in marked contrast to the smocks worn by Vermont's newest immigrants—its summer residents and artists. Their smocks, he wrote, "are not farmer's smock at all but artists' smocks, made not of brown or blue wool homespun, [but of] more fanciful, if less durable material."[10]

Glover was referring to the influx of artists in the Dorset/Manchester area—many associated with the Art Students League of New York—who were to band together formally in the early 1930s to form the Southern Vermont Artists Association. Founded in 1922 and known until

1933 as the Dorset Painters, these local and out-of-state artists exhibited their work for the summer tourists in the Manchester area, drawing their "inspiration from the mountains and meadows, hills and ridges of southern Vermont."[11] By the late 1920s, the summer exhibitions of the Dorset Painters were drawing national attention and receiving notice in the national art magazines.

Within Vermont, however, it was the "durable material" of Vermont farmers and the landscape which they had modified which particularly drew the attention in the late 1920s of the newly created Vermont Commission on Country Life.[12] Uppermost in the minds of the commissioners was how to stem the tide of emigration which seemed to pull particularly the talented and the ambitious. President Coolidge was only the most obvious example of such a native son who had left and flourished elsewhere. There were countless others whom the commission would recite.

The commission raised questions which today seem both inappropriate and out of place in their implicit discrimination:

> How may the best elements and qualities in the basic human stocks be conserved and improved? . . . Are summer visitors an economic asset? If so, are they a social and moral asset as well? What is the effect of their presence on the quality of the life of Vermonters? Is the answer to these questions the same for all classes of summer visitors? If not, which classes should be encouraged to come?[13]

The sixteen committees, which convened for a two-year period and presented their summary reports and recommendations as *Rural Vermont: A Program for the Future*, purported to use "the methods of scientific planning . . . as a means of ensuring progress."[14] The results, from today's perspective, offer a compelling explanation for the idiosyncratic nature of Vermont myths in the twentieth century. It is especially instructive to take a close look at the final chapter of *Rural Vermont*, which was prepared by the Committee on Vermont Traditions and Ideals.

Chaired by Professor Arthur Wallace Peach, the committee sought to present evidence of "pronounced traditional and idealistic qualities of mind and heart that give Vermont and Vermont folk their particular significance . . . "[15] Stephen Daye Press of Brattleboro published the committee's findings in four books, known as the *Green Mountain Series*. These included biographies of eminent Vermonters, a collection of prose writings, an anthology of Vermont verse, and most interestingly, a selection of Vermont folk songs and ballads. Together, the committee noted, the volumes "serve to give a 'habitation and a name' . . . to the traditions and ideals that have motivated Vermont life for over a century."[16]

The committee's report concluded by noting approvingly that, "The old stock is here still, in greater proportion to the total population than in any other commonwealth of the north." Among those characteristics of Vermont's "old stock" cited by the commission were "individualism, self-sufficiency, independence, courage, integrity, loyalty" and also,

> elements of isolation, factors of association and heredity involving the 'will-to-do' of a hardy, independent, liberty-loving, brave and individualistic people, still as stubborn as were their fathers in opposition to what they consider to be against their rights or whatever fails to appeal to their judgment and common sense.[17]

Like an anthropologist describing a lost race of people out of step with the rest of the world, the Commission on Country Life had seemingly turned Vermonters into a museum display of living artifacts from the past.[18]

Other clear images of such an anthropological point of view can be found in photographer Clara Sipprell's soft-focused portraits of the residents of Thetford Center in the 1920s. In *The Blacksmith Shop*, for example, Sipprell's camera is focused on an elderly man intent upon his craft and illumined by a soft, raking light (*Fig. 3.3*). Paradigmatically, it envisions an activity associated with a pre-industrial, agricultural past. The effect of her emphasis upon elderly Vermonters whose dress or activities recalled a bygone era was an iconography that would be repeated throughout the next decades.

The sesquicentennial celebrations of the Declaration of Independence and the founding of the Republic of Vermont similarly renewed interest in state and national history. Celebrated in 1926 and 1927, respectively, these anniversaries provided additional focus to and attention on the character and political identity that could be associated with the labels "American" and "Vermonter." The Vermont chapters of the Daughters of the American Revolution used the opportunities to place commemorative plaques in many Vermont towns and cities, for example, in the Elmwood Avenue Cemetery in Burlington, where the graves of notable Vermonters associated with both American and Vermont history were noted. The D.A.R had previously taken charge of the commission of a statue to the Green Mountain Boys by Raymond Porter. Placed on the green in Rutland in 1918, it was a Vermont variant of Daniel Chester French's *The Minuteman*, erected in 1875 at Concord, Massachusetts, for the nation's centennial celebrations. Similarly, James Wilbur of Manchester engaged sculptor Sherry Fry to render a full-length bronze statue of patriot and University of Vermont founder Ira Allen, which was installed on the university's green in 1925.

Fig. 3.3 Clara Sipprell.
The Blacksmith Shop.
c. 1925–30.
Courtesy, Special Collections,
University of Vermont.

The individual who stands out during this period as the most passionate historian of Vermont's past is John Spargo (1876–1966), director and founder in 1927 of The Bennington Museum. English-born, socialist in political persuasion, Spargo also served concurrently as the director of the Vermont Historical Society and as president of the Vermont State Sesquicentennial Commission. Among his credits was his 1925 history of the Bennington Battle Monument, written while he was serving as president of the Bennington Battle Monument and Historical Association. Spargo's energy and dedication to The Bennington Museum and to the acquisition of objects for it led Charles Crane to observe in 1937 that the collections of this new museum rivaled those of the century-old Vermont Historical Society.[19]

These institutions, as well as the emerging local and county historical societies, assembled a concomitant visual iconography of myth that would be perpetuated by artists in the future. The Green Mountain Boys were elevated to the stature of a Paul Bunyan, and the landscape of Vermont became an idyllic setting in which their histories were played out.

Vermont Artists and Regionalism

"Vermont is one of the most beautiful states in the Union," noted the Committee on Traditions and Ideals in 1931, "yet it has developed few artists; and the reasons why cannot be found in any popular explanation."[20] In the years ahead, that observation would be significantly altered. The catalysts were the creation of new museums devoted to contemporary art—particularly the Museum of Modern Art in 1929 and the Whitney in 1930, both in New York City—and the resounding belief stated in the writings of Vermont native John Dewey that art should play a significant role in everyday life. Locally, the Southern Vermont Artists Association incorporated in 1934 as an exhibiting organization, bringing together artists, both summer and permanent residents, throughout the state.

Luigi Lucioni was elected a member of the SVAA in 1935. Two years later he was hailed by *Life* magazine as the "painter laureate of Vermont." His reputation as the youngest American artist to have his work purchased by the Metropolitan Museum of Art gave a boost to the local art scene in Vermont, and his *Village of Stowe* (1931) remains one of the icons of the period (cat. 50). Crisply rendered, with an attention to technical detail that became Lucioni's trademark as a painter and etcher, *Village of Stowe* presents the viewer with an image of a timeless, unchanging country village. The appeal of such imagery was obvious, arriving on the scene as it did just one year after the Crash of 1929 and the erection of the streamlined Chrysler Building. Its image of sleepy, unchanged New England epitomized the virtues not just of Vermont but of an entire region north of Boston, virtues which many people argued were worth reassessing after the economic debacle that brought on the Depression.

The success of the SVAA led other artists to organize in the state. In Burlington, the University of Vermont's newly completed Robert Hull Fleming Museum, opened in June 1931, pledged part of its exhibition space to the Northern Vermont Artists Association and featured the prints and paintings of Luigi Lucioni in his first one-man Vermont exhibition a short fifteen months later. The NVAA's annual exhibitions, held in May or June, complemented the SVAA's annual exhibitions, held in August; for many years thereafter both exhibitions were listed on the state's calendar of events.

So, too, the previously established Wood Art Gallery in Montpelier began to actively exhibit and collect the work of Vermont artists in the mid-1930s. The gallery was named after and endowed by Montpelier-native Thomas Waterman Wood, a past-president of the National

Academy of Design in the 1890s, who gave it broad scope. According to a leading guidebook of the 1930s,

> In recent years the trustees have purchased, as extensively as their funds permitted, representative canvases of the best contemporary Vermont painters, including [John] Lillie, [Henry] Schnakenberg, [Luigi] Lucioni, and [Herbert] Meyer. In time, this section of the gallery should become the best permanent collection of paintings, watercolors, and etchings executed by Vermont artists, an interpretation in part, at least, of the scenic and social background of the state.[21]

Fueling this sudden outburst of interest in contemporary art in Vermont and throughout the country was a popular response to the writings of Vermont-born John Dewey. Dewey's philosophy of art, initially presented as the William James Lectures at Harvard University in 1931, was published as *Art as Experience* in 1934 and attracted national attention, just as had his earlier writings on his philosophy of education. The seventy-two-year-old philosopher argued eloquently for the integration of art with everyday experience.

Dewey viewed his lectures as attempts

> to restore continuity between the refined and intensified forms of experience that are works of art and everyday events, doings, and sufferings that are universally recognized to constitute experience.[22]

His aesthetic philosophy, mistakenly viewed by some as a denouncement of "abstract" art in favor of realism, spearheaded the arts education movement begun earnestly in the 1920s.

The response of colleges and universities in Vermont, as elsewhere, was to add fine arts courses to their curricula. At Bennington College, Paul Feely, Simon Moselsio, and Edwin Avery Park joined the faculty in the 1930s. Arthur Healy at Middlebury College and Francis Colburn at the University of Vermont, both of whom exhibited with the Northern Vermont Artists in 1935, established their reputations as "Vermont artists." Paul Sample played a particularly prominent role. A summer resident at Lake Willoughby in the 1930s, Sample exhibited with the Northern Vermont Artists in 1932. In 1937, he left his teaching position at the University of Southern California and joined the faculty of Dartmouth College as artist-in-residence. Three years later he taught briefly at the University of Vermont. In Sample's *Church Supper* (1933), as in much of his work, his subject was a contemporary genre scene couched in the "naive realism" of regionalist painters such as Grant Wood, Thomas Hart Benton, and John Stewart Curry (cat. 51). But stylistically, Sample borrowed the compositional devices of the Mexican muralists, such as Diego Rivera and José Clemente Orozco. Sample's Vermont images were among the first to attract national attention, and his iconography placed New England and Vermont within the national context of the regionalist movement in American art.[23]

Experiments in Public Art: The W.P.A. in Vermont

The creation of the federally funded W.P.A. arts programs initiated by the Roosevelt administration directly fulfilled Dewey's philosophy of art: Art should indeed be everywhere visible. Financial support for the artists would be provided by children's art classes, by commissions for murals and panels to be painted for federal buildings throughout the country, and by easel painting and graphic arts programs.

Unfortunately, records are virtually nonexistent for both the Federal Art Project (FAP) and

Fig. 3.4 Ronald Slayton. *Social Activities of the 30s. c.* 1937. Woodcut. Private Collection.

the related Treasury Relief Art Program (TRAP) in Vermont. A handful of artists throughout the state, including Cecil Grant, Ray Williams, Simon Moselsio, Francis Colburn, and Ronald Slayton participated in the easel painters' project, but only Slayton's work has survived.

Among the Vermont artists employed by the programs, Slayton alone seems to have attempted work with the theme of social protest. This was principally inspired by his visiting Orozco in 1933 while the latter was completing his murals for Baker Library at Dartmouth College in Hanover, New Hampshire. Under the circumstances, therefore, Slayton's work, such as his woodcut entitled *Social Activities of the 30s* (*c.* 1937), of a greedy Uncle Sam and a war-mongering soldier, seems curiously out of place in rural Vermont of the 1930s (*Fig. 3.4*).

Of the two federally funded art programs in Vermont, the Treasury Relief Artist Program (TRAP) produced more lasting results. In Rutland, the recently completed Beaux Arts Federal Building (1931–1933) was decorated with "six murals done by Stephen Belaski . . . portraying outstanding events in the history of Vermont."[24] Other murals in Vermont, some federally funded, some locally funded, were placed in the post office in White River Junction; in the village of Georgia; in the Fleming Museum (the geology panels); and along the walls of the children's room of the St. Johnsbury Athenaeum, where illustrative panels depict local residents in stories by Hans Christian Andersen.[25] In retrospect, however, these attempts at "public art" in Vermont, while innovative in placement, are as stylistically flat as the walls on which they were placed. If they established any precedent, it may have been for the paper "placemat histories" ("Did You Know?") which flourished for the next four decades in roadside diners and country restaurants for motoring tourists.

Unfortunately, Vermont artists on the federal payroll were never as organized or as able to realize their potential as were their fellow workers of the Federal Writers' Project. There, the collaborative efforts of Vermont writers produced in 1937 *Vermont: A Guide to the Green Mountain State*. In format and context, this now classic Baedekers offered both historical and contemporary commentary for the motoring tourist and provided a balanced view of Vermont in both text and photographs.[26]

In Vermont as elsewhere, however, photographs once again offer the most striking images of the decade. Fanned out across the country, photographers for the Farm Security Administration assembled a visual record of rural, agricultural America for the Department of Agriculture. Documentary as opposed to pictorial in format and intention, these photographs provided the most comprehensive look at America during the 1930s. Those shot in Vermont were no exception. The pathos and dignity of small-town Vermont life was captured in 1940 in a photographic series of Woodstock, Vermont, shot by Marion Post Wolcott. Her images of elderly, tight-lipped Vermonters at town meeting or of the state's ordinary folk conducting their daily affairs, such as *Peddler who goes from door to door, selling hardware and groceries. Woodstock, Vermont, 1940*, encompass both the myth and reality of living in a rural state.

The F.S.A. photographs of Vermont were not well known. They were eclipsed by the more severe images of depressed tenant farming in Alabama as documented by Walker Evans, and by the stark faces and conditions of migrant workers as recorded by Dorothea Lange. Vermont, as viewed by the photographers of the Farm Security Administration, was merely an anachronism, a place slightly out of step with other regions, even quaint in a picturesque way.

City dwellers found the Vermont scenes deceptively attractive. But for rural residents, the dignity of plain living came at the price of physical hardship. Many farmers in Vermont still relied on horse-drawn machinery to cultivate their fields. Moreover, Vermonters well knew that the state's abandoned farms (cat. 53) were not the result of insidious tenant farming but of the lure of greener pastures to the west. They also knew that if the images of Vermonters by Marion Post Wolcott, Clara Sipprell, and Paul Strand seemed to focus on an older generation, there was a reason: Vermont for sixty years or more had lost its most ambitious youth to cities and places beyond its borders, and now an unusually high proportion of elderly Vermonters was the result.

Motor Travel, Tin-Can Tourists, and Mass Culture

Vermont attracted national attention in 1936 when it rejected in a statewide referendum a federal offer of a parkway running the length of the state along the spine of the Green Mountains. Vermonters such as Charles Edward Crane reasoned that the Green Mountain Parkway was rejected by Vermonters because it would have "defiled" what was commonly viewed as a "sacred" landscape.[27] While the refusal to accept federal monies was cited as yet another example of Vermonters' rugged independence, a larger issue loomed in the thoughts of the Vermont Bureau of Publicity: What could Vermont offer to attract the increasing number of tourists traveling by private automobile?

Just four years earlier the state highway system had been officially created, but accessibility to the north country was a double-edged sword. Vermont's geographical remoteness contributed in part to its charm and gave validity to its new state slogan, "Unspoiled Vermont." However, unless tourists could travel easily to and within the state, they would not come in sufficient numbers to boost Vermont's economy. Conversely, if too many came or if immigration to the state increased too dramatically, the lure of scenic, uncrowded roads would be spoiled; Vermont would become less distinct and unique than it had hitherto been. Vrest Orton, the most articulate spokesman for environmental sanity in the state since George Perkins Marsh, referred to the parkway as "The White Elephant Road" and articulated the question that lay at the heart of the debate:

> Are we going to keep the greatest, and perhaps the only asset we have, our unique scenic beauty . . . or are we going loco, like Florida and California, and 'develop,' commercialize, exploit and 'improve' this asset for the benefit of the tin-can tourist?[28]

Orton's concern for the despoilment of Vermont was matched by Charles Crane's fear that Vermont's rural, even unique, way of life would eventually disappear. For Crane, it was only a question of time before the cultural hegemony of Vermont and its unspoiled landscape would be replaced by a uniform, nation-wide mass culture:

> Hearing, reading, seeing the same things, we are prone to think the same things . . . The little wedge-shaped state of Vermont, though subject to the same ether-waves [radio], the same cinema, and the same news dispatches, still presumes some semblance of the provincialism which she has had from the pioneer days . . . The automobile even more than the radio and the movies, is a breaker down of barriers.[29]

The architecture of Vermont was yet another reason for tourists to visit. A keen interest in preserving Vermont's architecture had been expressed in *Rural Vermont*. Specific buildings were in the process of being restored. One example was the First Church in Old Bennington, "for which thousands of dollars have just been raised . . . to make a sort of Westminster Abbey in Vermont."[30] By the mid-1930s, Herbert Wheaton Congdon, an architect and photographer from Arlington, had begun his "Old Buildings Project," an enterprise that led to the publication of *Old Vermont Houses* in 1940. Stimulated by W.P.A. programs such as the Index of American Design and sponsored by the University of Vermont's Robert Hull Fleming Museum, Congdon's photographic study of Vermont architecture prior to 1850 documented regional and local variants of national and period styles of building.[31] His images, informed by his own training as an architect, were formal, precise, and detailed, and represent the stirrings of a preservationist sensibility rather than the commercialism of pictorial advertisements for out-of-staters (cat. 52).

The appearance of *Yankee* magazine in October 1935 signaled the increasing association of Vermont with both the broader geographical region of New England and with a more extensive cultural life. From Dublin, New Hampshire, editor Robb Sagendorph argued that *Yankee* was published "in the interest of Yankee Traditions," because "the Yankee, like the Red Man, has become the Vanishing American."[32] The resurgence of New England reflected a new spirit of cooperative enterprise at the regional level, both culturally and economically, which helped to sell the state to tourists. Vermont as part of northern New England would emerge as a new iconography in popular culture.

"Before President Coolidge made the name of our state known to modern people," Dorothy Canfield Fisher noted in 1937, "we were so far in the past as to be practically invisible." In those days when she traveled to New York and gave her address as Arlington, Vermont, the author recalled, people thought it was "some fancy name for a new 'development' in the suburbs." But that had changed:

> Nowadays when you tell New York saleswomen that you live in Vermont they say, 'Oh, how nice! I envy you!' This change is not due to any sudden discovery of our virtues. It is caused by (a) the advent into fashionable favor of winter sports, Vermont sounding like a place where you can wear ski pants, and (b) the depression.[33]

The landscape as a setting in which recreational activities take place had been Vermont's selling point to outsiders ever since it started promoting itself in the years after the Civil War. But these activities had been principally associated with summer and fall. Now that, too, began to change after the winter Olympic Games were held across Lake Champlain in Lake Placid, New York, in 1932. The idea of winter recreation caught the imagination of the public. Virtually overnight, Vermont entrepreneurs began developing ski areas in Brattleboro, Woodstock, Pico, Bromley, Stowe, and Jay. The attendant social activities—from ski trains to ski lodges, complete with couples nestled by cozy fireplaces—became a stock in trade. Skiing was fashionable.

In an era faced with economic depression, the rise of fascism and communism, and the threat of America's imminent involvement in World War II, the need for a temporary escape was evident. What could be more temporary and exhilarating than a breathless run down the slopes! "In two or three decades," noted Charles Crane, "[skiing] has made the winter's snow on Vermont mountains almost as popular as summer surf at Atlantic beaches . . . It's not only amazing—this winter sports development—it's revolutionary."[34]

Crane's *Winter in Vermont*, published in 1941, gave credence to Fisher's observations that Vermont was finally being recognized. His book signaled a new and popular image of Vermont not rooted in the older myths of Vermonters or their history. The message was simple: Vermont offered a refuge and an escape, complete with a white blanket, to blot out the realities of a world gone askew.

Photographs by fashion photographer Louise Dahl-Wolfe accompanied Crane's text, including those that had recently appeared in a pictorial feature on Stowe in *Harper's Bazaar*. *Harper's* focus in photographs such as those of "Nose-Dive Annie" (cat. 55) and Lowell Thomas was clearly on the fashions and the celebrities of the slopes, not on the sport itself, but the effect was to create a new mythos, one that contrasted radically with the bleak and often severe contemporaneous images of the F.S.A. photographs of the state.

Irving Berlin's "White Christmas" perpetuated the new mythos (*Fig. 3.5*). Sung by crooner Bing Crosby in the 1942 Mark Sandich film, *Holiday Inn*, the song was an immediate success, winning an Academy Award and earning a place among the top ten songs of the year on the popular radio program, "Your Hit Parade." *Holiday Inn* was among the first of many Hollywood films described as "light-hearted, patriotic musicals" for war-time audiences.[35] Its New England setting, like the songs, was removed and remote from the hum-drum urban life of war-time America. Together they were a perfect recipe for sentiment and nostalgia, for evoking memories of the simple "good old days" of long ago.

The formula for *Holiday Inn* was repeated twelve years later in the 1954 film, *White*

Fig. 3.5 "White Christmas." Sheet music. 1942. Private Collection.

Christmas, with a setting reminiscent of *Holiday Inn* and with Bing Crosby again singing his rendition of "White Christmas." Referred to as an "Uncle Sam without whiskers," Crosby during the war years was seen as holding "a kind of national acceptance, affection, and esteem such as the American people have given to only one other entertainer . . . Will Rogers." He was viewed not only as "everyone's neighbor everywhere in the world," but as "a symbol of a kind of composite American."[36] Vermont, in turn, became everyone's neighborhood and fulfilled everyone's dream of a white Christmas, "just like the ones they used to know."[37] Now along with its snow, Vermont conjured up images of other "fundamentals . . . the Christmas tree and Christmas turkey . . . two essential items [which] are native products of Vermont, so much so that both the Vermont tree and the Vermont turkey are coveted far and wide."[38]

"Moonlight in Vermont" was first aired on "Hit Parade" in 1944. Composed by Karl Suessdorf and John Blackburn and made famous by Margaret Whiting, vocalist with the Johnny Mercer Orchestra, "Moonlight in Vermont" played upon the images made popular by *White Christmas* and added new ones. The lyrics spoke of the now popular "ski trails on a mountain-side," as well as of other seasons, such as summer and fall. To listeners under the song's spell,

Vermont now became a romantic all-season dreamland, especially when the moon was full. The world war in which the United States was then engaged created both the audience and the mood for such musical escapes:

> Men and women stationed all over the world were at war, and when they heard the record ["Moonlight in Vermont"], they liked it because it reminded them of home . . . the song was frozen in history.[39]

Military conscription, rationing at home, and an all-out war-time economy brought the nation together, creating ideal conditions for the further flowering of a mass-culture. Vermont and Vermonters were to figure prominently in the iconography of that culture.

Vermont as an Exemplar of National Ideals

Some of the best-known images of the war years depicted life in Vermont as an exemplar of national ideals. They were drawn by Arlington resident and illustrator Norman Rockwell. In the spring of 1943, Rockwell's illustrations for the *Saturday Evening Post* included renderings of President Roosevelt's "Four Freedoms" as outlined in the president's January 6, 1941, annual message to Congress: Freedom of Speech, Freedom to Worship in One's Own Way, Freedom from Want, and Freedom from Fear. (They were later to become the cornerstone of the Atlantic Charter that Roosevelt forged with Prime Minister Winston Churchill.)[40]

Rockwell's models for the "Four Freedoms" (cat. 54) were residents of and around Arlington, Vermont; real people from a real place. In *Freedom from Want*, for example, Rockwell illustrated a Thanksgiving dinner in Arlington. With its oblique compositional reference to a secular "Last Supper," Rockwell's image of Thanksgiving quickly became as potent an icon as George Henry Durrie's earlier painting, *Home to Thanksgiving*, published as a lithograph by Currier and Ives in 1866. But whereas Durrie had depicted a typical New England farm, with parents greeting their children on the front porch, Rockwell placed the viewer not in the landscape nor with reference to any specific region, but at the end of a Thanksgiving table presided over by a kindly grandma and grandpa.

In terms of existing images of Vermont, Rockwell's paintings were unique. For the first time an artist had depicted a cross-section of life in a Vermont town, showing children and young, old, and middle-aged men and women from all walks of life. Virtually overnight, small-town Vermont came to represent typical—which is to say ideal—small-town America. The landscape of Vermont, hitherto an important element of the rural, unspoiled mythos, was displayed by the everyday activities found in any small Vermont town.

The "Four Freedoms" quickly became national symbols more potent than those of a specific state or region. Ben Hibbs, who as the editor of the *Saturday Evening Post* had commissioned Rockwell to undertake the project, commented that

> Those four pictures quickly became the best-known and most appreciated paintings of that era. They appeared right at a time when the war was going against us on the battle fronts, and the American people needed the inspirational message which they conveyed so forcefully and so beautifully.[41]

Other images of Vermont and Vermonters depicted by Rockwell and published in the *Saturday Evening Post* during the period 1943–1948 also drew critical acclaim, but none achieved the fame of the "Four Freedoms," which continued to be popular throughout the late 1940s and into the 1950s as Americans entered the Cold War. While the abstract paintings of New York artists such as Jackson Pollock and Franz Kline were viewed as symbolic of the artistic (and hence, political) freedom of the West, Rockwell's images of Vermont concretely illustrated political freedom and democracy in everyday terms.[42] According to Dorothy Canfield Fisher, this was Rockwell's genius:

> In a period when wormwood and vinegar are the fashionable flavorings, it is genuine originality for Rockwell to dip his brush into the honey-pot of lovableness and zest in living.[43]

Anna Mary Robertson Moses, better known as Grandma Moses, rivaled Rockwell as a painter of Vermont and upstate New York, especially the region around Hoosick Falls and Eagle Bridge. Pictured in Rockwell's *Homecoming* painting of December 23, 1948, Grandma Moses recreated a naive vision of nineteenth-century rural New England that appealed to post-war America's fears of stockpiled atomic weapons and the sharp ideological differences that separated East and West. Paintings such as *Home for Thanksgiving*, inspired by Durrie's Currier and Ives lithograph, and *White Christmas* (1954) were child-like both in their technique and vision, but they spoke of an earlier, peaceful, pre-war era, and in that regard functioned in much the way had George Inness's *Peace and Plenty* (1865) at the end of the Civil War. *Bondville Fair*—described by the artist as a painting of "a little fair that is held up in Vermont one day in the year, when all of the natives come down from the mountain"—celebrates folk culture and activities that Grandma Moses and many other Americans realized were rapidly disappearing.[44]

Post-War Myths and Realities

The appearance of the first issue of *Vermont Life* in the fall of 1946 ushered in a new format for promoting tourism in the state (cat. 58). A quarterly magazine geared to the seasons, *Vermont Life* was originally published by the Vermont State Development Commission. It relied on text and photography to explore themes that touched on a cross-section of life in the Green Mountain State.[45]

In the mid-1950s, the back covers of *Vermont Life* displayed testimonials by well-known figures—historical and contemporary—who praised (usually in superlatives) the special qualities of life in Vermont. Juxtaposed with an equally perfect photograph of Vermont, the testimonials were evidence that the development commission had adopted the soft-sell advertising techniques of Madison Avenue. Their aim was to promote the state to outsiders, not just to the average motoring tourist. Indeed, the commission was looking for that special class of tourist—the well-educated professional—to whom Dorothy Canfield Fisher addressed her essay, "Vermont Summer Homes," in the spring 1949 issue. There she implored professionals, wherever they lived and regardless of their place of birth, to "come back home to live." By 1954, the commission had established a Vermont Information Center in Rockefeller Center in New York City, adjacent to Radio City Music Hall.

As the state's magazine pictured so clearly, Vermont after the Second World War was a place to experience firsthand, the small-town, New England life that had figured so prominently in the popular culture of the 1940s. Now, a new generation of travel books appeared, among them those by author and photographer Samuel Chamberlain. His *Six New England Villages*, published in 1948, stimulated travelers to see places such as Litchfield, Connecticut; Old Deerfield, Massachusetts; and Old Bennington, Vermont. He had other Vermont villages to recommend, too, some mere survivors of the past which progress had passed by and others carefully restored, such as Woodstock and Grafton.

There were also newly created "villages," such as the Shelburne Museum.[46] A manifestation of the vision of Electra Havemeyer Webb, the Shelburne Museum was founded in 1947 to provide a historical assemblage of American material culture (especially folk art) in an outdoor architectural setting. Collections with a Vermont focus assembled by Mrs. Webb ranged from quilts to decoys, from paintings to toys. Her intention, similar to the guiding principles of earlier outdoor museums, was

> To instill a deeper appreciation and understanding of our heritage . . . to show the ingenuity and craftsmanship of our forebears . . . to depict the manner of living during the early days . . . and to create an education project, varied and alive, intended to do something worthwhile for the State of Vermont.[47]

Americans welcomed the offering. The change and pace of their life had accelerated considerably after the Second World War. With a renewed belief in the inherent goodness of technological progress and the higher standard of living it promised, Americans found the need to reconstruct their history in museums such as the Shelburne, following the earlier models established in Colonial Williamsburg, Greenfield Village, and Sturbridge Village. For cultural historian Walter Karp, such historical reconstructions of the past were "nothing less than the grand contradiction of modern American life." He called the need that brought them into being

> . . . the San Andreas fault in the American soul—the schism between our faith in technological progress and our profoundly gnawing suspicion that the old rural republic was a finer, braver, and freer place than the industrial America that now sustains us.[48]

No one articulated those virtues of the "old rural republic" more clearly than Vermonters Dorothy Canfield Fisher and Robert Frost (cat. 59). Fisher's *Vermont Tradition: The Biography of an Outlook on Life*, published in 1953, is not only one of the most celebrated histories of the state but one of the most cogent personal affirmations of a unique Vermont way of life:

> The basic, primary concern of Vermont tradition is with the conduct of human life . . . based on the idea that group life should leave each person as free as possible to arrange his own life.[49]

Dorothy Canfield Fisher was Vermont's "First Lady," a Vermont version of Eleanor Roosevelt. Like Mrs. Roosevelt, she had an intense interest in global affairs and a commitment to human rights. At the same time, her allegiance to her native Arlington was unswerving. The Canfield family home was given to the village as a community center, and her last publication, *Memoirs of My Home Town* (1955), was sold for the benefit of the Arlington Historical Society. In many ways, Fisher's estimate of Robert Frost—"He is far too great a poet to be framed in by geographical boundaries"[50]—was an accurate epitaph for her own life, too. It was also an epitaph for the passing of "Old Vermont."

By the mid 1950s, the Vermont that Fisher wrote about could no longer be framed exclusively by the political and cultural boundaries of the past. The traditional, rural ways of life were slowly disappearing, eroded by the realities of a fast-paced popular culture and by new media such as television. Television would further diminish the geographical remoteness of the state, not only in relationship to the rest of the country but in relationship to the rest of the world. Politically and culturally, the new medium informed Vermonters about major issues facing all

Americans and every world citizen. By the late 1960s, the most pressing national concerns were the Vietnam War and the deteriorating environment. Vermonters would be at the forefront of the debates on both those problems.

The Green Revolution and the Green Mountain State

The long-standing effort by the state to sell Vermont as a sanctuary to outsiders based on the myths of home-spun virtue and rural living was successful. What had been perceived in the early 1940s as a kind of social and cultural polarity pitting the summer (i.e. tourists) against the winter (i.e. year-round residents) began to dissipate. Although Vermont's population had decreased in the decade 1930–40, it began to increase dramatically in the post-war period. In the decade between 1940 and 1950, the population swelled by almost 20,000 to 377,747. Over the next two decades, the state would gain again as many new residents as it had gained in the entire previous century.

Land speculation and development—both urban and rural—followed hard on the heels of the population boom in Vermont. Both were fueled by the commencement of the federal interstate highway system in the 1960s, which not only made travel within Vermont less arduous for residents and set the stage for bedroom communities and suburban living, but also made the state more accessible to tourists year-round. Now, the specter of unchecked land development loomed on the horizon. Tom Slayton, current editor of *Vermont Life*, dates the contemporary era in Vermont to a trip newly elected Gov. Deane C. Davis made through southern Vermont in 1969. Davis was shocked by the poorly planned and executed development he saw there. According to Slayton, "Davis's concern, publicity about the new developments, and a concerned state legislature combined in 1970 to create the landmark development-control law still known as Act 250."[51]

Act 250 immediately attracted nationwide attention as one of the country's most progressive attempts at regulating land use. But Vermont's legislators moved further. They also placed strict regulatory limits on billboards and implemented a container deposit law. Although Congress passed the Clean Air Act the same year, seeking to reduce hazardous emissions that were polluting the air, the small state of Vermont was clearly setting the nation's pace for protecting its natural resources. The Green Revolution had begun. Nowhere was its impetus more clearly focused than in Vermont.

"We do well to ask," wrote the author of *Small is Beautiful* in 1973

> why it is that all these terms—pollution, environment, ecology, etc.—have so suddenly come into prominence. After all, we have had an industrial system for quite some time, yet only five or ten years ago these words were virtually unknown.[52]

Arguing that we had failed to see "nature as capital" and that the increasing use of our non-renewable natural resources since World War II would quickly deplete traditional fossil fuels such as coal, oil, and natural gas, author Ernst Friedrich Schumacher proposed the development of what he called "intermediate technologies." He emphasized the use of renewable resources, such as wood and water; labor-intensive rather than exclusively machine-oriented production; and traditional ways of life, with their emphasis upon handicrafts. It was an approach to contemporary life that offered a global prescription for living "as if people mattered."

Schumacher's theories only seemed a revolutionary concept. In practice, it was a philosophy of living to which Vermonters had subscribed, out of necessity, for almost two centuries.

Agriculture survived in Vermont, for example, because climate, geography, and depressed economics had forced the farmers to be flexible and to diversify. With the legal constraints imposed by their tough environmental legislation, Vermonters understood Schumacher's observation that

> Among material resources, the greatest, unquestionably is the land. Study how a society uses its land, and you can come to pretty reliable conclusions as to what its future will be.[53]

Small-scale, self-sustained communities sprang up in Vermont in the 1970s, spurred on by Schumacher's vision and by the national and worldwide concern for the quality of the environment.[54] Intellectual communities offered opportunities for experimentation of "New Age" ideas. Goddard College in Plainfield supported social economist Murray Bookchin's program in social ecology (now the Institute of Social Ecology in Rochester). The University of Vermont commenced an environmental studies program under the leadership of Carl Reidel that helped to shape the state's future policies regarding land-use. Burlington architect John Miller proposed a geodesic dome that would enclose the entire former mill town of Winooski, and Futurist guru Buckminster Fuller, inventor of the geodesic dome, visited Winooski and lectured on its feasibility. Consumer advocate Ralph Nader also found a responsive audience in the Green Mountain State. Small-scale and cooperatively owned businesses emphasizing intermediate technologies surfaced or were revived. The "new" Vermonters read Barry Commoner, Loren Eiseley, and René Dubos; they perused Stewart Brand's *Whole Earth Catalogue* or the *CoEvolution Quarterly*, and generally agreed with Wendell Berry that there was a future in the axiom, Think Little. They also re-read the early attempts at self-sufficiency as practiced in Vermont by Helen and Scott Nearing in the 1950s. As writer Scott E. Hastings, Jr., commented,

> Over the last twenty years, the idea of 'Country Living' has become a hot item of urban culture . . . Once again some of the old hill farms resound to the cheerful tunk of the axe getting up firewood and the dulcet squirting of milk (often as not from a nanny goat) against the pail. There is, in fact, a proliferating industry geared to the greater satisfaction of this effort.[55]

The nationwide "back to the land" movement created a new market and a new consumer. Garden Way, with headquarters in Charlotte and a retail store in South Burlington, became the L.L. Bean outlet for new homesteaders. In North Troy, for a brief period, the Quadractor was manufactured, a log-skidding machine for owners of small woodlots that, unlike its commercial counterpart, would not damage the forest. Leader Evaporator of St. Albans, a long-time commercial manufacturer of sugar-making equipment, introduced a smaller line for backyard, even top-of-the-stove, do-it-yourselfers (cat. 62). Vermont Castings, in Randolph, offered a redesigned cast-iron wood-burning stove with a greater heating efficiency than had been imagined (cat. 65.1). The city of Burlington stopped burning coal and turned to the renewable resource of wood chips to generate electricity. Blair and Ketchum's *Country Journal* was born and flourished. From throughout the state came the ripe odors of new compost heaps and the shrill ring of chain saws.

Hand-Hewn, Handcrafted, Homemade

The revival of the handcrafted, traditional object using natural materials indigenous to Vermont was closely allied with those creative enterprises involving intermediate technologies. An object or a building homemade or hand-hewn was preferable to the mass-produced object or the pre-fabricated building. A new generation of woodworkers and carpenters appeared out of nowhere. Some had college degrees; some were trained, Foxfire-style, by apprenticing to a master. Still others were schooled in new crafts programs such as Boston University's Program in Artisanry, which emerged in the early 1970s. Vermont's wood-working industry, previously a staple in the Vermont economy, was given new life (cat. 65, 66, 67). Younger artists again began working in slate, marble, clay, glass, fine metals and natural fibers.[56]

This renewed interest in Vermont crafts was not solely an outgrowth of Schumacher's philosophy. The preservation of traditional folkways and crafts had been a specific recommendation of the Commission on Country Life in 1932. The founding of the Shelburne Craft School immediately after the Second World War and the initiation by the Vermont Department of Education of the State Arts and Crafts Service in the 1940s provided a historical basis for the renaissance in the crafts. As early as 1955, the non-profit Vermont Handcrafters was founded to promote hand-crafted Vermont products. Sixteen years later, a state-wide craft center at Frog Hollow in Middlebury was created to provide a sales gallery for some of the best crafts in Vermont. By 1975, Frog Hollow Craft Center had become an "official state craft center," and in the following year, a similar state craft center was opened across the state in Windsor. Craft fairs such as those in Burlington, Stowe, and Stratton Mountain became annual events for artisans, offering them an opportunity to present in a more formal setting what could be viewed as "grass-roots" crafts at the annual agricultural fairs across the state.

Culture and Politics

Vermont was in the vanguard of the Green Revolution. It was also in the vanguard of the cultural politics of the period. By 1964 federal legislation had created the National Endowment for the Arts and the National Endowment for the Humanities, thus providing at the state level public monies to support the arts and humanities. Following the Vermont grass-roots political model of the town meeting, the Vermont Council on the Arts and the Vermont Council on the Humanities and Public Issues implemented policies of state-wide, elected boards of trustees, thus running contrary to policies in many other states, where a majority of the trustees are politically appointed. By so doing, the broadest representation of the diverse cultural needs of Vermont citizens was met. In the years since, the V.C.A. has provided funds to help support individual visual and performing artists and nurtured community and regional arts councils throughout Vermont.[57]

The Vermont Council on the Arts has also funded exemplary projects that have expanded our concept of "art." The first state folklorist, for example, was hired by the Council on the Arts in 1978. Within four years, Jane Beck had organized a major exhibition, "Always in Season," which surveyed the folk art and folkways of Vermonters. In this exhibition, the richness of Vermont's folk culture was revealed for the first time. A particularly significant inclusion was the work of the "Original Vermonters," the Abenakis, which ethnologist John Moody observed, "has remained a living tradition passed down through family and communities to the present."[58] Three years later Beck surmised that "despite the influx of newcomers and the booming tourist industry, a traditional way of life still exists. This older way of life is rural and tied closely to the seasons."[59]

Like the discovery of the richness of the state's folk art, the revelation in the mid-1970s that Abenakis had been quietly living in Vermont and practicing their tribal language and customs for the past 200 years required a dramatic reassessment of the state's cultural history (cat. 57, 64). The new willingness of the Abenakis to affirm their presence in the state, after two centuries of invisibility, was rooted in growing pressures on the state's increasingly developed land and the Abenakis' need to reclaim tribal hunting and fishing rights within their ancient homelands if they were to preserve their traditional way of life. Meanwhile, scholars such as Marjory Power, William Haviland, and John Moody began publishing research that documented the Abenakis' claims and put to rest the long-accepted myth that Indians had never been permanent residents of the Green Mountain State.[60]

A broader and more inclusive vision of Vermont's cultural heritage was also the result of the enlightened efforts of the Division of Historic Preservation, formally created in 1975 as part of the state's Agency of Development and Community Affairs. (Although the Vermont Legislature established the Historic Sites Commission in 1947, it was the National Historic Preservation Act, passed by Congress in 1966, that provided federal funds and stimulated a nation-wide interest in architecture and archaeology.) The preservation and examination of Vermont archaeological sites, historic buildings, and districts, together with an aggressive policy of public education, have further enriched and extended our concept of Vermont's cultural history.[61]

In the past twenty-five years, the exhibitions organized by museums and art galleries in Vermont[62] have reflected these broader concepts of "cultural artifact." They have also reflected a spectrum of contemporary social and political issues and documented Vermont's rural culture and the gradual loss of the family farm.

Artists and artisans—avant-garde to anarchist—have found both an intellectual stimulus and an environmental sanctuary in the Green Mountain State. Academic communities throughout Vermont have fostered and supported the arts by means of annual festivals, institutes, conferences, and visiting artist programs.

The richness and diversity of artistic expression in Vermont should not be surprising for a state with a total population of just over half-a-million residents, given its proximity to such cultural centers as Boston and New York. The diversity of cultural politics in the state is simply a reflection of a lively political life unique to Vermont.

These are politics perhaps best understood by the people who live here. Vermont has at times been viewed as traditionally Republican. A more accurate view would assert that Vermonters are independent. It should be noted that both Senators Warren Austin and George Aiken favored bi-partisan unity on many issues, and especially in international affairs. These reasoned voices of elder statesmen were in keeping with one aspect of the Vermont myth: that the state was largely inhabited by older and more sagacious residents than those who lived elsewhere.

That image was to change dramatically after 1962, when young Philip H. Hoff was elected governor of Vermont. He became the first Democrat to hold that office in almost 100 years. In the mid 1970s, an elderly Senator George Aiken stepped down from office, and a young attorney, Patrick Leahy, was elected in his place. Leahy had come into prominence in part because of his strong prosecution of industries polluting Lake Champlain waters. In 1984 Madeleine Kunin, a Swiss-born immigrant, was elected Vermont's first woman governor. Bernard Sanders, former mayor of "The People's Republic of Burlington" (*Fig. 3.6*), has recently been elected to Congress running as an independent.

Just in the past decade, the Green Revolution has been brought into Vermont cities and towns. Third-party politics, employing strategies combining self-reliance, community organizing, and a new awareness of the state's cultural and historic fabric have given new life to Vermont towns as diverse as Brattleboro, White River Junction, Burlington, and Rutland. Urban homesteading has become an alternative to country living.

Vermont and the Global Village

Vermonters have established a new tradition of seeing themselves as part of a construct larger than the Green Mountain State. In the twentieth century, Vermont's cultural and economic identity has become regional, national, and even international in outlook. This is evidenced by Vermonters such as publisher Charles Tuttle, Jr., of Rutland, who established a unique book trade with Japan after World War II.[63] The Experiment in International Living, founded in Putney in the 1930s, came to maturity in the two decades following, offering Americans, Europeans, and Asians an innovative, in-depth experience in understanding one another.[64] The Fresh Air Fund, through which Vermonters have been sharing their homes with disadvantaged children from New York City for nearly forty summers, demonstrates a similar desire on the part of the state's residents to foster understanding and goodwill. In 1984, Mayor Bernard Sanders, acting with the unanimous support of the Burlington board of aldermen, initiated a sister-cities relationship with Puerto Cabezas, Nicaragua, which resulted in massive donations by Vermonters of medical supplies, food, clothing, and educational materials for that Central American city.[65] More recently, a sister-cities relationship has been established between Burlington and the Soviet Union city of Yaroslavl.

Vermonters have had a special interest in developing closer ties with the Soviet Union ever since exiled Soviet author Alexander Solzhenitsyn moved to Vermont in 1977. During the 1980s interested citizens from Middlebury developed a cultural exchange of children's art between the Soviet Union and the United States.[66] Project Harmony, a Vermont-initiated cultural experiment, has created an opportunity for school-aged students from the Soviet Union and Vermont to travel to each other's countries to present their music to enthusiastic audiences. Just recently, Ben & Jerry's Homemade, Inc., one of Vermont's most well-known entrepreneurial stories of the twentieth century, has been negotiating to open a scoop shop in Petrozavodsk (cat. 68, 73).

Evidence of Vermonters' international perspective is also found along the northern border of the state, where road signs are bilingual—French and English—reflecting the impact of the Quiet Revolution of the Francophone majority from the province of Quebec. A substantial part of Vermont's economy is dependent upon Canadian tourists. Hydro-Quebec, the province-owned power corporation, figures prominently in Vermont's future energy needs. Bombardier, a Quebec-based firm, established a transit coach plant in Barre. The recently negotiated Free Trade Agreement between Canada and the United States will most likely result in an increase in the number of Canadian businesses investing in the Vermont economy. Former Governor Kunin's trips to Japan and Eastern Europe to secure new trading markets for the state's businesses and industries continued those aggressive economic policies that successfully attracted I.B.M. to Vermont in the 1950s.[67] The number of individuals and small firms in Vermont doing business beyond the political boundaries of the state and region is astonishing, as is the range of services and the variety of products they offer.

Faced with the loss of Vermont's older mythic identity and the vigor of the new global perspective taken by the state's residents, visitors to the state continue to purchase staples they

Fig. 3.6 Garry Trudeau. *Doonesbury.* Sunday July 5, 1981. Syndicated Cartoon Strip. *Burlington Free Press.*
DOONESBURY COPYRIGHT 1981 G. B. TRUDEAU. Reprinted with permission of Universal Press Syndicate.
All rights reserved.

associate with a rural, agrarian past: maple syrup and cheddar cheese (cat. 76, 77). In reality,
however, those traditional Vermont products have been increasingly threatened with "pollution"
by ingredients originating outside the state and by acid rain—a more complex environmental
issue than development. Furthermore, Vermont is becoming associated with new products, such
as Ben & Jerry's ice cream (*Fig. 3.7*), Burlington Bakery Bagels, Catamount Amber Ale (cat.
74), Champlain Chocolates (cat. 78), Dog Team Sticky Buns, or Grafton Goodjam (cat. 75), as
well as hundreds of other products originating from the kitchens, basements, and tool sheds of
inventive Vermonters. The spirit of cottage industries still thrives but under a different banner
and capitalized by different means. However, neither this revival of cottage industries nor the
perspective of the global village is unique to Vermont. These are phenomena that can be found
throughout the country.

This was made clear to me recently when I visited Arizona. Flying into Phoenix, I was
struck by the image of tenuous patches of green and the horizontal development in the larger
landscape of brown, jagged, vertical mountains. The drive on the interstate from Phoenix to
Tucson seemed strange and unfamiliar. The sentinel saguaro cactus and sagebrush were as
pervasive to this muted and subtly colored desert floor as the maple tree and fern-filled forest
are to the variegated verdure of the Green Mountain State. The "dude ranch" and "resort"
vacation in Arizona, whether in Sedona or in Scottsdale, are simply the counterparts of the "bed
and breakfast" and "country inn" in Craftsbury Common or Woodstock. Whether one lives in
Carefree, Arizona, or Eden, Vermont, the gradual eroding and eradication of cultural, political,
and geographical boundaries temporally and spatially joins Vermonters and Arizonans together
with the rest of the country and the world. As Arizonan Jeff Smith asked himself recently,

So what is the state of the State of Arizona? . . . Taking the cosmic view, the Big
Picture if you will, Arizona is no more real than all the artificial boundaries and

distinctions that divide places and people. We are one world; we are one people. Arizona is America is Russia is the world.[68]

So it is with Vermont today.

Conclusion

Vermont is a "state of mind" as well as a geographical and political entity. Qualities that Americans generally and Vermonters specifically identify as "redemptive" and "unique" when referring to the state's landscape are deeply engrained in the national psyche. But we need to ask whether Vermont is different in that regard from other states. Charles Morrissey posed this question in his bicentennial history and reached an ironic conclusion:

> The trouble with Vermont is that Vermont isn't different enough . . . [It] is part of the modern world despite the rural landscape which belies the reality and the Currier and Ives imagery projected from the garish sides of maple syrup tins.[69]

Nonetheless, visitors to Vermont often edit out any images and experiences that fail to conform to their preconceived ideas of what Vermont should be. Year-round residents are wont

Fig. 3.7 Glenn Russell. *Ben Cohen and Jerry Greenfield* (Ben and Jerry) in front of their Cowmobile in Burlington prior to their cross-country Scoop-A-Thon. 1986. Courtesy, Glenn Russell.

Fig. 3.8 Erik Borg. *Shelburne Road, South Burlington, looking South.* 1991.

to do the same. Why? Because Vermonters need to perpetuate old myths and create new ones just like everyone, everywhere. Faced with its high taxes and high cost of living relative to wages; its long history of economic depression; its suburbanization and "malling," which threaten to make Vermont look like "Anywhere, U.S.A.," Vermont may even discover its need for myths is more acute (*Fig. 3.8*). Consider the homage that is paid these days to the state's Northeast Kingdom. In his preface to *The View From The Kingdom*, writer Noel Perrin calls the residents of the Northeast Kingdom "the most remote and Vermonty of all Vermonters."[70] For some at least, then, the Northeast Kingdom has become the last bastion and stronghold of the Old Vermont.

However, those who keep Vermont traditions alive and well today are not necessarily those who were born here. The myth that "real" Vermonters (i.e. natives) are endowed with qualities called "Vermonty" is just that. In reality, all the people who live here and participate in the social, political, economic, and cultural life of the state—regardless of their place of origin—make Vermont "a special place."

So, too, Vermont's size is a critical factor. Compared with populations in states in the rest of the country, the number of residents of the Green Mountain State remains small, just more than a half million souls. Historically, as Dorothy Canfield Fisher noted, "the life of Vermont men and women has always been colored by the absence of immense numbers of human beings. Our relations with each other have been individual and personal."[71] This is still true today.

And the landscape plays its part also. While our larger cities and towns continue to grow, particularly those linked by the interstate highway, Vermont still "retains a 'working' rural landscape—its farmland."[72] A majority of the state's 251 towns, gores, and villages have been relatively untouched by development. Moreover, a large portion of their historic architectural fabric is still intact, while beyond the farmland and villages are parts of Vermont still so heavily wooded and mountainous that they remain virtually inaccessible. Together, landscape and townscape conspire to provide a setting ripe for those afflicted with the malady of nostalgia.

Tourism may be the final critical factor. It continues to be, as it has for a century, an important industry in the economy of Vermont. As such, it provides the most compelling of reasons why Vermont myths need to be created in the first place: They are profitable.

But there need not be a disparity or a dichotomy between myth and reality. Both are necessary. "The world never ceases to feed on dreams . . . ," observed essayist Paul Fussell. "The world is a thing that has always required compensatory imagery to make it acceptable, and 'pastoral' is as good a word as any to suggest the form compensatory imagery is likely, universally, to take."[73]

After all is said and done, then, Vermont remains for most Americans a "pastoral Arcadia." Most Vermonters would agree. As such, the state holds a special place in the culture and cultural history of the nation. Perhaps this explains why Vermonters will continue to thoughtfully conserve their traditions and landscape, as they have in the past, even as they reach out to the rest of the world.

William C. Lipke

Notes

1. Charles T. Morrissey, *Vermont: A Bicentennial History* (New York: W.W. Norton; Nashville: American Association for State and Local History, 1981), pp. xiv–xv.

2. Morrissey, *Bicentennial History*, p. xi.

3. Charles Crane, "Our Famous Snowflake Man," *Winter in Vermont* (New York: Alfred A. Knopf, 1941), p. 36.

4. Stanley Mallach, "Child Labor Reform and Lewis Hine," *Photography and Reform: Lewis Hine and the National Child Labor Committee* (Milwaukee: Milwaukee Art Museum, 1984), p. 13.

5. Sara Cleghorn, *Portraits and Protests* (New York: Henry Holt, 1917). Robert Frost observed that "There is more high explosive for righteousness in the least little line of Sara Cleghorn's poem about the children work-ing in the mill . . . than in all the prose of our radical-bound boys pressed together under a weight of several atmospheres of revolution." Quoted in Marion E. Dodd, "Along New England Book Trails, II—Vermont," *Yankee*, 4, No. 7 (November, 1938), p. 22.

6. Wallace Nutting, *Vermont Beautiful* (1922; reprint ed., New York: Garden City Publishing Co., 1936), pp. 270–278.

7. Herbert Corey, "The Green Mountain State," *National Geographic*, 51 (March, 1927). Corey was also stating another frequently heard theme when he mused that "Vermont may continue to resemble Scotland in sending men from its rugged hills to take their place among the leaders of the Nation." p. 331.

8. Quoted in *Return to These Hills: The Vermont Years of*

Calvin Coolidge. By Will and Jane Curtis and Frank Lieberman (Woodstock, Vt.: Curtis-Lieberman Books, 1985), p. 94.

9. William Allen White, *Calvin Coolidge: The Man Who is President* (New York: Macmillan, 1923), pp. 238–245.

10. Waldo F. Glover, "On Smocks for Vermont Farmers," *The Vermonter,* 29, No. 9 (1924), p. 143.

11. Nancy Boardman, "The Southern Vermont Art Center," in *SVA Sixtieth Anniversary Festival of the Arts* (Manchester, Vt.: SVAC, 1989), p. 4. See also Margaret Sherwood Pierce, "In Retrospect," in *SVA: The Fiftieth Anniversary* (Manchester, Vt.: SVAC, 1979).

12. Two Hundred Vermonters, *Rural Vermont: A Program for the Future* (Burlington, Vt.: The Vermont Commission on Country Life, 1931), pp. 10–11. Several explanations have been given as to why such a commission was created. On the state level, it reflected general concerns raised by the American Commission on Rural Life regarding the continued nationwide emigration of rural residents to urban areas and the subsequent decline of abandoned rural areas. This trend was especially apparent in Vermont. According to the 1920 census, Vermont—for the first time in its history—had lost population (one percent) during the previous decade. Equally alarming was a trend among Vermont's small towns: 176 of them had lost a significant percentage of their populations in the years since 1850.

13. *Rural Vermont,* p. 3. The Commission on Rural Life was an extension of the University of Vermont's Eugenics Survey, conducted by Professor H. F. Perkins in 1925.

14. *Rural Vermont,* p. 2.

15. *Rural Vermont,* p. 372.

16. *Rural Vermont,* p. 374. "These four books were the inspiration of Professor Peach; now, they can be many people's inspiration," wrote Helen Hartness Flanders in "Prospecting for Folk Songs in Vermont," *The Vermonter,* 36, No. 9 (September 1931), p. 197.

17. *Rural Vermont,* p. 372.

18. Writing almost fifty years after the report, historian Charles Morrissey echoed this view when he noted that "traveling through Vermont is like visiting a vast outdoor museum, a countryman's Williamsburg, a Walt Disney world where elderly Vermont farmers and their wives go strolling like Mickey Mouse and Minnie Mouse against a stage set of white farm houses and village greens." Morrissey, *Bicentennial History,* p. 191.

19. Charles Crane, *Let Me Show You Vermont* (New York: Alfred A. Knopf, 1937), p. 321. For more information about John Spargo, see the papers of John Spargo, Special Collections. Bailey-Howe Library, University of Vermont.

20. *Rural Life,* p. 377.

21. Workers of the Federal Writers' Project of the Works Progress Administration for the State of Vermont, *Vermont: A Guide to the Green Mountain State* (Boston: Houghton Mifflin Co., 1937), p. 120.

22. John Dewey, *Art as Experience* (1922; reprint ed., New York: Capricorn, 1958), pp. 11, 2. For an assessment of Dewey as a Vermonter, see Dorothy Canfield Fisher, *Vermont Tradition: The Biography of an Outlook on Life* (Boston: Little, Brown & Co., 1953), pp. 366–383.

23. See in particular the most recent interpretation of Paul Sample's work by Robert McGrath, who viewed the artist's "spare and tightly rendered forms . . . [as] analogous to the tight-lipped, rock-ribbed speech and behavior of the mythical Vermont hill farmer." Robert McGrath, *Paul Sample* (Hanover, N.H.: University Press of New England, 1988), p. 40. For a less stark view of Sample's Vermont, see his watercolors, which were reproduced as illustrations for Katherine Hamill's documentary essay entitled, "A Vermont Farm," which appeared in *Fortune,* 19, No. 2 (May 1939).

24. *Vermont: A Guide,* p. 131. Belaski's narrative style was indebted to the work of N. C. Wyeth and other contemporary illustrators of popular children's books on American history and biography. The six panels, recently restored, represent some of the finest extant work in Vermont funded by the W.P.A. See also the impact of narrative mural painting on Paul Sample's commission by the National Life Insurance Co. of Vermont during the 1950s in its home office in Montpelier.

25. The largest body of work supported by W.P.A. funds existing in the state today was funded by the New York City W.P.A. and is part of the collection of the Wood Art Gallery in Montpelier. The collection was acquired through the help of former Wood Gallery trustee Edwin B. Clark of New York.

26. Many of the contributors to *Vermont: A Guide to the Green Mountain State* had worked together earlier as part of the Commission on Country Life. The photographs were taken by photograhers living in the state.

27. Crane, *Let Me Show You Vermont,* pp. 4–5.

28. Vrest Orton, "The White Elephant Road," *Yankee,* 2, No. 2 (February 1936), p. 39. Orton had recently founded The Countryman Press.

29. Crane, *Let Me Show You Vermont,* p. 18. Crane also argued that Vermont's "comparative isolation, involving more individual and less mass action, and a proximity to nature are among our influences, plus the hormones and traditions which we inherit from the pioneers, such as the Green Mountain Boys," p. 20.

30. Crane, *Let Me Show You Vermont,* p. 122.

31. Herbert Wheaton Congdon, *Old Vermont Houses* (1940; reprint ed., Dublin, N.H.: William L. Bauhan, 1973), p. xvii.

32. Contributors to early issues of *Yankee* included Dorothy Canfield Fisher and Vrest Orton. Until the appearance of *Vermont Life* after World War II, *Yankee* reached a broader, regional audience than did the waning state magazine, *The Vermonter.* Among the best of *Yankee's* articles about Vermont in the late 1930s was Marion Dodd's survey of contemporary writing in the state. "Along New England Book Trails, II – Vermont," *Yankee,* 4, No. 7 (November 1938).

33. Dorothy Canfield Fisher, "Vermonters" in *Vermont: A Guide to the Green Mountain State* (Boston: Houghton Mifflin, 1937), p. 4.

34. Crane, *Winter in Vermont*, p. 199.

35. Theodore Strauss, review of *Holiday Inn* in the *New York Times*, 5 August 1942.

36. Bing Crosby and the Andrews Sisters, *Merry Christmas*. Decca Records, No. A550, 1945 (1947). Album notes.

37. "I'm Dreaming of a White Christmas" underscores the important element of fantasy in myth. A dream is not reality. That quality was also stated in Crosby's popular rendition of "I'll Be Home For Christmas If Only In My Dreams." (1943) The "I" in both songs was originally the American G.I. Other songs recorded by Crosby which extolled the merits of the winter "dreamscape" were "Let It Snow" and "Winter Wonderland," both written in 1946.

38. Crane, *Winter in Vermont*, p. 44. Crane estimated in 1941 that "nearly two million families annually gather round Vermont Christmas trees."

39. Julie Becker, "Moonlight in Vermont," *Yankee*, 49, No. 10 (October 1985), pp. 18–19. For related popular songs with a Vermont theme, see the newly catalogued sheet music collection of the period 1820–1980 in the collections of the Vermont Historical Society, Montpelier, Vermont.

40. The "Four Freedoms" appeared in the February 20, February 27, March 6, and March 13, 1943, issues of the *Saturday Evening Post*. "Each was accompanied by a short essay by some well-known writer, saying in words what Rockwell was saying on canvas." Ben Hibbs, quoted in Norman Rockwell, *Norman Rockwell: My Adventures as an Illustrator* (New York: Doubleday & Co., 1960), p. 343. For other renderings of the "Four Freedoms," see "Artists Interpret the 'Four Freedoms,'" *Art Digest*, 17, No. 11 (March 1, 1943), p. 10. Rockwell had moved to Arlington in 1938, already a successful illustrator. His first cover for the *Saturday Evening Post* appeared in 1916. Among the colony of fine arts illustrators residing in Arlington was Rockwell, Mead Schaeffer, Jack Atherton, and George Hughes.

41. Rockwell, *My Adventures as an Illustrator*, p. 343. Editor Ben Hibbs noted that the "Four Freedoms" were reprinted in the millions and distributed both in this country and abroad. The Treasury Department "took the original paintings on a tour of the nation . . . to sell war bonds. They were viewed by 1,222,000 people in 16 leading cities and were instrumental in selling $132,992,539 worth of bonds." p. 343.

42. See Serge Guilbaut, *How New York Stole the Idea of Modern Art: Abstract Expressionism, Freedom, and the Cold War* (Chicago: University of Chicago Press, 1983). The more conventional interpretation of abstract painting during the post-war period was that it was politically subversive and un-American. The emergence of an American Modernist (abstract) avant-garde movement in painting was in sharp contrast to the dominant Regionalist (realist) painters of the previous decades associated with the rise of popular culture.

43. Dorothy Canfield Fisher, "Preface," in Arthur L. Guptill, *Norman Rockwell: Illustrator* (New York: Watson and Guptill, 1946), pp. viii-ix.

44. Louis Bromfield, "Introduction," in Otto Kallir (ed.), *Grandma Moses: American Primitive* (Garden City: Doubleday & Co., 1947), p. 12. It seems appropriate, given the references to a "mythic Vermont" in her paintings, that the largest public collection of Grandma Moses's works are in Vermont in The Bennington Museum.

45. *Vermont Life* was most closely modeled after the format of *Arizona Highway*, the successful monthly magazine published by the Arizona Highway Commission, beginning in the mid-1920s. *Vermont Life's* editorship has included Earl Newton; Walter Hard, Jr.; Brian Vachon; Charles Morrissey; Nancy Price Graff; and Thomas Slayton. Among its associate editors have been Arthur Peach, Ralph Nading Hill, Ronald Rood, Stewart Holbrook, and Stephen Greene.

46. Earlier "outdoor museums" where the past was reconstructed were: Colonial Williamsburg (begun in 1929); Winterthur (1926); Greenfield Village in Dearborn, Michigan (1929); and Storrowtown Village in Springfield, Massachusetts (1929). For an exhaustive analysis of the obsession with recreating the past see David Lowenthal on "Nostalgia," in *The Past is a Foreign Country*. For a general history of "outdoor museums," see *Art in America*, 43, No. 2 (May 1955).

47. Quoted in *Shelburne Museum: 1989 Annual Report*. (Shelburne, Vermont: 1989), p. 4. The most recent assessment of Electra Webb's achievement has been made by Benjamin L. Mason, "A 'Simple' Vision," in *An American Sampler: Folk Art From the Shelburne Museum* (Washington, D.C.: The National Gallery of Art, 1987). Today, the Shelburne Museum has grown to 37 buildings and includes some 80,000 artifacts. It attracts 175,000 visitors annually.

48. Walter Karp, "Greenfield Village," in *American Heritage*, 32, No. 1 (December 1980), p. 100. Officially opened on October 21, 1929, to commemorate the fiftieth anniversary of Thomas Edison's invention of the incandescent light, Greenfield Village was originally called "The Early American Village."

49. Dorothy Canfield Fisher, "Preliminary Remarks," *Vermont Tradition: The Biography of an Outlook on Life* (Boston: Little, Brown & Co., 1953), pp. 8–9. Published in October 1953, it was reprinted three times by the end of the month. At the time of her death, Fisher was one of the most popular women in the United States. She was a prolific author and lecturer who served on the editorial board of the Book-of-the-Month Club and was the recipient of countless honorary degrees. For a critical biography of Fisher, see Elizabeth Yates, *The Lady From Vermont: Dorothy Canfield Fisher's Life and World* (Brattleboro, Vt.: The Stephen Greene Press, 1971). The softcover edition reproduces Norman Rockwell's portrait of Fisher and her husband, John. The book was originally published by Stephen Greene Press in 1958 as *Pebble in a Pool*.

50. Fisher, *Vermont Tradition*, p. 383. Fisher surmised that Robert Frost's poems "tell us that no matter how

inept our efforts, we do well to try to time human life to the slow, in-the-end triumphant pace of growth," p. 385.

51. Tom Slayton, "The Question of Development," in *Finding Vermont* (Montpelier, Vt: Vermont Life, 1986), p. 66.

52. Ernst Friedrich Schumacher, *Small is Beautiful* (New York: Harper and Row, 1973), p. 16.

53. Schumacher, *Small is Beautiful*, p. 95. Schumacher's concept of enlightened management of natural resources was not new. Vermonter George Perkins Marsh had argued for a similar rational approach to the conservation and preservation of natural resources in his revolutionary *Man and Nature*, published in 1864. The heightened awareness of world-wide environmental issues was due also in part to a number of seemingly disparate circumstances. The concept of the earth as a self-contained, interdependent eco-system was brought home by the photographs of earth from space taken by NASA's Apollo and Gemini missions in the 1960s and 1970s. The phrase "Mother Earth" was given new currency. Suddenly, many people realized that the destruction of natural resources in one part of the world could be as detrimental to the balance of nature as was the annihilation of human lives by famine or war.

54. Utopian communities in Vermont ranged from the sophisticated, family-managed agricultural estate of Shelburne Farms to Earth People's Park in the Northeast Kingdom. Educational experiments in Vermont which emerged in the early 1970s and which responded to issues of environmental quality and self-sufficiency included the creation of both Sterling College in Craftsbury Common and the Center for Northern Studies, based in Wolcott. See Jack Cook, "Sterling College," *Country Journal*, 10, No. 9 (September 1983), pp. 76–82, and Jack Cook, "Scholars of the Far North," *Country Journal*, 13, No. 2 (Februrary 1986), pp. 70–75.

55. Scott E. Hastings, Jr., "Farmstead and Family Life: One for the Blackbird," in *Always in Season: Folk Art and Traditional Culture in Vermont*. ed. Jane C. Beck (Montpelier, Vt.: Vermont Council on the Arts, 1982), pp. 78, 81.

56. The Bennington Potters was one of the most successful examples of the commercial revival of the crafts in the 1960s. See Jane F. McCullough, "The Bennington Potters," *Vermont Life*, 26, No. 2 (Winter 1961).

57. Stephen Reiner, "The Vermont Council on the Arts," *Vermont Life*, 31, No. 3 (Spring 1977).

58. John Moody, "The Native American Legacy," in *Always in Season: Folk Art and Traditional Culture in Vermont*. ed. Jane C. Beck (Montpelier, Vt.: Vermont Council on the Arts, 1982), p. 64.

59. Jane C. Beck, *Always in Season: Folk Art and Traditional Culture in Vermont*. (Montpelier, Vt.: Vermont Council on the Arts, 1982), p. 18. Most recently the Vermont Folklife Center has opened its doors in Middlebury.

60. Tom Slayton, "The Vermont Abenaki Are Visible Again," *Vermont Life*, 36, No. 3 (Spring 1982), pp. 51–57.

61. For an excellent history of historic preservation and archaeology in Vermont, see *Historic Preservation in Vermont*. ed. Paul Bruhn (Montpelier, Vt.: The Preservation Trust of Vermont, 1982).

62. For a comprehensive list of museums and galleries in Vermont see *Vermont Museums, Galleries, and Historic Buildings*. ed. Christine Hadsel (Montpelier, Vt.: The Vermont Museum and Gallery Alliance, 1988).

63. Jacob L. Chernofsky, "Charles E. Tuttle and the Japanese Connection," *Antiquarian Books* (September 17, 1990).

64. For the history of the Experiment in International Living see Donald B. Watt, *Intelligence is Not Enough* (Brattleboro, Vt.: The Experiment Press, 1967) and Donald B. Watt, et al., *Letters to the Founder* (Brattleboro, Vt.: The Experiment Press, 1977).

65. A visual record of the Puerto Cabezas-Burlington relationship was documented by photographer Dan Higgins. See *Sister Cities: Side By Side* (Burlington, Vt.: Green Valley Film and Art, Inc., 1988), photographs by Dan Higgins and foreword by Alexander Cockburn.

66. The exhibition "Child to Child: American-Soviet Children's Art Exchange" was toured nationally by the Smithsonian Institution's SITES program. On Solzhenitsyn, see Andrew Nemethy, "The Solzhenitsyns of Cavendish," *Vermont Life*, 38, No. 1 (Autumn 1983), pp. 20–27.

67. According to August St. John, "The immediate issue in Vermont in 1990 is not education. Not the environment. But the deficit . . . A deteriorating economy will not preserve the environment, it will merely build pressures to relax land-use controls and encourage commercial development." Quoted in Peter Horton, "Dr. Doom and Dr. Gloom," *Vermont Magazine*, 2, No. 4 (July/August 1990), p. 70.

68. Jeff Smith, "Taking a Holiday From Racism," in the *Tucson Weekly*, 7, No. 14 (May 23–29, 1990), p. 3.

69. Morrissey, *Bicentennial History*, p. 22.

70. Noel Perrin, "Introduction," *The View From the Kingdom* (New York: Harcourt Brace Jovanovich, 1987), p. 8. Photographs by Richard Brown, essays by Reeve Lindbergh.

71. Fisher, *Vermont Tradition*, p. 188.

72. Slayton, *Finding Vermont*, p. 36.

73. Paul Fussell, "On the Persistence of Pastoral," *Thank God for the Atom Bomb and Other Essays* (New York: Ballantine, 1988), pp. 170–177.

Contributors to the Catalogue

LJB   Lauren J. Barth
Assistant Curator of Decorative Arts
Shelburne Museum
Shelburne

DAD   David A. Donath
Director
Billings Farm and Museum
Woodstock

WNH   William N. Hosley, Jr.
Curator of Decorative Arts
Wadsworth Atheneum
Hartford, Connecticut

JMH   John M. Hunisak
Professor of Art
Middlebury College

WCL   William C. Lipke
Associate Professor of Art
University of Vermont

JRM   J. Robert Maguire
Shoreham

CYO   Celia Y. Oliver
Curator
Shelburne Museum
Shelburne

KEP   Karen E. Petersen
Director
Rokeby
Ferrisburgh

RHS   Richard H. Saunders
Director
Middlebury College Museum of Art
Middlebury College

VMW   Virginia M. Westbrook
Exhibition Curator
Crown Point, New York

FMW   Frederick M. Wiseman
Ambassador for Scientific and Cultural Affairs
Abenaki Nation at Missisquoi
     AND
Associate Professor
Department of Humanities
Johnson State College

CZ   Catherine Zusy
Curator of Decorative Arts
The Bennington Museum
Bennington

7 *Desk*; attributed to Asa Loomis (1793–1868); Shaftsbury, *c.* 1815; Private Collection

16 *Receiver*; attributed to Vermont Glass Factory; Salisbury, *c.* 1814; Private Collection

18 *Thirteen-Inch Terrestrial Globe*; James Wilson (1763–1855); Barnard, *c.* 1810–1817; Vermont Historical Society

20 *Chest of Drawers*; George Stedman (working in Vermont 1816–1822); Norwich, *c.* 1816–1822; The Henry Francis du Pont Winterthur Museum

21 *Titus Hutchinson Family*; Thomas Ware (1803–1826/7); *c.* 1820–1825; Woodstock Historical Society; formerly in the collection of the Ottauquechee Chapter, D.A.R. Museum, Woodstock

27 *The Haymakers, Mount Mansfield, Vermont*; Jerome Thompson (1814–1886); 1859; Manoogian Collection

31 *A Marble Quarry*; James Hope (1818/19–1892); 1851; Museum of Fine Arts, Boston; M. and M. Karolik Collection

37 *Chapel Organ*; Jacob Estey Organ Company; Brattleboro, 1884; Old Stone House Museum, Brownington

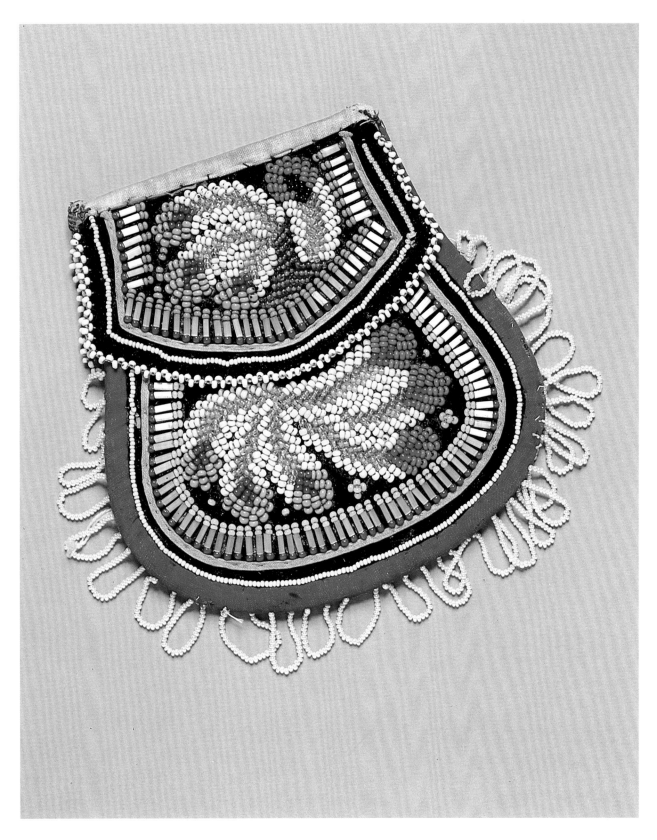

46 *Beaded Reticule*; Abenaki (?), Found in Tunbridge, *c.* 1880; Abenaki Cultural Center, Swanton

50 *Village of Stowe, Vermont;* Luigi Lucioni (1900–1988); 1931; The Minneapolis Institute of Arts. Gift from the Estate of Mrs. George P. Douglas

51 *Church Supper*; Paul Sample (1896–1974); 1933; Museum of Fine Arts, Springfield, Massachusetts; The James Philip Gray Collection

61 *Peace Hand Puppet*; Bread and Puppet Theatre; Glover, *c.* 1972; Bread and Puppet Theatre, Glover

Catalogue of the Exhibition

Notes to the Catalogue

Each of the catalogue entries in this volume provides primary information about the object in a heading. Detailed information here consists of the form, object's maker or attribution (where known), place of manufacture and date, materials, signature or inscription (if any), dimensions, collection, and credit line. Each artist's or maker's vital dates are given. If the maker is unknown, the first line of the heading is omitted. Height (H), length (L), width (W), circumference (C), depth (D), and diameter (DIAM) are overall measurements unless otherwise noted.

1 *Musket*

c. 1770
Hickory, brass, and iron
L: 67⅝ inches
Engraved (on lockplate): "Ethan"
Ownership attributed to Ethan Allen
(1773–1789)
Vermont Historical Society, Montpelier

Of the many forms of myth that a culture weaves for itself, the most moving and vivid are those that wrap around the shoulders of a hero. When Ethan Allen led the Green Mountain Boys to wrest Fort Ticonderoga from an unsuspecting British garrison in May of 1775, he transformed a heretofore defensive resistance to English tyranny into an offensive quest for freedom and democracy. By his daring at a crucial moment in American history, he attained a stature larger than life and earned for himself a spot high in the pantheon of American Revolutionary War heroes.

More than 200 years later, Ethan Allen's name continues to reverberate with almost sacred intonation. What care Vermonters that in his day he was called a "ringleader of the Bennington

Mob,"[1] "ruffian," or a dozen other defamatory names? He acted precipitously to wrest home rule from a distant despot. We don't need to know any more—not even what he looked like—for Ethan Allen to carry the meaning of our memory of the revolutionary struggle for freedom.

It is no more essential to know with certainty whether Ethan Allen really owned this gun. Certainly, the gunstock is old enough, and it closely resembles the work of gunsmiths working in the Connecticut Valley, the center of firearm production in the colonies.[2] It is possible that Allen brought the gun with him from Connecticut when he first explored the New Hampshire Grants around 1766 or that he obtained the gun once he arrived here, but in either case it is unlikely that Allen scratched his name in the lockplate. We do know that the rifle was left with Captain Abram Underhill at Dorset, Vermont, early in the Revolutionary War and that it passed through his family until it was presented to the Vermont Historical Society in 1876.

Regardless of whether this rifle belonged to Allen, it is symbolic of our struggle to gain control of our own affairs. The reminder works, however, only as long as the mythology passes on in the fabric of the culture. Every generation has done its part by retelling the story of Ethan Allen, each time retooling it to fit the learning style of the times, first in the state's early formal histories;[3] later in biographies; later still in the state's literature;[4] and most recently by recreating historical space at the Ethan Allen Homestead. This gun continues to bear testimony silently, but only as long as we keep retelling the heroic story.

VMW

1. Affidavit in Support of the Petition of Rev. Benjamin Hough, March 7, 1775, *The Documentary History of the State of New York*, vol. 4 (Albany, N.Y.: Charles Van Benthuysen, Public Printer, 1851), p. 539.

2. M. L. Brown, *Firearms in Colonial America: The Impact on History and Technology* (Washington, D.C.: Smithsonian Institution Press, 1980), p. 318.

3. See, Kevin Graffagnino, "The Vermont 'Story:' Continuity and Change in Vermont Historiography," *Vermont History*, 46, No. 2 (Spring, 1978), pp. 77–99.

4. See John McWilliams, "The Faces of Ethan Allen: 1760–1860," *The New England Quarterly*, 49 (1976), pp. 257–82.

2 Certificate of Punishment of Rev. Benjamin Hough

Sunderland, January 30, 1775
Ink on paper
H: 12¾ inches W: 7½ inches

J. Robert Maguire

Nowhere on the New Hampshire Grants was resistance to New York authority more tenaciously maintained by the Green Mountain Boys than in Socialborough, a town settled under New York land titles and covering much of the present day limits of Rutland. Here, early in 1773, there appeared an intrepid Anabaptist minister named Benjamin Hough, who as justice of the peace and magistrate under a commission from New York posed a no less-determined resistance to the Green Mountain Boys. Following repeated confrontations with local resisters, the New York Assembly on petition by Hough passed an act against "tumultuous and riotous assemblies" in which certain acts were declared to be felonies punishable by death. Named in the act as ringleaders of recent disturbances were Ethan Allen, Seth Warner, and six other leaders of the Green Mountain Boys. A warrant was issued for their arrest and a reward offered for their apprehension.

Retribution was soon visited upon Hough, who was taken from his home "by about thirty persons a Number of whom were armed with Firelocks Swords and Hatchets." Hough was bound, forced into a sleigh, and carried to Sunderland for trial, where he was informed that "he could not have his Trial till the Monday following because they intended to send for Ethan Allen and Seth Warner who were then at Bennington and who are two of the principal Ringleaders of the Bennington Mob." At his trial, Hough unflinchingly admitted the three charges against him to be true, namely, that he "had complained to the Government of New York . . . had dissuaded and discouraged the people from joining the Mob in their proceedings [and] . . . had taken a commission of the peace under the Government of New York, and exercised his office as a Magistrate."

Following deliberation by the seven judges, "who acted in the double office of Accusers and Judges," Allen pronounced sentence: Hough "should be tyed up to a Tree and receive two hundred lashes on the naked Back, and then as soon as he should be able, should depart the New Hampshire Grants and not return again upon pain of receiving five hundred Lashes." Thereupon, Hough "immediately had his Clothes taken off and he was stripped to the skin, and four persons being by the said pretended Court appointed to carry the said sentence into Execution [he] accordingly received the two hundred Lashes on his naked Back with whips of cords; which Lashes were inflicted by each of the said Executioners giving [him] alternately a Number of Lashes." Hough was "very much wounded and bled considerably by the said abuse."

After execution of the sentence, he was given this certificate of punishment, and "having recovered his strenth the next Day [he] proceeded on Foot on his Journey towards the City of New York," where, "destitute of the means of Support," he was granted a license to solicit alms from the public. The punishment of Hough appears to have been the final, and most violent, act of personal injury inflicted by the Green Mountain Boys in the jurisdictional controversy with New York.[1]

JRM

1. Hough's account of his abduction, trial, and punishment is told in his own words in his affidavit dated March 7, 1775, in support of his petition for relief to the Governor's Council of the Province of New York. *The Documentary History of the State of New York.* vol. 4 (New York, 1851), pp. 539–542.

REFERENCES

Hall, Hiland. *The History of Vermont from Its Discovery to Its Admission into the Union in 1791* (Albany, N.Y., 1868), pp. 178–190.

Sunderland January the 30th Day AD 1775
This may Certify the Inhabitants of the ~~Island~~
New Hampshire Grants that Benjamin
Hough hath this Day Recd a full Punish-
-ment for his Crimes Committed Heretofore
Against this Country and our Inhabitants
are Ordered to Give him the Huff a free
and Unmolested Passport Toward the
City of NewYork or to the westward of
our Grants he Behaving as becom-
-eth Given Under our Hands the Day
and Date Aforesaid.

Ethan Allen
Seth Warner

3 *Green Mountain Frontier*

c. 1690–1760

From *The Western Abenakis of Vermont, 1600–1800*, by Colin G. Calloway. Copyright © 1990 by the University of Oklahoma Press.

Early New Englanders found Vermont to be both a forbidding wilderness and a Native American stronghold. During much of the seventeenth and eighteenth centuries their experience was that of tentative trespassers. They encountered native inhabitants descended from aboriginals whose presence can now be traced back through the Woodland Period (1600 B.C. to 1000 B.C.) to the beginning of the Archaic Period (7000 B.C. to 1000 B.C.) and whose maize agriculture, hunting, fishing and gathering activities were all developed. These Western Abenakis, who numbered approximately 10,000 at the start of the seventeenth century, inhabited an area that stretched from Lake Champlain on the west to the White Mountains in the east, and from southern Quebec to the Vermont-Massachusetts border. Key Native American communities were located at Squakeag (Northfield, Massachusetts) and Cowass (near modern-day Newbury, Vermont) on the Connecticut River, as well as at Winooski and Missisquoi on Lake Champlain.

As European settlements increased in southern New England throughout the 1600s and 1700s, Native American refugees from Connecticut and Massachusetts moved northward, helping to replenish a population reduced by famine, disease, and warfare and reaffirming aboriginal claims to land, especially in the northern half of Vermont (cat. 3.1). However, European settlers followed them in increasing numbers after 1760 and ultimately undermined the hunting, fishing, and trapping potential of the land for the native inhabitants.

Myth and irony contributed significantly to the European colonists' image of the Abenaki, and ignorance has compounded the problems of our understanding today. Confronted by settlers who threatened their land claims and way of life, these Native Americans responded defensively. Even-

tually, war assumed a disproportionate importance in Native American societies and produced a distorted image of Abenakis as warlike. Written records exacerbated this image as the English wrote about the Abenaki as a military threat and the French reported on them as allies against the English. In reality, Western Abenakis fought to survive in a dangerous new world.[1]   RHS

1. This summary is compiled from Colin G. Calloway, *The Western Abenakis of Vermont, 1600–1800* (Norman and London: University of Oklahoma Press, 1990), Chapter 1 "The Green Mountain Frontier: Conflict, Coexistence, and Migration," pp. 3–33.

Cat. 3.1 Daniel Friedrich Sotzmann. *Vermont.* 1796. Hamburg: Carl Ernst Bohn. Engraved by Paulus Schmidt. Courtesy, Special Collections, University of Vermont.

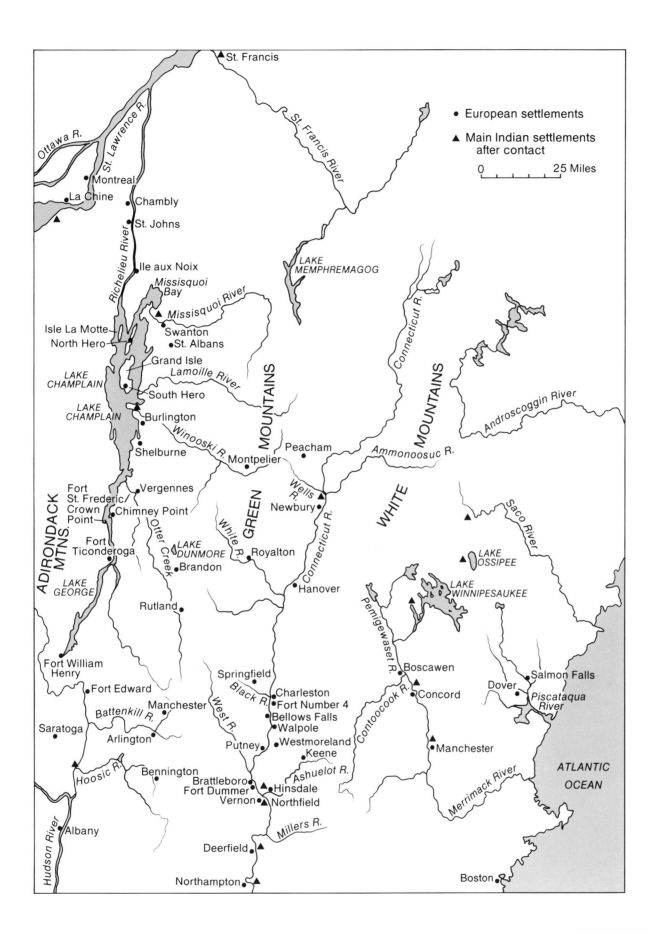

St. Francis

European settlements

Main Indian settlements
after contact

0　　　　　　　25 Miles

Ottawa R.

St. Lawrence R.

Montreal

La Chine

Chambly

St. Johns

Richelieu River

Ile aux Noix

LAKE
MEMPHREMAGOG

St. Francis River

Missisquoi
Bay

Missisquoi River

Isle La Motte

Swanton

North Hero

St. Albans

Grand Isle

Lamoille River

LAKE
CHAMPLAIN

South Hero

LAKE
CHAMPLAIN

Burlington

Connecticut R.

Androscoggin River

Shelburne

Winooski R.

Montpelier

Peacham

Ammonoosuc R.

GREEN MOUNTAINS

WHITE MOUNTAINS

Fort
St. Frederic/
Crown
Point

Vergennes

Wells
R.

Newbury

Chimney Point

ADIRONDACK MTNS.

Otter Creek

White R.

LAKE
DUNMORE

Royalton

Connecticut R.

Saco River

Fort
Ticonderoga

Brandon

LAKE
OSSIPEE

LAKE
GEORGE

Hanover

Pemigewaset R.

LAKE
WINNIPESAUKEE

Rutland

Fort William
Henry

Boscawen

Fort Edward

Springfield

Black R.

Charleston

Fort Number 4

Dover

Salmon Falls

Concord

Piscataqua
River

Manchester

Battenkill R.

West R.

Bellows Falls

Walpole

Saratoga

Arlington

Putney

Westmoreland

Keene

Manchester

Hoosic R.

Bennington

Brattleboro

Fort Dummer

Vernon

Hinsdale

Northfield

Ashuelot R.

Contoocook R.

Merrimack River

ATLANTIC
OCEAN

Hudson River

Albany

Deerfield

Millers R.

Northampton

Boston

4 *Colchester Jar*
St. Lawrence Iroquois style (?)
c. 1400–1500
Clay
H: 7 inches DIAM: 5 inches C: 27 inches
Robert Hull Fleming Museum, University of
Vermont, 1827.1

The Colchester Jar, discovered in Colchester, Vermont, in 1825, has long been the center of controversy concerning the eastern or southeastern boundary of the Iroquoians. Archaeologist James Pendergast, in a well-researched and documented argument published in 1990, concluded that the Colchester Jar represents an Iroquoian presence on the eastern side of what the Abenaki called the "lake between" (Lake Champlain). Other scholars believe that the jar represents stylistic diffusion resulting from intercourse and trade among tribal nations rather than the actual presence of Iroquoians. Both these scholarly models imply that the Iroquois somehow have "stylistic ownership" of the attributes of the jar.

The controversy that has swirled around this jar in recent decades is not a result of any problems inherent in the jar itself but with our perception of it. Archaeologists use a ceramic terminology that applies the "type site"—the name of the place where a ceramic style was first discovered—as part of a shard's name; hence, this jar is called the "Colchester Jar." Thus, if early research by ceramicists was carried out in the Iroquoian area, all ceramics discovered there would bear St. Lawrence or New York names, regardless of any shard's true place of origin. Such a methodology may mistakenly suggest that a cluster of style names (which are, of course, really Euroamerican perceptions) implies an Iroquoian "heartland," whose ceramics are necessarily distinguished by those characteristics represented in the shards. When a Colchester Jar is found at the perceived edge of this heartland, people assume that its style somehow radiated from the Iroquoian heartland into a darkened Vermont periphery.

This darkness is the result of the same scholarly neglect and misunderstanding that caused such otherwise astute Vermont historians as the late Dorothy Canfield Fisher and Ralph Nading Hill to cast Vermont as a Native American "no man's land." However, if Vermont had not been so neglected by earlier professional archaeologists—and New York and the St. Lawrence region less archaeologically attractive—the situation may have been reversed: An Abenaki heartland would have been documented in Vermont early on, and any pottery discovered in New York bearing any similarity to that found in Vermont would be considered as peripheral to Vermont.

Historical accidents in Northeastern archaeology are not necessarily bad, but they have been used by the state of Vermont in an attempt to extinguish Abenaki rights to land that has been theirs for 10,000 years. Therefore, the Colchester Jar represents both myth and reality: Its stylistic attributes are real, but what Euroamericans hold as truth about the jar's provenance is belief. And of course, the long-held myth that Vermont was never a permanent residence for Native Americans is based partly on that belief. This nomenclature carries profound moral implications when it fosters beliefs that deny the rights of a native people to their homeland and their ancestral way of life. FMW

5 *A South View of the New Fortress at Crown Point, with the Camp, Commanded by Major General Amherst in the Year 1759*
Thomas Davies (c. 1737–1812)
Watercolor on paper
H: 14¾ inches w: 21 1/16 inches

Henry Francis du Pont Winterthur Museum

At Crown Point, "where [Lake] Champlain's lizardlike length suddenly pinches into a thin tail,"[1] the French built Fort St. Frederic in 1731 in order to assure their control of this water highway through the American wilderness. For nearly thirty years the French maintained their control, first with Fort Frederic alone, and after 1755 with a second fort a dozen miles south at Ticonderoga. When Amherst's 1759 expedition ended the seventy-year contest for control of the Champlain Valley and drove the French northward, the British general ordered that a new fort be built on the Crown Point peninsula. Thomas Davies,

lieutenant of artillery, recorded the early stages of construction with the precision he had learned as a cadet at the Royal Military Academy in Woolwich.[2]

As Davies began to sketch the encampment at Crown Point, General Amherst dispatched a party of Provincials to construct a road eastward to Fort Number 4 on the Connecticut River in Charlestown, New Hampshire. Rangers and Redcoats, scouts and settlers traveled the Crown Point Road or hauled supplies over it. Many liked the look of the territory and returned after the Revolution to carve the first farms out of the forest. Some of these founded memorable Vermont lineages, such as Captain John Coolidge, who used his mustering-out scrip to buy a parcel of land in southern Plymouth Township (then called Salt Ash) just a few miles west of "26-Mile Camp" in the northwest corner of Cavendish.[3]

Although Davies frequently indulged his painter's prerogative, embellishing the foreground with native people, plants, or animals, his groupings in this view of "Hutts of Rangers & Indian Wigwams," with their inhabitants, were probably quite true-to-life. Gathered at the periphery of the construction were the present and future inhabitants of the Champlain basin: Iroquois, who were allies of the British, and the farmer/soldiers from Amherst's army.

While 3000 men labored to construct Fort Crown Point, Amherst sent his officers on exploratory forays. He ordered Thomas Davies to investigate likely locations for waterfalls,[4] in the hope that he would find a suitable location for a sawmill. His view, *The Falls of Otter Creek*, (cat. 5.1) painted in 1766, suggests that his quest was successful. The falls powered a gristmill, burned by the Green Mountain Boys in 1773 during their raid on New York settlers, as well as an iron furnace and foundry that produced cannonballs for the War of 1812. The settlement on the site was incorporated as a city in 1788, when it was named Vergennes, in honor of the French minister of foreign affairs.[5]   VMW

Cat. 5.1 Thomas Davies. *The Falls of Otter Creek, Lake Champlain, with a Saw Mill.* 1766. Watercolor on paper. Courtesy, Royal Ontario Museum, Toronto, Canada.

A South View of the New Fortress at Crown Point, with the Camp, Commanded by Major General Amherst in the Year 1759

Drawn on the Spot by Thos. Davies. Capt. Lieut. of the Royal Artillery

A the New Fort. B Ruins of the Old Fort
C Light Infantry of the Army Fort
D Grenadier Fort
E Gages light Infantry Fort

F A Redoute
G Sloops of War
H Sutts of Rangers & Indian Wigwams
I Part of Lake Champlain

K Roads from Ticonderoga

1. Frederick Van de Water, *The Reluctant Republic: Vermont, 1724–1791* (1941; reprint ed., Taftsville, Vt.: The Countryman Press, 1974), p. 135.

2. R. H. Hubbard, "Thomas Davies, Gunner and Artist," *Transactions of the Royal Society of Canada*, 4th Series, Vol. IX (1971).

3. Blanche Brown Bryant and Gertrude Elaine Baker, *Genealogical Records of the Founders and Early Settlers of Plymouth, Vermont* (Delano, Fla.: The E.O. Painter Printing Co. 1967), p. 98.

4. R. H. Hubbard, Ed., *Thomas Davies in Early Canada* (Oberon Press, 1972), p. 24.

5. J. Kevin Graffagnino, *Vermont in the Victorian Age: Continuity and Change in the Green Mountain State, 1850–1900* (Rutland, Vt.: Vermont Heritage Press and the Shelburne Museum, 1985), pp. 95–97.

6 *Chest of Drawers*

Probably Temple, New Hampshire, *c.* 1780
Brought to Andover, Vermont *c.* 1785
Cherry and pine
H: 59¾ inches W: 39 inches D: 21½ inches

Farrar-Mansur House, Weston

Furniture and heirlooms brought to Vermont by eighteenth-century immigrant families were among the most poignant reminders of the world they had left behind. A quilt woven from wool raised at home or a chest made by a former neighbor evoked memories that eased the burdens of dislocation and mobility. However, these objects also highlighted the cultural differences among settlers. Like variations in building styles, home furnishings, speech, and even methods of laying out fields and fencing, they dispel the myth that Vermonters of the late eighteenth century were a homogeneous mix of displaced Connecticut Yankees.[1]

The Mansur chest is a remarkable artifact. American eighteenth-century furniture in better condition does not exist. Its finish and hardware are original and unrestored. Moreover, it is as sound in structure and as potent in style today as it was 200 years ago when it was new and new to Vermont. Such care is usually the hallmark of an object esteemed as a significant family relic.

This chest belonged to John Mansur (1765–1851), who along with Oliver Farrar and several others emigrated from Temple, New Hampshire, and settled in the Andover-Weston area. Mansur was a farmer, the second son of William Mansur, a Revolutionary War veteran from Temple, whose war pension may have made possible his son's emigration. John Mansur's farm was located north of the Simonsville district of Andover on a hillside, from whose height it was possible on a clear day to see the tower of the Temple meetinghouse, about sixty miles to the east.[2]

The chest is plain compared with the work of New England's eighteenth-century master craftsmen, but it represented luxury and status to hill-farm families, such as John Mansur's, who settled much of Vermont during the 1780s. It also represented the family and friends Mansur left behind, and thus it helped bridge the distance between one home and the next and strengthened the presence of diverse regional cultures on the Vermont frontier. The degree to which it was cherished by the Mansur family is demonstrated by its scrupulous preservation and ultimate enshrinement in a museum.   WNH

1. Some of the best published work on the folkways and vernacular expressions of Vermont's early inhabitants was written by Stewart G. McHenry; a representative example is "Eighteenth-Century Field Patterns as Vernacular Art," *Old-Time New England*, 69 (Summer-Fall 1978), pp. 1–21.
2. Mary R. Ellis, *The House of Mansur* (Jefferson City, Missouri: Mary Ellis, 1926); Henry Ames Blood, *The History of Temple, New Hampshire* (Boston: George C. Rand & Avery, 1860), pp. 97, 102, 104; John Mansur, Estate Inventory, 1852, Windsor District Probate Court Records, vol. 21, pp. 562–563; Interview with Robert H. Graham (Mansur family genealogist) of Naples, Florida (December 28, 1990). Mansur's son, Franklin, moved to Weston after his father's death and later owned the "Farrar-Mansur House," the house museum that now owns the Mansur chest.

7 *Desk*

Attributed to Asa Loomis (1793–1868)
Shaftsbury, *c.* 1815
Curly maple and pine
H: 42¾ inches W: 41⅜ inches D: 19 inches
Private Collection

Zadock Thompson's widely influential *History of Vermont* (1842) devoted more space to describing Vermont's sugar maples than to any other native tree. Noted as "one of our most common and valuable forest trees," the sugar maple, according to Thompson, was "used by chair makers and cabinet makers in many kinds of their work." Most notable was the "curled maple," an "accidental" aberration in the formation of annual rings which cabinetmakers employed to "advantage for manufacturing beautiful articles of furniture."[1] It is Vermont's most distinctive indigenous wood.

Not surprisingly, curled maple furniture was more popular in Vermont than elsewhere in New England, and some of the best American cabinetwork manufactured from the wood was Vermont-made. It was used throughout the state in detailing for architecture and as a furniture wood, but it appears to have been particularly favored in Bennington County.[2] This desk originally belonged to Lemuel Buck (*ca.* 1765–1840), one of the founding settlers of Arlington and later a resident of Shaftsbury, where the desk was made.[3] Although it is not signed, it is closely related to a curled maple chest of drawers made, signed, and dated (November 1816) by Asa Loomis, a prominent cabinetmaker in Shaftsbury.[4] It also shares with the chest of drawers an idiosyncratic arrangement of upper interior drawers, a feature that be-

came identified with Vermont furniture of the later eighteenth and early nineteenth centuries. With its heavy pine stock interior wood and its opulent exterior of cuts of curled maple, this desk epitomizes the flamboyant use of native woods commonly found in early Vermont furniture.

WNH

1. Zadock Thompson, *History of Vermont, Natural, Civil and Statistical* (Burlington, Vt.: Chauncy Goodrich, 1842), p. 209.

2. Outstanding examples of early Vermont-made curled and birds-eye maple furniture may be seen in the following public collections: tall clock case, "Rokeby," Ferrisburgh; birds-eye maple veneered card table, Community House, Middlebury; bureau signed by Abel Rideout of Weston, Farrar-Mansur House, Weston; birds-eye maple veneered card table signed by Royal H. Gould of Chester, The Art Institute of Chicago; sideboard attributed to Vermont, Museum of Fine Arts, Springfield, Massachusetts; fancy chair attributed to Prosper Millington of Shaftsbury, Shaftsbury Historical Society; chest of Drawers, Dan Foster House (Weathersfield Historical Society); bureau signed and dated (1836) by Dexter Durby of Bridport, Sheldon Museum, Middlebury. Several more examples from private collections are documented in the "Early Vermont Furniture Archive," compiled by the author.

3. Interview with Anson Hawkins, Shaftsbury, Vermont. July 12, 1979. The desk entered the Hawkins family of Shaftsbury during the 1850s.

4. The related bureau has an identical skirt and bracket foot construction, exhibits the same idiosyncratic arrangement of drawers, and is made from brilliantly figured curled maple. It descended in the Loomis family and currently belongs to a descendent in Ohio. My thanks to Catherine Zusy, curator at The Bennington Museum, for this information. Loomis married Clarissa Cross three weeks before he completed the bureau, suggesting its likely use as a bridal gift.

8 Coverlet

Maker unknown, initialed "E. K."
Danby, Vermont, 1821
Wool woven in strips, sewn together
H: 81⅞ inches W: 87 inches

The Woodstock Historical Society, Woodstock, Vermont, Gift of Mr. and Mrs. Laurance S. Rockefeller

The Danby coverlet speaks eloquently of the state of mind in rural Vermont in the early 1820s. The poem woven into the border captures the spirit of optimism and nationalist fervor that gripped the entire nation in the first decades of the nineteenth century. Prose and poetry proclaiming the virtue of the new United States of America had been produced by the yard since the end of the Revolutionary War.[1] Patriotic symbols proliferated in every medium, gracing china, signage, even machinery, but in 1821 nationalistic slogans incorporated into coverlets were something relatively new.[2]

On the surface, the poetry of prosperity supports the view of America that Francis Wright described as "a spirit of daring enterprise."[3] But the reference to agriculture and manufactures indicates the tensions that produced hot debate in the years following the War of 1812, as divergent interests struggled to determine whether the United States would continue to export raw materials and import finished products or institute tariffs to protect and encourage its own manufactures.[4] Weavers found themselves in the middle of the conflict. They needed both raw materials and protection for their product. By weaving such slogans into their designs, weavers could appeal to patriotic fervor while furthering their own political agenda.

Danby, Vermont, was in a central position in this struggle. This region enjoyed the highest wool production in the country, making the Vermont Wool Growers Association a significant political force. The 1820 census of manufactures indicates that the entire textile industry had declined drastically during the previous decade. The year this coverlet was woven, one Danby woolen mill failed as another went into production.[5] Although we do not yet know the identity of the person who wove this piece, the political orientation of the poem suggests it was a man. Further information about this fascinating object will come as a result of the inquiries launched as part of Vermont's bicentennial celebration.   VMW

1. In the 1790s, a group of writers became known as "the Connecticut Wits" for their efforts to supply America with its own epic poetry. Any of them (Barlow, Dwight, Humphreys, Hopkins, or Alsop) could have penned these words. More likely, a latter-day imitator published them in the popular press. See Vernon Louis Parrington, *The Connecticut Wits* (New York: Harcourt, Brace, 1926).

2. The earliest example of this form appears in a coverlet made in New Jersey in 1818. That border slogan reads, "Agriculture and Manufacture are the Foundation of Independence."

3. Francis Wright, *Views of Society and Manners in America* (Cambridge, Mass.: Harvard University Press, 1963), p. 100.

4. George Dangerfield, *The Awakening of American Nationalism, 1815–1828* (New York: Harper Torchbooks, 1965).

5. J. C. Williams, *History of Danby* (Rutland, Vt.: 1869).

9 *Park Family Gravestone*

Attributed to Moses Wright, Jr.
  (working in Vermont 1790–1810)
Burgess Cemetery, Grafton, 1803
Slate, southern Vermont
H: 37 inches W: 38¾ inches
Photograph, 1990

Reproduced as a photomural in the exhibition

Vermont's early slate gravestones include some of the most intriguing examples of folk carving produced anywhere in America during the early national period. With the industry centered in the Connecticut Valley, slate stones produced in Brattleboro, Westminster, Rockingham, and as far north as Thetford and Newbury exhibit such peculiar ornamentation and stylistic exuberance that they represent a milestone of Vermont art during the early national period. Among the various shop traditions and local styles, none surpasses the work of the Rockingham carvers, a multi-generational craft dynasty dominated by the Wright family of Rockingham from about 1788 until 1820.[1] The stone marking the graves of the wife and children of Thomas K. Park of Grafton is one of the most original and spectacular examples of Moses Wright's work. Wright's moon-shaped spirit effigy, or death head, is a masterful example of aesthetic power achieved by the most economical means. This basic moon-faced image, incised from lines laid out with a simple compass and square, was the hallmark of Wright's style, repeated over and over on more than seventy-five stones in the Rockingham, Chester, Westminster, and Grafton area.

Much has been written about the Park stone over the years, making it Vermont's most famous slate gravestone.[2] Although unique in size and for the number of moon-faced soul effigies incised on it, the stone is surprisingly representative of its maker's persistent experimentation. No two of Wright's stones are exactly alike, even though the lettering, ornament, and incised faces on all of them are handled in an unmistakably similar manner. Few Vermont artists or craftsmen of the period are documented by so large and diverse a

body of work, a fact that further heightens Moses Wright, Jr.'s, significance in the arts of early Vermont.

The story of Thomas K. Park (1761–1826) and his family is an inseparable element of the gravestone's meaning. Between the ages of twenty-five and sixty-two, Thomas Park sired twenty children by three wives, the first fifteen by his first wife, Rebecca Gibson Park (1763–1803). Such fecundity was unusual enough, but the fact that fifteen of Park's children died young and only four out-lived him in adulthood is extraordinary. No other gravestone in New England memorializes losses on such a scale, and Wright's handling of the memorial by engraving fourteen death heads hanging like pendants from a tree of life is indeed evocative.

Park was born and raised in Preston, Connecticut, and participated in the first settlement of Grafton (then known as Thomlinson) around 1785.[3] Grafton's rank among Vermont towns peaked around 1810, when it hovered at the cusp of the most populous upper third, but by 1840 it had dropped to the middle. Despite his losses, Park remained in Grafton (the few of his children who reached adulthood all moved West) until 1826, when he died, a relatively prosperous farmer in a middling Vermont town. Today the gravestone he commissioned for his deceased wife and children is a poignant monument to Vermont as most people experienced it during the early years.[4]

WNH

1. William N. Hosley, Jr., "The Rockingham Stonecarvers: Patterns of Stylistic Concentration and Diffusion in the Upper Connecticut River Valley, 1790–1817," *Puritan Gravestone Art II* (Boston: The Dublin Seminar for New England Folklife and Boston University, 1978), pp. 66–78.

2. David Watters, "The Park and Whiting Family Stones: The Iconography of Church Covenant," *The Canadian Review of American Studies*, IX, No. 1 (Spring 1978), pp. 1–15; Allan I Ludwig, *Graven Images* (Middletown, Ct.: Wesleyan University Press, 1966), pp. 116; Peter Benes, "The Rockingham Carvers: Folk Ecclesiology in the Upper Connecticut River Valley, 1786–1812," *New England Historical and Genealogical Register*, 132 (April 1978).

3. Correspondence with Helen Pettengill of Grafton (August 12, 1990) provided genealogical information on Thomas K. Park and his family. Additional details are included in Helen M. Pettengill's *History of Grafton, Vermont, 1754–1985* (Grafton, Vt.: Grafton Historical Society, 1985), p. 93.

4. Zadock Thompson, *History of Vermont, Natural, Civil and Statistical* (Burlington: Chauncy Goodrich, 1842), pp. 209–210; Thomas K. Park, Estate Inventory, 1826, Windham District Probate Court Records, vol. H, pp. 276–278. Park's estate was valued at $937.69 and included a yoke of oxen, forty sheep, a small number of cows and sheep, tools for livestock and grain farming, and such luxury items as a "clock and case" ($7), silver spoons, two bureaus ($10 and $12), a "locker" ($11)—a type of sideboard popular in Vermont, and a pantry furnished with pewter, glass, and ceramic tableware.

10 *Lieutenant Colonel Joseph Wait*
     Gravestone
     North Clarendon, 1808
     Marble, Rutland County
     H: 45 inches W: 24 inches
     Photograph, *c.* 1923
     Reproduced as a photomural in the exhibition

The smiling little figure with up-raised sword and the martial air of a toy soldier marks the burial place of Joseph Wait, one of the most active military figures on the northern New England frontier. One of seven brothers from Brookfield, Massachusetts, all of whom became soldiers, he was one of the four among them who died in military service. He joined the Provincial Army in 1754, when he was twenty-one, and took part in the major campaigns of the French and Indian War, serving in the final years of the war as captain of a company of Rogers' Rangers.

With the coming of peace and the opening of settlement on the New Hampshire Grants, Wait played a prominent role as a captain of the Green Mountain Boys under Ethan Allen in resisting the jurisdictional claims of the Province of New York. In company with a younger brother, Benjamin, who had served under him as an officer in Rogers' Rangers and who later gave his name to the town of Waitsfield, he was one of the first settlers of Windsor, Vermont. Appointed lieutenant colonel of a regiment of New Hampshire Rangers in the Continental Army during the Revolution, he served in Canada and on Lake Champlain until his death in September 1776. He was mortally wounded when struck in the head by a splinter from a gun carriage in the skirmishing on Lake Champlain that preceded the Battle of Valcour. In the care of some of his men, he started homeward to the Connecticut River Valley by way of the old Crown Point military road, but he died along the way in the present town of Clarendon. There "his remains were deposited in the intervals of the late Jonathan Parker, Esq.," according to an early newspaper account written when many of those who had served with him were still living.[1]

Frontier leaders such as Joseph Wait, schooled in the stern discipline of a rough and perilous service, could not have expected to be universally loved by the men they commanded. To Frye Bailey of Newbury, who served under him as a private soldier in the chaotic retreat from Canada and subsequently on Lake Champlain, he was "the most sovereign Tyrant, and cruel scoundrel I ever saw . . . a haughty, proud Tyrant." Bailey, on his own homeward journey "afoot and alone" to Newbury from Mount Independence, passed the place where Wait lay dying. "As I was going by," he recalled years later, "the man of the house hailed me, after enquiring who I was and receiving an answer, he said my Col was in his house, and he thought him dying. He desired me to go and see him, I said I did not owe him so much service, that I was glad the World was likely to be rid of such men."[2]

The gravestone was erected in solemn commemorative ceremonies held on July 4, 1808. Convening "at the late public house, late of the said Jonathan [Parker], now of Mr. Robert Wilbur, . . . a procession was formed and a statue of marble, honorary and to perpetuate the memory of Col. Wait, was escorted by a number of the patriots and heroes of our revolution, to a grove, near the tomb of the late Jonathan Parker, Esq." An old comrade-in-arms, former Green Mountain Boy Isaac Clark "pronounced a concise, appropriate and martial eulogy, biographical of the deceased warrior. . . . In procession the statue was conveyed to the solitary dead, and erected over the tomb, under a discharge of minute guns. The procession then repaired to the bowery and partook of a repast," in the course of which the following toast was drunk to the memory of Col. Wait: "May his Tomb no longer be forgotten, whilst there remains an American officer to the millioneth generation, to pay due honors to the man and hero, who fought with Montgomery before the walls of Quebec."[3]   JRM

Our common Country
Claims our aid.
Living or dying
I will defend Her.

1. "Independence at Clarendon," *Vermont Rutland Herald*, 28 July 1808.

2. "Colonel Frye Bailey's Reminiscences," *Proceedings* (Montpelier, Vt.: Vermont Historical Society, 1923–1925), p. 45.

3. *Vermont Rutland Herald*, 28 July 1808.

REFERENCES

Wait, Horatio Loomis. *Memorial of Joseph Wait, Lieutenant Colonel Continental Army* (Privately printed, Chicago, 1899). The author was the great-grandson of Joseph Wait.

Spargo, John. *Lieutenant Colonel Joseph Wait of Rogers' Rangers and the Continental Army, Freemason and Pioneer Vermont Settler* (n.p., 1942).

11 *Stove*

G. H. Iron Company
Brandon, *c.* 1840–1850
Cast Iron
H: 41½ inches   W: 25¾ inches   D: 17½ inches
Shelburne Museum, Gift of David Wells

Iron mining was an industry in Vermont from the end of the eighteenth century through the Civil War era. Crockett's *History of Vermont* states that in 1810 eight blast furnaces and twenty-six forges were in operation throughout the state. Though it seems unlikely today, towns such as Bennington, Ludlow, Shaftsbury, and Brandon all were sites of deposits and were once important for the industrial manufacture of iron goods and tools.

The iron industry in Vermont was established in Brandon as early as 1797, when town foundries processed ore mined in nearby Forestdale. The furnaces at Brandon melted ore for stoves, cannon, tools, and kitchen equipment for trade across New England and were respected for the high iron content (30 percent) which they produced. In 1820, John Conant of Brandon built and manufactured his "Conant Stove," the first cook stove made in Vermont. In 1845 the town furnaces produced 1200 tons of workable iron, but the industry declined after mid-century, when transporta-

tion costs fell and it became cheaper to import stoves and iron goods from Troy and Albany, New York, the region's largest producers of such items.

More elaborate parlor stoves were manufactured in the state as early as the 1830s and were intended for use in the formal rooms of the house. This parlor stove, with its Corinthian columns and fleur-de-lis, echoes the predominantly Greek architectural taste of the era. Aside from their decorative purpose, the columns were also practical: The increased surface area distributed heat from the fire more efficiently and helped the stove warm the enlarged spaces of Greek Revival parlors. A teapot or kettle of boiling water on the element above the fire chamber was a precursor of today's humidifier.   LJB

REFERENCES

Brandon, Vermont: A History of the Town, 1761–1961 (Brandon, Vt.: Town of Brandon, 1961).

Groft, Tammis Kane. *Cast With Style: Nineteenth Century Cast-Iron Stoves From the Albany Area* (Albany, N.Y.: Albany Institute of History and Art, 1981).

Jacobs, Elbridge. "Iron in Vermont—A Glance at its Story," *Vermont Quarterly*, 21 (April 1953), pp. 128–131.

Pierce, Josephine. *Fire on the Hearth: The Evolution and Romance of the Heating Stove* (Springfield, Mass.: Pond-Ekberg Co., 1951).

12 *Covered Jar*

Hinesburg, *c.* 1790
Glazed Earthenware
H: 9¾ inches DIAM: 8 inches

Rokeby (Ancestral Estate of Rowland Evans
Robinson), Ferrisburgh

Found among the collection of eighteenth- and
nineteenth-century formal china and stoneware in
the old family homestead of Rowland E. Robinson, Vermont's foremost Victorian author, were
two redware jars of almost identical size and proportion. Their simple lines and utilitarian shape
illustrate redware's indispensable role in early Vermont kitchens.

Redware—made from the same reddish-hued
clays used for bricks and roofing tiles—was manufactured for use in the kitchen and dairy from the
seventeenth to the early twentieth centuries.[1]
Ovoid jugs and jars such as this covered jar were
the most common form of early American pottery. The jars served a variety of purposes, frequently storing preserved meats, pickles, fruit
butters, and pickled eggs.[2] Most dry goods, such
as sugar, flour, and meal would have been purchased and stored in larger quantities.

Both the date of the jars' origins and the name
of the potter who created them are unknown.
Available evidence suggests there were few commercial redware manufacturers in Vermont in the
late eighteenth century. John Norton of Bennington (cat. 35), Charles Bailey of Newbury,
Samuel Woodman in Poultney, and Moses Bradley at Chimney Point (Addison) all produced redware products prior to 1795, but most earthen and
stoneware production sites were established after
1800.[3] As the number of settlers in Vermont increased and opportunities to barter and trade expanded, Vermont farmers often supplemented
their farming operations with income from other
types of production. Women spun or sewed; men
created handmade products such as furniture or
simple earthenware pots and jugs—all of which
would have been useful for trade in lieu of cash.

This jar may be the work of Ebenezer Bostwick, a member of a large clan of Bostwicks living
in Hinesburg in the 1790s. In May 1793, Bostwick
traveled to Thomas Byrd's store in Vergennes,
where he purchased one pound of tea, three
pounds of indigo, and 51¾ pounds of lead, an essential ingredient in earthenware. Thomas Richardson Robinson, Rowland Robinson's grandfather, was a new emigrant from Rhode Island
who also shopped at Byrd's store. In an early
Robinson family account book, receipt of pottery
from Ebenezer Bostwick is noted in exchange for
grain.[4] Regardless of whether Bostwick was a
commercial or sometime potter, however, or
whether he made this jar, the exchange alone helps
us to understand earthenware's importance as a
trading commodity in Vermont's early domestic
economy.   KEP

1. Elisabeth Cameron, *Encyclopedia of Pottery and
Porcelain, 1800–1960* (New York: Cameron Books,
1986), p. 184.

2. Georgeanne H. Greer, *American Stonewares* (Exton,
Penn.: Schiffer Publishing Ltd., 1981), p. 87.

3. Unpublished letter from Catherine Zusy to Karen
E. Petersen, 29 October 1990.

4. Thomas Byrd, Day Book, 1792–1793, in Robin-
son-Stevens Family Papers in the Rokeby Museum Archives (May 29, 1793).

13 *Tall Clock*

Works by Nathan Hale (1771–1849)
Case attributed to Julius Barnard
(working in Vermont 1801–1809)
Windsor, *c.* 1805
Cherry and pine case; steel and brass
eight-day movement
H: 92 inches W: 19½ inches D: 11 inches
Private Collection

This clock was made about 1805 for Barnabas Ellis, a Weathersfield, Vermont, saddler whose Rutland County descendents still care for it. Its maker, Nathan Hale, was the first clockmaker to advertise in Vermont's newspapers.[1] He was trained and practiced briefly in his native town of Rindge, New Hampshire, before migrating in 1796 to Windsor, Vermont—the state's fastest-growing commercial center—where he made clocks and sold dry goods in partnership with his brother Harry until about 1805. Around 1810, Hale moved north to Chelsea, where he operated a tavern and invested in real estate.[2] Nathan Hale exemplifies the restless and entrepreneurial spirit frequently encountered in Vermont boom towns of the early national period. His account book, a rarely surviving document, provides a window into the world of Vermont's artisan culture. It chronicles his business activities while shedding light on the complex web of suppliers and sub-contractors employed by inland New England clockmakers at the time.[3] Hale bought clock faces, parts, and partially assembled clock movements from a variety of Boston and unidentified regional suppliers. Although not a prolific clockmaker, Hale nonetheless attracted customers from as far away as Bath, New Hampshire, and Hartford and Hartland, Vermont. He traded parts and occasionally sub-contracted work to the Woodstock, Vermont, clockmaker Russell Cheney, and paid William Robinson—possibly a journeyman or apprentice—for clock work.

Clockmakers were higher up the retail chain than cabinetmakers, and it was common for them to supply both clocks and cases, the clock and the case being valued about equally. Nathan Hale's clocks varied in price, the most expensive costing almost sixty dollars, but he did not make his own clock cases, relying instead on local cabinetmakers such as Julius Barnard and William Rodgers.[4] Unfortunately, the manufacture of clock cases is hard to document. This example was probably made by Julius Barnard, the local cabinetmaker who advertised most frequently in the Windsor newspapers during Hale's active years and the best candidate on stylistic grounds.

This cherry case, with its prominently scalloped waste molding, belongs to the tradition of lower Connecticut Valley cabinetwork in which Barnard was trained. Having been reared in Northampton, Massachusetts, where he began to practice before moving north to take advantage of Windsor's booming economy, Barnard mastered the fashions popular in the older valley settlements.[5] The clock is further distinguished for exhibiting one of the earliest applications of the Vermont State Seal as an ornamental device. The painter of the lone pine and cow on the dial is unknown. John Wilder, a Windsor chair and sign painter, had extensive business relations with Hale but was never explicitly paid for painting clock faces. What is certain is that by 1805 Vermont's artisan class—men such as Barnabas Ellis and Nathan Hale—embraced Vermont statehood by assimilating its symbol as part of the ornamental vocabulary of their private lives.   WNH

1. *Spooner's Vermont Journal,* 24 June 1796.
2. *Spooner's Vermont Journal,* 5 May 1817. "Nathan Hale informs his friends and the public, that he has commenced Tavern-keeping . . . in Chelsea, Vermont." He died there in 1849.
3. Nathan and Harry Hale, Account book, Windsor, Vermont, 1803–1807, Windsor Public Library.
4. William Rodgers, Account book, Hartland, Vermont, 1798–1812. Private manuscript collection, courtesy of Roy C. Kulp. Transactions with Barnard are cited in Hale, Account book, p. 11, and it was from Hale that Barnard acquired his shop in the brick commercial block built in Windsor in 1804. Windsor Land Records, 8, pp. 214–215 (July 6, 1805).
5. William N. Hosley, Jr., "Vermont Furniture, 1790–1830," in *New England Furniture, Old-Time New England,* 72, No. 259 (Boston: Society for the Preservation of New England Antiquities, 1987), pp. 248, 268.

14 *Bottle*

Attributed to Vermont Glass Factory,
   East Middlebury
c. 1814–1815
Soda lime Glass
H: 13 inches W: 9 inches

Sheldon Museum, Middlebury

15 *Breast Pump*

Attributed to Lake Dunmore Glass
Company, Salisbury

c. 1835

Soda lime Glass

H: 1¼ inches W: 3¼ inches

Sheldon Museum, Middlebury

In 1814, shortly after the Vermont Glass Factory began operating one of the state's first glassworking furnaces in Salisbury, the company erected a second glassworks in East Middlebury. Directors Epaphras Jones and Samuel Swift believed that an ideal combination of circumstances warranted such speedy expansion: The national embargo on imported goods during the War of 1812 precluded competition from abroad. More importantly, the materials for glassmaking were locally available: sand from the shores of Lake Dunmore; charcoal and potash from local forests; and lime from the ledges. The most costly material, clay for making crucibles, had been found in nearby Monkton, where a deposit of "Monkton Porcelain Earth" was being used in pottery.[1] A growing market and the new glassworks' location next to one of only a handful of roads crossing the Green Mountain range seemed to guarantee success.

The circular brick building in East Middlebury housed one furnace with the capacity of three "pots," or crucibles, for melting glass. Water power from the Middlebury River powered three blowers to raise the temperature in the furnace.[2] The East Middlebury works specialized in bottle production, while the factory in Salisbury was equipped to make window glass. These two commodities made up the bulk of the business, although workers were known to produce other items as "off-hand" work. The company paid its employees with bank bills, issued on the Farmer's Bank of Troy, which illustrate the factory buildings (cat. 16.1).

Differences in glass color result from the pres-

ence of impurities in the "frit" or mixture of raw materials. Workers made no effort to remove these from bottle glass because bottles were often used to hold a variety of household liquids that benefited from an absence or low level of light. Window glass, however, needed to be translucent, but not perfectly colorless; hence the pale green shade of the glass produced in Salisbury. Fine glassware and utilitarian objects like this breast pump called for extra refinement to make them perfectly clear.

The promise of profit in glassmaking was short-lived. The Salisbury works suffered a fire in 1815, just as the war and the embargo ended and European goods flooded the American market. The Vermont Glass Factory quickly rebuilt but never recovered financially. The East Middlebury furnace closed down in 1816, the Salisbury works a year later. In 1832, however, the old Salisbury works reopened as the Lake Dunmore Glass Company and operated successfully for ten years.[3]

The provenance of both the bottle and the breast pump are unclear. An old tag attached to the bottle and the bank note claim that the bottle is the only one known to have been made by the "bottle factory at East Middlebury." It was purchased in 1886, presumably by Henry Sheldon, an inveterate collector of Middlebury artifacts and founder, in 1882, of the "Sheldon Art Museum, Archaeological and Historical Society." It is quite likely that Sheldon collected the breast pump as an example of the glass manufactured by the Lake Dunmore Glass Company.   VMW

1. Henry R. Schoolcraft, "An Account of the Vermont Glass Factory," *The Literary and Philosophical Repertory*, Vol. 1 (Middlebury, Vt.: T. C. Strong, Dec. 1813), p. 64.

2. Samuel Swift, *Literary and Philosophical Repertory*, Vol. II, p. 316, as quoted in an unpublished paper by Peter H. Templeton, "Glassmaking in Addison County, Vermont" (1978) in the Sheldon Museum, Middlebury.

3. Ken Wilson, *New England Glassmaking* (New York: Thomas Y. Crowell Co., 1972), pp. 99–100.

16 Receiver

Attributed to Vermont Glass Factory,
Salisbury
c. 1814
Soda lime Glass
H: 3⅜ inches W: 3¾ inches L: 5¾ inches
Private Collection

During his tenure in the chemistry department of Middlebury College, Dr. Perley Voter enjoyed prowling around the northeast shore of Lake Dunmore on the site of the old Vermont Glass Factory, later the Lake Dunmore Glass Company. There, he picked up pieces of "cullet," chunks of raw glass of the same pale green color of this receiver. Over the years he assembled a small collection of ink wells whose color matched some specialized handblown equipment in the college laboratory. When the chemistry department modernized, replacing all its laboratory glass, Professor Voter salvaged a few pieces of the old equipment. This receiver was one of the pieces he rescued. Professor Voter shared the traditional belief that Henry Schoolcraft made the equipment while superintending the glassworks at Lake Dunmore, but the attribution remains unverified.

Henry Rowe Schoolcraft's reputation as an explorer, Indian agent, and author of some of the earliest descriptions of native people of the Midwest has thoroughly obscured his early career as a glassmaker, a trade in which he was trained by his father. He hired on as superintendent of the glass factory in Salisbury in October 1813,[1] at which time the company was advertising window glass in ten standard sizes in the Vermont Mirror.[2] With capital from investors in Troy, New York, tax breaks from the state legislature, and the participation of prominent Middlebury men, The Vermont Glass Factory enjoyed an auspicious beginning.

Schoolcraft came to Salisbury with a working knowledge of glassmaking, but in order to obtain a better understanding of the chemistry involved, he enrolled as a student of Professor Frederick Hall at Middlebury College. Professor Hall had joined the college faculty in 1806 after studying under Yale Professor Benjamin Silliman, one of the leading chemists of the day, who was then putting together one of the earliest collections of lab equipment in the country. However, Hall left Middlebury immediately after he arrived for a two-year tour of study in Europe. When he returned to the college, he was brimming with new ideas and bore a compound microscope to supplement the college's small collection of "philosophical apparatus."[3] He must have welcomed the arrival of a glassmaker as a student. Under Hall's tutelage, Schoolcraft systematized his study, "perfected the arts" of his trade, and prepared his research for publication "under the name of Vitriology,"[4] or "glass chemistry." Unable to gather subscriptions to publish his work, Schoolcraft ultimately took an assignment to search for minerals in the West and abandoned his efforts to illuminate the science of glassmaking.

Receivers such as this were used for qualitative analysis in glassmaking and other branches of chemistry to determine the impurities in molten liquids. The process is crucial to glassmaking because impurities are responsible for glass color; those glassmakers who aspire to achieve a high degree of clarity in order to make windows, for example, need to be able to analyze the contents of the sand, lime, charcoal, and silicates which are among the materials used to make glass. Thus, although this particular receiver cannot be tied to Schoolcraft directly, the attribution may well be accurate given Schoolcraft's interest in glass

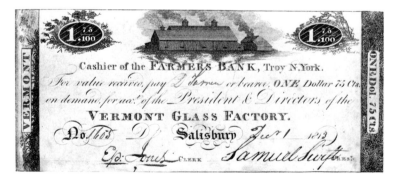

Cat 16.1 One Dollar and seventy-five cents bank note. Vermont Glass Factory, Salisbury. 1813. Courtesy, Sheldon Museum, Middlebury.

chemistry, his involvement with the Vermont Glass Factory, and his study under the first Middlebury College professor interested in developing a collection of lab apparatus.   VMW

1. Vermont Glass Factory records in the Sheldon Museum, Middlebury.

2. *Vermont Mirror*, 20 October 1813. For a full description of the Lake Dunmore Glass Co.'s works, see Ken Wilson, *New England Glassmaking* (New York: Thomas Y. Crowell Co., 1972), pp. 94–100.

3. David Stameshkin, *The Town's College, 1800–1915* (Middlebury, Vt.: Middlebury College, 1985), pp. 40–42.

4. Henry R. Schoolcraft, *Thirty Years With the Indian Tribes* (Philadelphia: Lippincott, and Grambo and Co., 1851), p. XXXV.

17 *Revolving Hydraulic Engine*

Asahel Hubbard (1787–1845)
Windsor, Patented 1828
Cast and machined iron with brass fittings
H: 17⅜ inches W: 8 inches

Old Constitution House, Windsor

Asahel Hubbard's name keeps company with an impressive parade of inventive mechanics featured in the pages of Windsor history. The mechanical design innovations throughout the nineteenth century of men such as Hubbard, George Hubbard, Nicanor Kendall, James Hartness, and Richard Smith Lawrence helped to give the region from Windsor south to Springfield the nickname of "Precision Valley" and furthered the myth of Yankee ingenuity that lives on today.

The myth conjures up images of inventors working late alone in their shops, but the mechanics of Windsor did not operate in a vacuum. Their genius was that of incremental improvement, often to machines first developed elsewhere. Asahel Hubbard's success, for example, came at the expense of Messrs. Cooper, Phelps, and Campbell, whose rotary gear pump could not hold up in service. Hubbard studied the design of their gear pump, whose principle had been illustrated as early as the 1620s, determined a way to improve it by adjusting the shape of the interior teeth, secured his patent in 1828, and then went looking for capital to put the Revolving Hydraulic Engine into production.[1]

Jabez Proctor, father of United States Senator Redfield Proctor, supplied Hubbard with more than financial backing. He also arranged Hubbard's appointment as warden of the state prison in Windsor. In 1829 the National Hydraulic Company was organized, and Hubbard moved his shop inside the prison walls so he could take advantage of the captive labor force. The engine's reliability depended on Hubbard's ability to machine the parts to very close tolerances, and it quickly earned a national reputation.

Powered by hand, kitchen-well pumps such as this could produce a stream of water an inch in diameter and worked flawlessly for years. A similar pump in Hubbard's brother's house was still working 150 years after it had been installed. Larger models, powered by teams of people, proved useful for fire and bilge pumping. Large-capacity, steam-powered pumps became primary movers for municipal water systems. A twenty-horsepower pump for the waterworks of St. Louis enabled the sleepy river town to grow into a major midwestern city. In 1833, Hubbard sold manufacturing rights to Fales and Jenks Machine Company in Pawtucket (which continued to produce pumps based on Hubbard's design for more than a century)[2] and retooled the prison shop for a more lucrative trade: arms manufacture.

Windsor's reputation as a leading center of early mechanical design in the young nation dates from the invention of Hubbard's revolving hydraulic pump, but the pump's true importance lies in the sequence of businesses it spawned. In 1835 Hubbard's son-in-law, Nicanor Kendall, patented his own innovation, the underhammer-lock rifle, and suggested that the prison shop manufacture them. N. Kendall & Company in turn hired Richard S. Lawrence, who designed and produced specialized machines for the making of weapons parts. Lawrence's lathes, milling machines, and other precision-machining equipment made it possible to produce identical components and laid the foundation for what became known as the American System of Manufacturing, more commonly called "interchangeable parts."[3] In 1845 Lawrence went into partnership with S. E. Robbins, and together they built their own rifle manufacturing business. Less than twenty years later, Lawrence and Connecticut Governor Oliver Winchester founded the Winchester Repeating Arms Co., which eventually developed the widely popular Winchester repeating rifle.[4]

Hubbard's design solution has been in continuous use since 1828. Today, automobile oil pumps operate on the gear pump principle he perfected, while the original pumps, as well as examples of other designs from Windsor's "family" of machines, are on display at the American Precision Museum in one of the former Robbins & Lawrence Armory buildings in Windsor. VMW

1. Katherine E. Conlin, Wilma Burnham Paroto, Stella Vitty Henry, *Chronicles of Windsor, 1761–1975* (Taftsville, Vt.: The Countryman Press, 1977), pp. 230–236.

2. Guy Hubbard, "Leadership of Early Windsor Industries in the Mechanic Arts," *Vermont Historical Society Proceedings, 1921, 22, 23*, (Montpelier, Vt.: Vermont Historical Society, 1921–1923), pp. 159–182.

3. Joseph Wickham Roe, *English and American Tool Builders: The Men Who Created Machine Tools* (Bradley, Ill.: Lindsay Publications, 1987). See also, Hounshell, *From the American System to Mass Production, 1800–1932* (Baltimore: Johns Hopkins University Press, 1984), p. 71.

4. Merrit Roe Smith, *Harpers Ferry Armory and the New Technology: The Challenge of Change* (Ithaca, N.Y.: Cornell University Press, 1977), pp. 19, 289–290.

18 *Thirteen-Inch Terrestrial Globe*

James Wilson (1763–1855)
Bradford, *c.* 1810–1817
Paper-faced ash wood, brass quadrant
H: 18¾ inches W: 18 inches
Printed on globe: "A NEW / TERRESTRIAL
GLOBE, / on which the / TRACTS and NEW
DISCOVERIES / are laid down / from the
Accurate Observations / made by / Cap.⁵
Cook, Furneux, Phipps & C. / By
J. WILSON, VERMONT.

Vermont Historical Society, Montpelier

Early Vermonters demonstrated an interest in geography that foreshadowed the global awareness they would exhibit in the late twentieth century. They set up district schools to teach reading and ciphering, and then instituted private academies to teach Greek, Latin, geography, and rhetoric. In 1800, Vermont had three such academies. Thirty years later, every county could claim at least one.[1] Vermont's academies followed the model of those in Boston and Philadelphia, where exercises were offered in the use of globes, both celestial and terrestrial.

Globes were not a new teaching tool in the early years of the nineteenth century, but they were costly. Benjamin Franklin had asked his agent not to spend more than eight guineas for the pair he ordered from London in 1753.[2] A century earlier Joseph Moxon had begun making globes in London with his father, printer James Moxon. The Moxons published a book explaining the use of their globes, and it went through five editions by 1699. Globe study at that time was primarily a mathematical exercise dedicated to navigation and astronomy.[3]

James Wilson saw his first globes at Dartmouth College shortly after he moved to Bradford, Vermont, in 1797, and he immediately set about trying to duplicate them. First he had to learn geography, however, which he accomplished by purchasing an *Encyclopaedia Britannica* from Hugh Somers in Ryegate.[4] He then went looking for instruction in copperplate engraving. Wilson invested ten years of study and consultation with

experts such as author and geographer Jedediah Morse before he was able to produce a globe whose meridians were aligned and whose engravings matched in quality those produced in London. Wilson's first globes sold for $50 a pair in 1810 and offered a more accurate representation of the North American interior than the European competitors could accomplish for a much higher price.

Wilson handled all the steps in the production process. He learned all he could about inks and varnishes, constructed his own lathes and presses, and solicited the help of a local papermaker to develop a firm paper that would not stretch when applied to the globe. He continued to improve registration techniques while his sons supervised the outfitting of a new factory in Albany, New York. In 1817, he stopped producing globes in Bradford and began globe production at his new factory at 110 Washington Street. Wilson remained active in the firm until he finished a thorough revision of all three sizes of globes in 1827.

The University of Vermont, Houghton Library at Harvard, Princeton, Yale, and the Library of Congress all own Wilson globes.[5] But this specimen and the one at Latham Memorial Library in Thetford suggest the impact that Wilson's globes had on shaping the image of the world for generations of Vermont students and teachers. VMW

1. David Ludlum, *Social Ferment in Vermont 1791–1850* (Montpelier, Vt.: The Vermont Historical Society, 1948), p. 228.

2. LeRoy E. Kimball, "James Wilson of Vermont, America's First Globe Maker," *Proceedings of the American Antiquarian Society*, 48 (April 1938), p. 30.

3. Helen M. Wallis, "Geographie is Better Than Divinitie. Maps, Globes and Geography in the Days of Samuel Pepys," in *The Compleat Plattmaker: Essays on Chart, Map and Globe making in England in the Seventeenth and Eighteenth Centuries*, Norman J. W. Thrower, ed. (Berkeley: University of California Press, 1978), pp. 1–6.

4. *Encyclopaedia Britannica* (Edinburgh, 1788–1797). Wilson's set, along with the desk he built to house it, is now in the collection of The Bennington Museum.

5. Richard J. Fowle, "James Wilson's Globes, An Anniversary Report and Appeal," *Proceedings of the American Geographical Society* (1960), p. 249.

19 *Coat of Arms*

Augusta Crafts (1773–1861)
Craftsbury, 1795
Silk embroidered with metallic threads
H: 16 inches W: 16½ inches
Embroidered: "Augusta Crafts 1795"

Mr. and Mrs. Fredrick W. Lapham III

Few objects better convey the pretensions of some Vermonters than this lozenge-shaped panel embroidered in 1795 in Craftsbury, then one of the northernmost settlements in the state. Its maker, Augusta Crafts, was the daughter of the founder of Craftsbury, Ebenezer Crafts. The elder Crafts, a land speculator, had brought his family north from Sturbridge, Massachusetts, in 1791. They brought with them their portraits (cat. 19.1) by Winthrop Chandler, the brother of Ebenezer Crafts's wife Mehitable. As a Yale graduate (1759) and distinguished Revolutionary War soldier,

Cat. 19.1 Winthrop Chandler. *Mrs. Ebenezer Crafts (Mehitable Chandler, 1741–1812) and daughters, Matilda (1771–1848), and Augusta (1773–1861).* c. 1781. Oil on canvas. Courtesy, Public Library, Craftsbury Common.

Crafts was, at the time of his arrival, one of the most prominent settlers in Vermont. This coat of arms, or hatchment, was woven two years after Augusta Crafts married Dr. James Paddock, who became the town's first physician.

Hatchments were a curious development in American society during the colonial period and first years of the Union. Sometimes painted but frequently embroidered, such as this one, they depict family coats of arms. More often than not in American society they were produced by families not entitled to them.[1] They first appeared in the seventeenth century, most frequently as mourning symbols displayed with caskets in funeral processions, but by the time Augusta Crafts created this example, they had become decorative embellishments for homes. Their purpose was primarily to remind those who saw them of the owners' lineage and distinction. Such an aristocratic affectation must have seemed anomalous to many in the small hamlet of houses built by the Crafts and their fellow settlers.

Embroidered hatchments appear to have been a New England phenomenon. Fewer than one hundred examples survive, many of them made in Massachusetts, where in 1769 Amy and Elizabeth Cummings advertised that at their school for needlework they would "instruct young ladies in embroidery, coats of arms. . . ."[2]

The Latin verse "Quo Fata Vocant," translated, means "whither the fates call." Stylistically Augusta Crafts's hatchment is related to a second hatchment, made by her cousin, Anna Maria Chandler, in 1797.[3] Chandler's is the only other hatchment known to have been made in Vermont.

RHS

1. *The Great River: Art and Society of the Connecticut Valley, 1635–1820*, exhibition catalogue (Hartford, Conn.: Wadsworth Atheneum, 1985), p. 402.
2. *Boston Chronicle*, 1 May 1769, quoted in Ethel Stanwood Bolton and Eva Johnston Coe, *American Samplers* (1921; reprint ed., New York: Dover Publications, 1983), p. 40.
3. *Important Americana* (auction catalogue), Sotheby's, New York, January 28–30, 1988, lot 1568.

20 *Chest of Drawers*

George Stedman
    (working in Vermont 1816–1822)
Norwich, *c.* 1816–1822
Cherry and pine with cross-bandings of
    mahogany, light wood stringing, and
    inlays
H: 34⅞ inches W: 41¾ inches D: 20⅛ inches
Inscribed on drawer: "Made by G. Stedman
    Norwich Vermont"

The Henry Francis du Pont Winterthur Museum

Among furniture historians Vermont was traditionally known as New England's lost region.
None of the early surveys of New England furniture included work attributed to Vermont, and
even more recent surveys, in which it attains token
representation, tend to emphasize the odd and eccentric aspects of the Vermont tradition. So it was
of some interest when the Winterthur Museum in
1966 first published a photograph of this chest
with a note of the discovery of a period inscription
on its interior that read "made by G. Stedman
Norwich Vermont," a man described by the author as a cabinetmaker "about whom nothing is
known."[1] Since then the Stedman chest has been
cited as proof-positive of Vermont's claims to
skilled cabinetmakers fully able to help create new
styles for a young nation.

Alas, G. Stedman remained a mystery until
1986, when David Hewett finally unraveled his
story, proving without doubt that the chest was
the work of a Chester, Vermont, cabinetmaker
named George Stedman.[2] Hewett, an antiques
writer and Vermont resident, conducted an exhaustive search for professional and biographical
information about Stedman. Stedman was identified as a man born in Chester, Vermont, where
he almost certainly apprenticed to Sampson
Warner, whose shop he acquired in 1816 at the age
of twenty-one. Warner headed west to greener pastures, a pattern of mobility that became routine
among Vermont's most skillful and ambitious
cabinetmakers. Stedman was no exception, hence
the puzzling inscription citing Norwich by a cabinetmaker whose only proven working address in

Vermont was Chester.[3] Stedman is also believed
to have worked in Shaftsbury, Vermont, before
his permanent move at the age of twenty-seven to
New York State. A quasi-transient, itinerant life
was thus not uncommon among journeyman artisans and makes it easy to imagine Stedman
spending time in any number of Vermont locations, including Norwich.

The Stedman chest, now known to be just one
of several Stedman pieces, including a similar
chest on display at The Bennington Museum, is a
remarkable and inventive piece of cabinetwork. It
is a sophisticated adaptation of a style first popularized in New England with the 1794 publication of
George Hepplewhite's *The Cabinet-Maker and Up-
holsterer's Guide.*[4] Its bombé front harks back to an
earlier style while the use of mixed woods and
neoclassical inlay and banding was fully à la mode.
The chest is just as inspiring and delightful now as
it was a quarter century ago when it was first
brought to the public's attention. The man "about
whom nothing was known" developed a style
that has enticed lovers of history and antiques ever
since, triggering a search for Vermont furniture
that adds perspective on Vermont's character
while explaining the background of one of its native arts.   WNH

1. Charles F. Montgomery, *American Furniture: The
Federal Period, 1788–1825* (New York: Viking Press and
the Winterthur Museum, 1966), pp. 189–190.

2. David Hewett, "G. Stedman—The Elusive Vermont Cabinetmaker," *Maine Antique Digest*, xiv, No. 3
(March 1986), pp. 1D–4D.

3. Although the chest is a stylish and technically com-
petent piece of cabinetwork, its presumed date of origin
during the late 1810s hardly suggests cutting-edge
work. Comparable—indeed, more classically derived—
Federal-style cabinetwork was being produced in more
cosmopolitan centers like Windsor and Rutland, Vermont, as early as 1800. Both Norwich and Chester were
towns of secondary commercial importance, and it is
not at all surprising to learn that a cabinetmaker such as
Stedman had a tough time making a go of it there. It is
rather more surprising that work of such significance
was ever produced in Chester. Stedman was not alone.
A remarkable Federal-style card table at the Art Institute
of Chicago is signed by another Chester cabinetmaker,
Royal H. Gould, who may have made it as late as 1820.

4. Although first published in 1789, Hepplewhite's book only became readily available in interior New England a decade later. A Hartford, Connecticut, bookstore advertised the book in the *Connecticut Courant* on December 9, 1799, and it is likely that Vermont cabinetmakers were aware of the book or work influenced by it by 1805.

21 *Titus Hutchinson Family*

Thomas Ware (1803–1826/7)

c. 1820–1825

Oil on canvas

H: 31 inches L: 125 inches

Woodstock Historical Society, formerly in the collection of the Ottauquechee Chapter, D.A.R. Museum, Woodstock

Prior to 1850 painting activity in Vermont was sporadic, and no town could boast the presence of a resident artist for more than a few years. Most painting that took place consisted of portraits, and those painters who achieved any level of success were either itinerant artists, such as William Jennys (active 1802), or locally developed artists such as Thomas Ware, the painter of this family portrait. In either case, painters were hard pressed in Vermont's small communities to find sufficient demand (i.e. wealth) to keep them busy for any extended length of time.

Although portraits of some of Vermont's first leaders (such as Ethan Allen) have never been uncovered, paintings of people of influence were the rule rather than the exception by the 1820s, when Titus Hutchinson (1771–1857) assembled his family for this portrait. Depicted here are Titus Hutchinson, third from the left, and his wife Clarissa Sage, flanked by their daughter Clarissa Sage (born 1814) and their sons Edwin (born 1803), Oramel (born 1804), Henry (born 1806), Titus (born 1809), and Alexander (born 1816).

Hutchinson, son of the Pomfret minister Rev. Aaron Hutchinson, was graduated from Princeton (1794) before returning to Vermont and becoming a lawyer in Woodstock. There he became the town's leading citizen and in succession was appointed U.S. Attorney for the state (1813), judge of the Supreme Court (1825) and chief justice (1830–32). He owned one of Woodstock's most prominent houses (still standing at the town's center), became local representative to the state legislature (1804), held a seat as director of the state bank (1806), and acquired extensive land holdings.[1] Although the painting has traditionally been dated *c.* 1820, it is conceivable it was done as late as 1825 to celebrate Hutchinson's appointment to the Supreme Court.

Ware was the painter of record in Woodstock for his brief career (1820–1825), and more than forty paintings are now attributed to him.[2] With the exception of this painting—his most ambi-

tious work (and probably the longest family portrait painted in the state during the nineteenth century)—all his other work consists of single portraits. His style, like that of many "plain painters" of portraits in nineteenth-century America, is marked by stiff postures, angular features, serious expressions, and sharp value contrasts.[3] Clearly this commission put all Ware's abilities to the test, and ultimately what makes the portrait so delightful and remarkable to our eyes is the refreshing directness with which he lined the family up like a chorus line. But while this element is appealing to the twentieth-century eye, it would have been frowned upon by Ware's contemporary academically trained portrait painters of America's art centers, such as New York.

The number of portraits painted for Vermont's leading families in the early nineteenth century is a reflection of a national phenomenon. Portraits, like many other personal possessions, were frequently symbolic of financial prosperity and social prominence. Many Vermonters, perhaps more out of necessity than by choice, lived modestly, and their personal life style did not imply any degree of significant wealth. Others, like Hutchinson, desired and could afford the very best that Vermont society had to offer, which is reflected in the houses they built, the furniture they utilized, and the portraits for which they posed.   RHS

1. Henry Swan Dana, *History of Woodstock, Vermont* (Boston and New York: Houghton, Mifflin and Company, 1899), pp. 331, 474, 580.
2. Arthur B. & Sybil Kern, "Thomas Ware: Vermont Portrait Painter," *Clarion* (January, 1984), pp. 36–45, who explain that Ware was taught by the itinerant Abraham Tuthill (1776–1843) and was a boyhood friend and Pomfret neighbor of Benjamin Franklin Mason (1804–1871), perhaps the most successful Vermont portrait painter of his generation.
3. John Michael Vlach, *Plain Painters: Making Sense of American Folk Art* (Washington, D.C.: Smithsonian Institution Press, 1988), pp. xv, 1–86.

22 *Dr. Jonathan Blackmer Gravestone*

Elijah Sikes (working in Dorset 1808–1818)
1813
Marble, Dorset
H: (headstone) 59 inches W: 27 inches
    D: 3 inches
H: (footstone) 26 inches W: 14¼ inches
    D: 1¾ inches
Photograph, 1990
Reproduced as a photomural in the exhibition

The discovery of marble in Bennington County during the 1780s attracted some of Massachusetts's and Connecticut's most talented stonecutters. Men such as Zerubbabel Collins (who arrived as early as 1778), Samuel Dwight, and Elijah Sikes created various styles of folk carving in marble that can be found today throughout Bennington County.[1]

Elijah Sikes was a member of a prolific family of stonecutters from the lower Connecticut River Valley who emigrated to Dorset from Chester, Massachusetts, in 1808. There, on the east side of Dorset Mountain, he opened a quarry, and for the next ten years he was Dorset's most active gravestone manufacturer.[2] Although the style of his Dorset work differs from that of the folk carvings he produced in Belchertown (ca. 1790–1795) and Chester (ca. 1795–1808), it is no less expertly crafted or designed.

The head- and footstone Sikes made and signed for Dr. Jonathan Blackmer in 1813 are extraordinary on several counts. Well preserved, rich in iconography, and strong in historical associations, these monumentally scaled and deeply carved stones are testimonials to Sikes's sculptural expertise. The Blackmer stone is a catalogue of ornamental techniques in marble: Its smooth, raised oval panel, deeply fluted columns, boldly articulated urns and rosettes, sharply beaded edge, and pronounced symmetry are the hallmarks of a master craftsman. Imagine how the stone would have looked one hundred and seventy-five years ago, when it was smoothly polished, unweathered, and possibly accented with gold-leaf.

Dr. Blackmer died young but not before leaving his mark in Dorset. In an age when membership roles in Vermont's many Masonic lodges read like a "who's who" of Green Mountain elites, Blackmer was a prominent Freemason, a fact which he took proudly to his grave by authorizing Sikes to decorate his gravestone with the Masonic compass and square and its emblems of officership: the treasurer's crossed keys and the senior warden's level. Approximately 450 townsmen and acquaintances were indebted to Blackmer at the time of his death—presumably for medical services rendered—but typical of the times, Blackmer's estate shows a man more involved in real estate and development and commercial agriculture than in his chosen profession. He raised sheep, pigs, and horses commercially, kept a few cows, maintained an orchard, and raised grain on a home lot and associated land parcels that totalled more than 400 acres.[3] By working both sides of the street in the new state, Blackmer gained wealth and prestige, a fact abundantly suggested by his remarkable gravestone.   WNH

1. William E. Harding, "Zerubbabel Collins's Successor and His Work in Bennington County, Vermont," *Puritan Gravestone Art* (Boston: Boston University and the Dublin Seminar for New England Folklife, 1976), pp. 14, 15, 19–22; Nancy Buckeye, "Samuel Dwight: Bennington County Stone Carver," *Vermont History*, 43, No. 3 (Summer 1975), pp. 208–216.

2. F. W. Beers, *Atlas of Bennington County, Vermont* (1869; reprint ed., Rutland, Vt.: Charles E. Tuttle Co., 1969), p. 9. My thanks to Bob Drinkwater of Northampton, Massachusetts, for bringing this gravestone to my attention and for background details on Sikes's career.

3. Jonathan Blackmer, Estate Inventory, Manchester District Probate Court Records, May 5, 1813.

23 *George West House*

Irasburg, 1824–1834

Photograph, 1990

Reproduced as a photomural in the exhibition

Although Vermont claims textbook examples of most of the classic architectural styles of the nineteenth and twentieth centuries, its vernacular architecture is a singular heritage. These local and regional styles of building are peculiar to Vermont. At least a dozen Vermont-based housing styles can be cited.

Between about 1830 and 1855, Vermonters from one end of the state to the other built houses featuring upper-story recessed porches. This is one of the state's most intriguing vernacular building styles.[1] By 1860 Vermont contained perhaps seventy or more buildings of this design, including such prominent examples as the original Pavilion Building in Montpelier (demolished) and grand inns or taverns in Saxtons River (demolished) and Simonsville. Today, examples survive in the upper Connecticut Valley towns of Saxtons River, Windsor, Hartford, Bradford, and Newbury (and across the river in the New Hampshire towns of Charlestown, Lebanon, and Claremont); in the hill towns and minor valley regions of eastern Vermont, in towns such as Grafton, Simonsville, Ludlow, Cuttingsville, Shrewsbury, Pittsford, Brookfield, Royalton, and Waterbury; and in the Northeast Kingdom, in the towns of Canaan, Cabot, and Irasburg, where some of the best and earliest examples can be found. Examples west of Route 7 are unknown. Most of the houses with recessed porches have few other overt features in common except their gable fronts; and although rarely dated or exactly datable, they generally manifest subordinate details confirming the peak popularity of the style during the Greek Revival period of the 1840s.

The George West House in the Northeast Kingdom town of Irasburg is one of the best surviving examples. It is prominently situated at the south end of the town green in what was in the 1820s and 1830s the most significant settlement in Orleans County. Set in the gable's peak is a plaque dated 1824, apparently original to the house.[2] However, George C. West, the lawyer/banker for whom the house was built, cannot be linked to the property until 1834.[3] On stylistic grounds, the house is one of the earliest examples of its type. If the date 1824 is accurate, it raises intriguing questions about whether the style originated in the Northeast Kingdom or was imported from Canada.

The front lower floor of the West house features a double parlor flanked by two wings, which were reputedly built as a music room for West's daughter and as an office for his law practice. Upstairs the spaces are small, but the entire width of the front is filled by the original master bedroom, a large and elegant room that communicates directly with the porch via a coved ceiling that carries through the exterior wall to make up the roof of the porch. The effect is to make the room commune with the outdoors like the rooms of few other houses of its period.

Architectural and cultural historians have naturally asked where and when the style began and what was its purpose. Unfortunately, these questions still beg to be answered. However, the desire for a well-ventilated master bedroom may have been what inspired the development of the recessed porch. Its advent coincided with a national obsession with interior ventilation and fresh air.[4] Unfortunately, until these fascinating buildings are studied in depth or until first-hand recollections of them are found, this is simply the best available explanation for a curious architectural phenomenon that is one of Vermont's own.   WNH

1. Nell Kull, "Recessed porches," *Vermont Life*, 21 (Spring 1967), pp. 47–50. This article was the first to note and describe Vermont's "recessed porch" houses, a topic surprisingly overlooked by Vermont's eminent architectural historian, Herbert Wheaton Congdon.

2. Special thanks to Curtis Johnson, architectural historian at the Vermont Division for Historic Preservation, for his help in retrieving information about recessed-porch houses catalogued in the Vermont Register of Historic Sites.

3. Marjorie A. Orcutt and Edward S. Alexander, *A History of Irasburg, Vermont* (Rutland, Vt.: Academy Books, 1989), p. 35.

4. Harvey Green, *Fit for America: Health, Fitness, Sport & American Society* (New York: Pantheon Books, 1986), pp. 77–100. My thanks to Christine Ermenc, director of education at the Connecticut Historical Society, for suggesting this interpretation.

24 *Kellogg Farm and Law Office*

Benson, 1790s–1830s
Photograph, 1990
Reproduced as a photomural in the exhibition

The Kellogg house, farm, and law office is one of Vermont's outstanding historic building compounds. The house and its adjoining buildings represent an unbroken accumulation, rich in architectural distinction and long in historical associations. The story of the property and the family which developed it marks the convergence of the architectural and legal professions with the world of agriculture in rural Vermont during the 1820s.[1] The mansion house that fronts the property was built in 1826 for John Azur Kellogg (1786–1852), a newlywed lawyer who was already one of Benson's most prominent citizens. Kellogg had left his native Amherst, Massachusetts, in the spring of 1805 to deliver a horse to an uncle in Weybridge, Vermont. Once there, he was welcomed into a community of cousins and former neighbors who sponsored his apprenticeship at law in the Middlebury office of Loyal Case. For the next five years Kellogg was engrossed in the whirl and dazzle of Middlebury's booming early years. Reading law first under Case, who died in 1808, and subsequently under the future United States Senator Horatio Seymour, Kellogg earned his way by serving as door-keeper during the 1806 session of the Vermont Legislature, as a clerk in the Middlebury branch of the Vermont State Bank, and by assisting Seymour in his role as postmaster. After being admitted to the bar in 1810, Kellogg cast about for a suitable place to practice. He selected Benson, the southern-most port on Lake Champlain and one of Rutland County's richest and fastest-growing agricultural regions.

In the years ahead, Kellogg, like many men of his era, was quick to realize the benefit of a professional life in a rural town. He cleverly parlayed his income as an attorney into vast landholdings on which he and hired men primarily raised sheep, which were then the Champlain Valley's most profitable form of agriculture. In 1829 he built a

law office on the corner of the Kellogg home lot at the center of the main crossroad in Benson. He continued to practice law until 1840, when he turned the business over to his son, Loyal Case Kellogg, but he continued farming until his death in 1852.

The mansion was built after the death of Kellogg's first wife and his remarriage to the daughter of one of Benson's most influential founders.[2] Although the house manifested Kellogg's increasingly lofty status in town, its classic country Palladian style (the Victorian porch is a later addition) was better a reflection of the style popular in Amherst twenty years earlier than of contemporary styles in more urban areas. However, in spite of being somewhat out of date in 1826, the house may have been designed by Thomas Dake, a talented architect from nearby Castleton, who pioneered work with this vocabulary earlier in his career. Certainly, the interior of the Kellogg

house features one of Dake's signature details— the double-vaulted center stairhall.[3]

Although the design cannot be firmly attributed, the house remains one of the architectural jewels of Rutland County. The farm around it changed and grew over succeeding generations. When it was recently retired, it was a dairy farm. Today, with almost a dozen barns and out-buildings in addition to the law office and mansion, the site is a remarkable document of Vermont's past.

WNH

1. John A. Kellogg, Manuscript daybook (1835–1852) and autobiography as cited in Charles G. Kellogg's, "History of the Kellogg Family" (Benson, Vt.: unpublished ms., 1984), pp. 9–20 & 28–33. My thanks to Charles Kellogg for sharing the fruits of his gleanings from the family papers.
2. Kellogg, "History," p. 23.
3. Herbert Wheaton Congdon, *Dake of Castleton: House-Joiner Extra Ordinary* (Montpelier, Vt.: Vermont Historical Society, 1949).

25 *L. Ransom Inn Sign*

Castleton, 1808
Oil on panel
H: 60 inches W: 29½ inches
Courtesy of Ransomvale Farm, Castleton

This simple sign identified the Ransomvale Farm in Castleton as part of a complex transportation network that criss-crossed Vermont with horse, wagon, and stage at the turn of the nineteenth century. The route has long been abandoned, but when it was in use, the stage from Castleton to Florence passed this way, stopping at Lemuel Ransom's inn for fresh horses before tackling the steep climb over Pittsford Notch.[1] The farm did not take overnight guests, but it often served meals to passengers, drivers, and horses alike. Thanks to the fertility of North Brittain Brook Valley, Ransomvale Farm was able to sustain itself on its agriculture when the railroads arrived in Vermont in the late 1840s, diverting traffic to a redesigned statewide transportation network that frequently bypassed small towns such as Castleton. The way station on the far side of the notch was less fortunate and fell to ruin.

This sign tells us that one of the travelers along this early route was likely an itinerant sign painter, because an almost identical sign once hung before T. L. Chipman's Inn[2] in Shoreham, just twenty miles to the north. Both signs have similar paint and lettering. The turned uprights and the carved scroll design at the top also closely resemble elements on signs from Salisbury, Connecticut,[3] indicating that the artist may have been one of many Connecticut peddlers who made yearly forays through Vermont. However, the eagles differ somewhat, suggesting that the sign painter carried examples of several designs from which proprietors could choose.

Motivated by pride in the new nation, artists and clients in the late 1700s and early 1800s frequently chose the eagle for an emblem. By 1810, the popularity of the eagle image surpassed all others and penetrated every level of American iconography.[4] It appeared on carvings, coverlets, crockery, and china as well as on tavern signs. A very early example appears on the gravestone of Lucinda Day, who died in Chester, Vermont, in 1800.[5]

This eagle displayed on the Ransomvale sign is the one adopted by Congress for the Great Seal of the United States in 1782. The American bald eagle, a native species renowned for its strength and independence, reminded the fledgling republic of its aspirations. To Lemuel Ransom, this eagle expressed his pride in belonging to a united and growing nation that triumphed in integrating the divergent manners and sentiments of Vermont's—and every state's—early inhabitants.[6]

VMW

1. Eleanor Toth Anderson, "The History of Ransomvale," American history term paper, Castleton State College, n.d.

2. Vermont Historical Society collections.

3. Erwin O. Christensen, *The Index of American Design* (New York: Macmillan, 1950).

4. Louis Jones, *Outward Signs of Inner Beliefs: Symbols of American Patriotism* (Cooperstown: New York State Historical Association, 1975).

5. Philip Isaacson, *The American Eagle* (Boston: New York Graphic Society, 1975), pp. 10–11.

6. Jedediah Morse, *The American Universal Geography* (Boston: J. T. Buckingham for Thomas & Andrews, 1796), p. 355.

26 *Seal of Vermont*

Charles Lewis Heyde (1822–1892)
Burlington, *c.* 1862–1863
Oil on canvas
H: 23¾ inches W: 18 inches
Shelburne Museum. Gift of Vanderbilt Webb, 1955

The elements which make up the seal of Vermont have been standard since 1821, when legislation was passed that stipulated what would be portrayed on the seal but not any particular design. In the years to come, there were many combinations of the mountain landscape, lake, pine tree, the sheaves of wheat, a dairy cow, and a stag, all underscored with the motto "Freedom and Unity." Debate centered particularly on whether the cow should face to the left or right, a controversy that may have prompted the 1862 legislation which finally codified the state seal.

According to the *Vermont Legislative Directory* of 1943, in 1862 or shortly thereafter "a painting intended to be the official version [of the seal] was made by Mr. Heyde of Burlington and placed in the custody of the Secretary of State." Unfortunately, this image was lost after being replaced in 1898, but a detailed description of the Heyde painting exists and has been matched with this painting. The mountains depicted by the artist are Camel's Hump and Mount Mansfield from the shore of Lake Champlain opposite Burlington. Heyde went to great lengths to perfect the raised position of the deer head, studying scientific drawings and a mounted trophy.

Charles Heyde came to Vermont in the 1850s and set up a studio on Church Street in Burlington by 1863. He was a prolific artist and painted landscapes featuring the Green and Adirondack mountains, Lake Champlain, and northern Vermont towns. Ever sensitive to the wants of patrons of art in northern Vermont at the time, he often completed several canvases of his most popular scenes, a practice illustrated by his three versions of Shelburne Point now in the collection of the Shelburne Museum. Heyde's life was complicated by his own alcoholism and the emotional instability of his wife, Hannah Whitman, sister of the poet, Walt Whitman. The less accurate perspective and the unsettled, thin brushwork in the painter's later works have been attributed to his inability to cope with these personal issues.

However, Heyde's great strengths as a painter were his abilities to faithfully transcribe Vermont's scenery and to convey the intensity of his feeling toward his surroundings. As he wrote of the Vermont landscape in October of 1852,

> Nothing can exceed the wild, bold, natural beauty of this place at present. The hues are incomparable and the artist who in his studio imagines himself a creator or interpreter of nature and her glorious beauties, here finds himself humbled . . . a child in power, only possessing wonder, admiration and the conviction of his weakness.[1]

LJB

1. Alice Cook Brown, "Charles Lewis Heyde: Painter of Vermont Scenery," *Antiques* (June 1972), p. 1025.

REFERENCES

Brown, Alice Cook. "Charles Lewis Heyde: Painter of Vermont Scenery," *Antiques* (June 1972), pp. 1024–1029.

Muller, Nancy. *Paintings and Drawings in the Shelburne Museum* (Shelburne, Vt.: The Shelburne Museum, 1976).

Vermont Legislative Directory. (1943), pp. 186–187.

27 *The Haymakers, Mount Mansfield, Vermont*

Jerome Thompson (1814–1886)
Oil on canvas
H: 30 inches W: 50 inches
Signed and dated, lower left:
    "Jerome Thompson 1859"

Manoogian Collection

As American landscape painters in increasing numbers found their way to Vermont beginning in the late 1840s,[1] they were frequently preoccupied by the interaction of man and nature, rather than by nature itself. In *The Haymakers*, one of a spate of Vermont subjects he painted in the 1850s,[2] Jerome Thompson focused on a haying scene set against the background of Mount Mansfield, Vermont's tallest peak.

The farm in the scene is set high on a hillside, typical of the hundreds of small hill farms that dotted the state by this time. The painting was done in the decade of the maximum rural population in Vermont and during the years when the viability of the hill farm reached its zenith.[3] However, farms such as this were only marginally profitable for hay or any other crop, and haying in the 1850s, as Thompson depicts, was a labor intensive activity that put heavy demands on a farmer and his family. Within a few years, the introduction of mechanized agricultural equipment proved the unsuitability of much of Vermont's land for contemporary farming. Hillside meadows such as this one were converted to pasture or fell into disuse, and the number of hill farms began to decline.

But such practical matters were probably of little concern to Thompson, who chose to extol the virtues of rural life. One contemporary critic probably correctly hit upon the artist's intention when he described the painting as "a genuine summer idyll, which all can feel and enjoy who have had a childhood experience in country life."[4] The contented expression of the hill farmer's spouse belies the life of toil that befell most farmers' wives, who, of necessity, supplied most of the meager wants of their families.

The specific details of Thompson's visit to Vermont from New York City, where he maintained his studio, are unknown. Certainly the arrival of the railroad in the late 1840s made locations such as the one pictured here far more accessible to the short-term visitor. But the train that probably brought Thompson to Vermont also contributed to the decline of the hill farm he depicted, as railroads enabled the farms of the Midwest to become formidable rivals in the production of the agricultural staples upon which both kinds of farm depended.[5]
                                                                    RHS

1. Other painters of national reputation who visited Vermont in the 1840s and early 1850s included Frederic Church (1849), Asher B. Durand (1849), John F. Kensett (1851), and Sanford Gifford (1858).

2. Thompson's other Vermont subjects included: *Recreation, or a Pic Nic Scene in Vermont*, 1857 (The Fine Arts Museums of San Francisco); *The Belated Party on Mt. Mansfield*, 1858 (Metropolitan Museum of Art); and *A Pic-Nic, Lake Bombazine, in Vermont*, date unknown (unlocated). See Lee M. Edwards, "The Life and Career of Jerome Thompson," *The American Art Journal* (Autumn 1982), pp. 12–17.

3. Harold F. Wilson, *The Hill Country of Northern New England: Its Social and Economic History 1790–1930* (1936; reprint ed., New York: AMS Press, Inc., 1967), pp 27, 53.

4. "Fine Arts: National Academy of Design," *The Home Journal* (June 4, 1859), p. 2, as quoted in Edwards, p. 15.

5. Wilson, *The Hill Country*, p. 65.

28 *Noted Spanish Merino Stock Rams*

Luther Allison Webster (1858–1944)
c. 1880–1890
Engraving
H: 12¾ inches W: 17⅝ inches
Vermont Historical Society, Montpelier

In the late nineteenth and early twentieth centuries proud sheep breeders often commissioned portraits of their prize stock for publication and display in their home or office. Livestock artists such as L. A. Webster of Shoreham, Vermont, traveled across the nation stopping at state and country fairs to produce portraits. Webster achieved national recognition for his work, which was published in Merino sheep breeders' journals and other livestock manuals, in state and county directories and gazetteers, and in such agricultural journals as *Moore's Rural New Yorker,* the *American Sheep Breeder,* and the *Nebraska Farmer.*

The Stickneys of East Shoreham were among Webster's long-term customers. Webster, who was reared on the next farm, worked for them as a boy and began drawing portraits of their stock in the late 1880s. According to his son, Harold, who traveled with his father in the 1910s, Webster sketched portraits in pencil at the farms and then returned home to make the engravings. Although some artists began using photographs to produce their engravings, many owners did not like this technique because it revealed an animal's defects. Webster solved that problem by cutting defects from the negative, rebuilding the image, and then making a print.

Vermonters raised sheep in the 1700s for mutton and wool for home use. This continued until the early 1800s, when the textile factories springing up around Vermont and New England created a demand for good quality, long-staple wool suitable for weaving cloth and blankets. In response to this demand, Vermont farmers developed their sheep flocks as a primary source of farm income.

They were aided immeasurably by the introduction of Merino breeding stock to Vermont in 1811. Merinos were known for producing wool ideally suited to the needs of the burgeoning textile industry and quickly proved to be especially well adapted to Vermont's agricultural conditions. In a short time, Vermonters became world famous for their Merino sheep. Improved breeding techniques increased the number of folds of skin and the amount of lanolin secreted, both of which increased the weight of an average fleece, while the cool climate encouraged a heavier and thicker wool fleece. By 1840, Vermont had 1,681,000 sheep—almost six sheep per person—with the industry concentrated in the Champlain and Connecticut Valleys.

Sheep farming began to decline in Vermont in the mid-nineteenth century. Major factors contributing to the decline were the removal of the protective tariff on wool in 1846 and increased wool production in the West. The opening of the Erie Canal in 1825, the Ohio Canal in 1832, and the Pennsylvania Canal in 1834, as well as the development of a nation-wide railroad system brought wool cheaply to the eastern markets and reduced prices.

By 1870, the Vermont sheep population had declined by 64 percent. However, although the number of sheep decreased significantly, wool production fell less dramatically because refined breeding had doubled and even tripled the weight of an average fleece. This increased yield allowed Vermont's large sheep breeding operations to compete with the western wool market, but it could not save breeders of small flocks from having to find other ways to sustain their agricultural incomes.

Ironically, even while the state's sheep population was declining, Vermont's reputation as a breeder of high-quality Merino stock was spreading worldwide. Western sheep breeders, particularly, provided a ready market for Vermont's superior Merino stock, but sheep breeders as far away as Australia—whose vast plains were just being settled in the mid 1800s—relied on advertisements like this one to locate stock for their own rapidly expanding sheep industry.   CYO

NOTED SPANISH MERINO STOCK RAMS,

BRED AND OWNED BY

E. E. STICKNEY, EAST SHOREHAM, VT., U. S. A.,

NOW THE PROPERTY OF SAMUEL McCAUGHEY, COONONG, NEW SOUTH WALES, AUSTRALIA,

NO. 62 SIRED BY JAY EYE SEE.   NO. 124 SIRED BY COMMENDABLE.   NO. 122 SIRED BY WALL STREET.

" 146   "   "   "   " 134   " "   "   JAY EYE SEE & COMMENDABLE BY WALL ST.

REFERENCES

Hastings, Scott Jr., and Geraldine Ames. *The Vermont Farm Year* (Woodstock, Vt.: Billings Farm and Museum, 1983).

"Interview: Harold Webster on his Father, Himself, and Others," *The Valley Voice*. 18 June 1975.

Meeks, Harold A. *Time and Change in Vermont: A Human Geography* (Chester, Ct.: Globe Pequot Press, 1986).

Russell, Howard, S. *A Long, Deep Furrow: Three Centuries of Farming in New England* (Hanover, N.H. and London: University Press of New England, 1982).

29 Cow Weathervane

Found on a Colchester barn, *c.* 1850–1900
Copper
H: 12 inches   W: 24 inches
Shelburne Museum

Cow, sheep, fowl, horse, and swine weathervanes were often used by farmers to identify their livestock specialty. Early vanes were made of wood, iron, or tin by local craftsmen or the farmers themselves. In the mid-nineteenth century, numerous commercial weathervane companies elsewhere in the East began mass-producing three-dimensional, hollow-bodied vanes, made of copper or zinc, in a variety of livestock models. Affluent farmers now were able to choose and order from a manufacturer's catalogue. As livestock farming became more complex and specialized, vanes, too, became more specialized to differentiate among breeds or were custom-made to depict a prize-winning horse, cow, or sheep.

This manufactured cow weathervane might represent a generic "good dairy cow" or one of the specialty breeds imported to improve Vermont dairy stock in the late nineteenth century. For decades it stood atop a dairy barn in Colchester, Vermont, where presumably it acquired its numerous bullet holes.

By the mid-nineteenth century in Vermont, sheep farming was declining and farmers were switching to dairy and cattle. Many factors contributed to this change: Western competition made sheep farming in the state less profitable; the growing cities in southern New England and New York created an expanding market for butter, cheese, and milk; improved refrigeration technology made it possible to begin to ship fluid milk; and developing railroad transportation made it possible for farm products to reach markets in New York and New England in a day rather than a week. Soon, improved breeds of dairy cows could yield as much as 70 percent more at market than sheep, and the new state agricultural societies, dairy associations, and national periodicals, such as *Moore's Rural New Yorker*, provided farmers with information regarding more sophisticated farming techniques.

Until the early nineteenth century, the emphasis of cattle breeding was on beef and draft qualities. With the development of a specialized dairy industry in the mid-nineteenth century, farmers began to pay more attention to the quality and quantity of milk their cows produced and to import a variety of European cows and bulls to improve the breeding stock. Herefords, first imported as dairy cattle, proved to be more valuable for beef. Shorthorns and Jerseys, the most popular milk cows because of the high butterfat content of their milk, were generally replaced in the mid-twentieth century by Holsteins, which produced milk in far greater volume.

By the 1880s a system of central creameries largely took over the production of butter and cheese from the local farms. Farmers delivered their milk directly to the creamery and were paid for the cream content. In the 1890s, St. Albans, Vermont, had the largest butter creamery in the world. Dairy products shipped from St. Albans to major northern cities tripled between 1850 and 1870; butter alone rose from 1,149,225 pounds shipped annually to 3,270,182 pounds. As Vermont farmers began to focus on the sale of fluid milk, they worked to develop more efficient means of production, to improve breeds of milk cows, and to maintain constant production year-round by developing herd management practices and providing abundant high-quality feed.

More than a century after dairying began to dominate the state's agricultural economy, Vermont has a worldwide reputation for the quality of its milk, its dairy products, and its cows. Although the number of dairy farms in the state has declined steadily since 1920, the amount of milk produced in Vermont has increased because of sophisticated selective breeding techniques and excellent herd management. Today in Vermont, agriculture directly contributes only approximately 3 percent of the gross state product, but the cow and the endangered dairy farm are potent symbols of the state, which alone among the fifty states honors a cow on its state seal (cat. 26).   CYO

REFERENCES

Bishop, Robert and Patricia Coblentz. *A Gallery of American Weathervanes and Whirligigs* (New York: E. P. Dutton, 1981).

Hastings, Scott, Jr., and Geraldine Ames. *The Vermont Farm Year* (Woodstock, Vt.: Billings Farm and Museum, 1983)

Meeks, Harold A. *Time and Change in Vermont: A Human Geography* (Chester, Ct.: Globe Pequot Press, 1986).

Russell, Howard W. *A Long, Deep Furrow: Three Centuries of Farming in New England* (Hanover, N.H. and London: University Press of New England, 1982).

30 *Cooley Creamer*

(probably a salesman's sample)
Vermont Farm Machine Co.
Bellows Falls, 1883
Painted wood and metal
H: 16⅜ inches W: 21⅜ inches D: 15½ inches
Vermont Historical Society, Montpelier

In the 1880s, the Cooley Creamer set the standard of creamery practice just as commercial dairying was becoming a mainstay of American agriculture, not only in Vermont but throughout the United States. Invented by a Vermonter and perfected and distributed by a Vermont manufacturer, the Cooley system facilitated the rise of centralized, "associated" creameries and the marketing of high-quality "creamery" butter.

William Cooley of Waterbury patented his new water-seal process for raising cream in 1877. Cooley's invention totally immersed a deep-setting pan in cooling water, an arrangement that encouraged rapid and uniform cream raising and protected the cream's purity. In subsequent years, the Vermont Farm Machine Company of Bellows Falls made several versions of the Cooley Creamer and sold them in the emerging dairy regions of the country.

The Cooley Creamer quickly became a popular piece of creamery equipment in the Northeast and the Midwest. In 1889, the Green Mountain Stock Farm in West Randolph won world honors at the Paris Exposition for the high quality of its butter, made using a Cooley Creamer. Even as the Cooley was being eclipsed in the 1890s, it remained the quality standard against which newer, faster centrifugal-type cream separators were judged.

The Cooley Creamer encouraged the application of industrial organization to dairy farming. The Vermont Farm Machine Company promoted the "Cooley cream gathering system," in which cream was separated at the farm and collected by centralized creameries and cooperatives. The Cooley system paid farmers for butterfat, rather than by milk weight, and helped to standardize quality. By 1889, two-thirds of all New England creameries used the "associated" Cooley system.

The Cooley Creamer arrived on the scene shortly after painters such as Jerome Thompson (cat. 27) had popularized a romantic image of the yeoman farmer. Few farmers or their families, however, could see the romance of their rural isolation or the grueling routine of their lives. Those who adopted industrial improvements like the Cooley system expressed their faith in the late nineteenth century progressive ideal. DAD

REFERENCES

Armsby, H. P. "The Cooley System of Creaming Milk," University of Wisconsin Agricultural Experiment Station, *Bulletin No. 7* (Madison, Wis.: 1885), pp. 9–13.

Cooley, William. "Improvement in Obtaining Cream From Milk," United States Patent Office, Specification for Patent No. 187,516 (February 20, 1877 [filed October 27, 1876]).

McKay, G. L. and C. Larsen. *Principles and Practice of Butter-Making* (New York, 1908), pp. 123–128.

Myrick, Herbert. "Associated Dairying in New England," in *Agriculture* [Volume 5], *Reports of the United States Commissioners to the Universal Exposition of 1889 at Paris* (Washington, 1891), V, pp. 565–575.

"Premium List, 1889," [supplement to] *American Agriculturalist* (November 1888), p. 546.

Tinkham, O. N. "Theories and Methods of Setting Milk," *Sixth Report upon Vermont Agriculture by the Superintendent of Agricultural Affairs* (Montpelier, Vt.: 1880), pp. 268–279.

Vermont Farm Machine Co., No. 67. *Illustrated Catalogue and Price List of Cooley Creamers Giving Full Information Regarding the Celebrated Cooley System* (Bellows Falls, Vt., n.d. [1894]).

31 *A Marble Quarry*

James Hope (1818/19–1892)

Oil on canvas

H: 18 inches W: 24 inches

Signed and dated lower center:
    "J. Hope 1851 / Pinxt"

Museum of Fine Arts, Boston.
M. and M. Karolik Collection. 62.275

At the time James Hope painted this view of Sheldons and Slason's Marble Quarry, West Rutland, the marble business was about to become one of the state's leading industries. During the 1850s there were numerous quarries in operation, and they were largely confined to a band running from Isle La Motte and Swanton in the north, southward through Middlebury, Shoreham, Brandon, Rutland, and Proctor to Danby and Dorset. It was in the latter town that Vermont's marble industry began when Isaac Underhill established North America's first commercial marble quarry there in 1785.[1] By 1890 Vermont ranked first in marble production, producing 62 percent of the nation's output.

This painting is one of three the artist did for the quarry's owners[2] (Charles Sheldon, Charles H. Slason, and John A. Sheldon) in 1851. The paintings were most likely commissioned that year to commemorate the completion of the railroad, which replaced the labor-intensive and costly method of transporting their finished marble by teams to the Champlain Canal at Whitehall, New York, the nearest shipping point, a distance of twenty-five miles.[3]

Hope has depicted the entire marble operation. On the left crews of cutters using "ball drills" extract large blocks of stone which are raised by a wooden lift and pulleys. Blocks were then stacked, before teams of oxen hauled them into the adjoining mill by means of stoneboats on wooden rollers. The large mill, constructed in 1850, contained steam-driven "gangs" of iron saws which cut the stone into slabs. Much of the quarry's output was dedicated to funerary monuments, which dot the yard.

Sheldons and Slason's Quarry became well known and was the subject of both prints (cat. 31.1) and photographs (cat. 31.2). By 1881 the quarry was among the largest in the state, employing 350 men. In addition to the vast amount of marble the quarry's employees worked up on their own, the quarry relied on the nearby railroad to ship annually many thousands of tons of marble for other Vermont mills.[4] In May 1873, for ex-

ample, the quarry shipped 110 railway cars of marble.[5]

The block of stone being lifted out of the quarry is marked "Washington Monument" and was probably intended for the obelisk in Washington upon which construction had begun in 1848. While the primary stone was granite quarried at Vinal Haven, Maine,[6] the exterior of the monument is sheathed in marble. In addition, each of the states was asked to contribute a memorial stone, and Vermont's may well have come from this quarry.

Hope was one of the few artists resident in Vermont during these years with the ability to paint pictures such as this. He was also conveniently located in Castleton, a few miles away. A native of Drygrange, Roxburghshire, Scotland, Hope had come in 1834 to Fair Haven, where he apprenticed himself to a wagon-maker and attended nearby Castleton Seminary for a year. By 1843 he had established himself as a portrait painter in West Rutland, and two years later he taught painting at the seminary. At least ten paintings by Hope survive. Most are Vermont landscapes from the

1850s (his most productive period), and this is perhaps his most compelling painting.

Ironically, the type of marble use documented here is today a minor portion of Vermont's marble industry. Most is now ground to a fine powder (calcium carbonate) for use in the coating of paper, as a filler in paint, and as an additive in fortified breakfast cereals.   RHS

1. J. Kevin Graffagnino, *Vermont in the Victorian Age* (Bennington and Shelburne, Vt.: Vermont Heritage Press and Shelburne Museum, 1985), p. 67.

2. *Rutland, in Retrospect*. Robert E. West, ed. (Rutland, Vt.: Rutland Historical Society and Academy Books, 1978), p. 56. Hope's second view of the quarry is owned by the Rutland Historical Society; a third is in a private collection.

3. Hamilton Child, *Gazetteer and Business Directory of Rutland County, Vt., For 1881–82* (Syracuse, N.Y., 1881), p. 208.

4. Child, *Gazetteer*, p. 208.

5. Abby Hemenway. *The Vermont Historical Gazetteer*. 5 vols. (Claremont, N.H.: Claremont Manufacturing Company, 1877), vol. 3, p. 1067.

6. Museum of Fine Arts, Boston. *American Paintings in the Museum of Fine Arts, Boston* (1969), vol. 1, p. 151.

32 *Picture Frame*
Worker from Eureka Quarry,
   North Poultney, *c.* 1900
Slate
H: 15½ inches W: 11½ inches D: 1 inch

The Bennington Museum, Gift of
Edith Temple Jones, 1983.66.

Made of Vermont purple slate by an unknown worker, this carved frame was a gift to Richard Temple Jones (1869–1941), long-time superintendent of the Eureka Quarry in North Poultney. The frame holds a photograph of William T. Williams, who was also a quarryman. The Eureka Quarry, organized in 1878, employed sixty-five men by 1886. Located on thirty-two acres, it was considered one of the finest of many quarries in the slate region, which includes Fair Haven, Castleton, Poultney, Wells, and Pawlet, Vermont, as well as Salem, Granville, and Hampton, New York. Most of the slate excavated from these sites was used to make roofing, but it was also used to produce fireplace mantels (which were often marbleized), billiard table beds, table tops, hearths, blackboards, tile, flagging, and steps.

The New England Slate Company quarried slate in Guilford, Vermont, as early as 1812, but Colonel Alonson Allen, of Fair Haven, is credited with quarrying the first slate from this region in 1839. Allen began by making school slates, but was soon producing roofing slate exclusively. By 1850, word of the discovery of slate in Fair Haven had spread to workers at the famous Penrhyn slate quarries in Caernarvon, Wales, and hundreds of Welshmen and their families emigrated to Vermont's slate region. Many of these men were known for their industry, thrift, and piety, and quickly worked their way up to positions of authority in Vermont. Such was the case with Richard Temple Jones, who started out at the Eureka Quarry as a laborer at the age of twenty and advanced to superintendent.

By 1872, slate quarrying had become the most prominent industry of the region. Two hundred boxcar loads of roofing slate were shipped from Poultney station each month. By the end of the decade, one-third of the nation's ninety-four slate quarries were located in Vermont. In 1886, the financial firm of John M. Bradstreet reported that Vermont's slate industry was "of considerable importance and much interest." Of Fair Haven, it stated that "It is no exaggeration that the 3,000 people of this little town live on slate." Today this corner of the state is renowned for its distinctive and colorful slate roofs.

The punched background and flat carving on this frame are characteristic of Welsh ornamental slate work of the late nineteenth century. Quarrymen in Wales are known to have made a wide range of slate curios to relieve the tedium of their regular hard work and as evidence of their skill. This frame was undoubtedly made by such a worker who emigrated to Vermont.   CZ

33 *Bowman Mausoleum*

G. B. Croft (architect)
Giovanni Turini (sculptor, 1841–1899)
Laurel Glen Cemetery, Cuttingsville,
     1880–1881
H: 18½ feet L: 25½ feet
Photograph, 1990

Reproduced as a photomural in the exhibition

The Laurel Glen Mausoleum in Cuttingsville, Vermont, is an extraordinary monument that documents late nineteenth century attitudes toward death and commemoration of the dead. It was begun in 1880 by John Bowman to receive the remains of his wife Jenny, who had died the previous January; his daughter Ella, who had died the summer before her mother; and his daughter Addie, who had died in infancy twenty-six years earlier. Eventually, he, too, would be interred there beside his wife and daughters. This mausoleum would have been extravagant in any context, but located as it is in a small cemetery in rural Vermont, its effect overwhelms the beholder to this day. A crew of 125 workmen labored for a year, and Bowman's total cost for this undertaking was approximately $75,000, a staggering expense in 1880–1881.

The mausoleum is at once a deeply personal expression of grief and an iconographically complex funerary monument totally in keeping with the imagery of mortuary art in the western world at the end of the nineteenth century. Bowman planned this imagery as carefully as he oversaw the construction of the mausoleum itself. Around the outside of the structure, horticultural experts transformed the landscape into a recreational destination, complete with symbolic plantings and curved walkways designed to supply contemplative vistas.

Laurel Glen is a self-contained architectural unit which encloses an invented realm of the dead. Today we must peer inside through a metal grate even during the months when the monumental granite door is open, but originally, visitors were allowed to walk inside for a more thorough experience of the sepulchre and even to sign a guest

Cat. 33.1 Interior of the Bowman mausoleum. Courtesy, Slide Library, Art Department, Middlebury College.

book. In appearance, this mausoleum is a Victorian hybrid of classical and Egyptian forms, combining a Greco-Roman entablature and walls that flare dramatically outward at the base. This is the characteristic profile of ancient Egyptian temple architecture, which was extremely popular for tombs and cemetery entrances throughout the western world during the nineteenth century.

The interior appears like a formally elegant, but not unfriendly, Victorian sitting room, exhibiting a fanciful mélange of classical Greco-Roman and Egyptian elements in addition to pedestals with busts of the Bowmans and their elder daughter, plus a full-figure statue of their dead infant playfully reaching upward. In the corners are large mirrors in marble frames which reflect the interior space and its contents *ad infinitum*. When we peer through the metal grate, we see that the child's gesture appears directed toward the reflected image of her mother's bust, which is actually located behind her (cat. 33.1).

The very notion of a realm of the dead that mimics a domestic interior probably alludes to

Cat. 33.2 Guglielmo Corti. *Corti Monument.*
Hope Cemetery, Barre. 1903.
Courtesy, Aldrich Public Library, Barre.

ancient Egyptian burial practice, and the architect, G. B. Croft, of New York City, who was a specialist in mortuary art, surely was familiar with the interiors of Egyptian tombs and explained their symbolism to his client. The marble figures were all designed by Giovanni Turini, also of New York City (1841–1899), and carved by professional stonecutters, as was customary in nineteenth century sculptural practice.

Outside the mausoleum is another Turini statue, a somewhat over-lifesize, free-standing figure of John Bowman himself, who climbs the exterior steps to pay a visit to the tomb and leave a wreath with a ribbon inscribed "to my wife & children." After the mausoleum was completed, Bowman built a large house, Laurel Hall, across the road; he moved there in 1887 after retiring from the tanning business in which he had made his fortune. We can imagine that from then until his death in 1891, Bowman crossed the road daily to visit the mausoleum and mounted the steps just as his portrait statue still does today. With this last touch—a marble effigy of a grieving survivor

climbing the same steps as we do—Turini created a figure which blurred distinctions between art and life in a peculiarly nineteenth century manner.

Although work on the Bowman mausoleum was done primarily, if not exclusively, by artists and artisans from New York City, skilled stonecutters by the thousands were emigrating from Italy and Spain in the late 1800s to work in Vermont's developing granite and marble industries, particularly those in and around Barre and Rutland. Many died prematurely here of silicosis contracted in the poorly ventilated stonecutting sheds, but they also quickly established reputations that rivaled those of the artisans of New York for the quality of their work. Their legacy today is visible in cemeteries such as those in Barre and Montpelier, where granite carvers memorialized the tragic, early deaths of their friends and co-workers with remarkable tombs and sculptures (cat. 33.2).

JMH

34 *Birds Eye View of Burlington and Winooski, Vermont*

Published by J. J. Stoner, drawn by
    E. Meilbek; Shober and Carqueville, Lith.,
    Chicago
1877

Photograph, Special Collections,
University of Vermont
Reproduced as a photomural in the exhibition

At least two decades before the nation's centennial celebration triggered a flurry of interest in recording the accomplishments of a hundred years of progress, birds-eye view artists were combing the country sketching town portraits for proud citizens of the nation's thriving communities. These elevated-perspective portraits caught the adolescent nation in its youthful glory. At least fifty views were done of close to forty Vermont towns and cities in the half century between 1850 and 1900; and untold numbers of residents of the

Cat. 34.1 Thomas Waterman Wood. *The Village Post Office.* 1873. Oil on canvas. Courtesy, New York State Historical Association.

Green Mountain State paid anywhere from two to five dollars for a print, which was usually in duotone and only rarely in color.

The majority of the Vermont views were published by the L. R. Burleigh Company of Troy, New York, or the George E. Norris Company of Brockton, Massachusetts, but many other firms were also engaged in this work. J. Stoner Company, of Madison, Wisconsin, was one of the most highly regarded, and capitalized on civic pride by publishing birds-eye views of prominent cities across the country.[1] In Vermont, only four communities were awarded the honor: Burlington and Winooski, Bennington, Brattleboro, and St. Albans.

Artist Edward Meilbek distilled the essential element of success for Burlington and Winooski when he sketched the flanking waterways providing waterpower on the Winooski River and trade access to the world from the Lake Champlain shore. All the residents who paid five dollars for this view took pride in their own small corner of the city and their place in the big picture. Hanging on a parlor wall, the lithograph offered a tangible antidote to memories of the depression just past (1873) and underscored the reality of thriving commerce, the vital university complex on the hill, and the cultural benefits and public conveniences of modern civilization.[2]

Modern viewers, spared the starry-eyed pride of the nineteenth-century consumer, can still find in this view the keys to Vermont's relationship with the rest of the nation and with the province of Quebec to the north. A variety of industries are engaged in finishing Canadian timber into doors, boxes, furniture, lumber, and Venetian blinds. Marble and granite works are transforming Vermont bedrock into monuments and mantels, curbstones and bridge abutments. Soapworks continue a tradition established in 1791 with the issuance of the first U.S. patent, to a Vermonter for the manufacture of potash. Riding the growth curve of the American northeast, Burlington's population had swelled to 12,000, and Winooski was earning a reputation as a major manufacturing center.

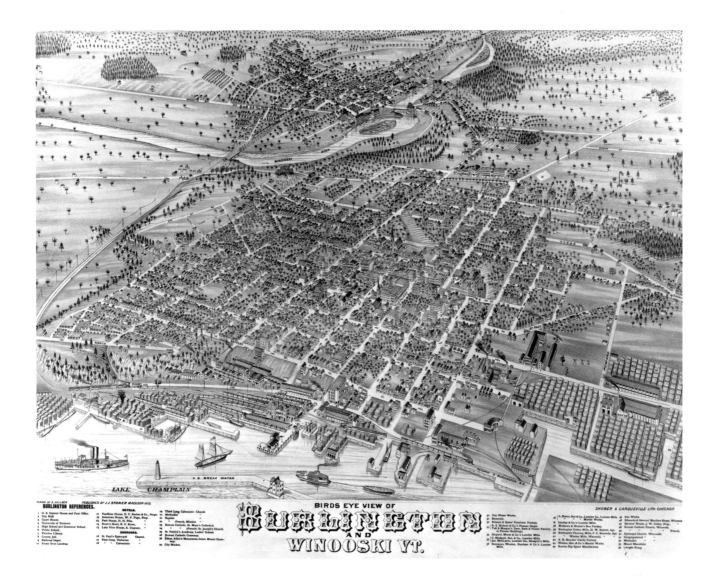

Burlington and Winooski residents cherished this evidence of their modern prosperity, but at the same time they, like all Vermonters, were probably comforted by the nostalgic perspective of Montpelier artist Thomas Waterman Wood (1823–1903). Wood enjoyed wide-reaching popularity in his time, in part because he painted precise details of rural life, composing them in vignettes that read like stories of a way of life that was fast disappearing.[3] *The Village Post Office* (cat. 34.1), completed just three years before the Burlington view, captures real people—Wood's Uncle Zenas and other Montpelier friends—in an ordinary moment in a familiar rural institution, mod- eled on the general store in Williamstown, Vermont. The myth perpetuated by Wood's paintings and others like them helped to assuage confusion caused by the whirlwind of change in late nineteenth-century America.   VMW

1. John William Reps, *Views and Viewmakers of Urban America* (Columbia, Mo.: University of Missouri Press, 1984), pp. 209–212.

2. J. Kevin Graffagnino, *Vermont in the Victorian Age: Continuity and Change in the Green Mountain State, 1850–1900* (Rutland, Vt.: Vermont Heritage Press and the Shelburne Museum, 1985).

3. Wood Art Gallery, *Thomas Waterman Wood PNA* (Montpelier, Vt.: Wood Art Gallery, 1972), pp. 13–19.

35 *Jug*

E. & L. P. Norton
Bennington, 1864
Salt-glazed stoneware with cobalt decoration
H: 24¼ inches DIAM: 15¼ inches
Impressed in roundel: "CALVIN PARK /
  1864 / MEMBER FROM WOODFORD"
Inscribed in cobalt: "George J."

The Bennington Museum. Bequest of
Mrs. Elmer H. Johnson, 66.2

This twelve-gallon cooler was one of two jugs presented in 1864 to Calvin Park of Woodford, Vermont, to celebrate his election to the Vermont state Legislature. Reputedly "a large-hearted, learned, liberal, and peculiar man," Park was extremely proud of his horses, which may explain why a prancing stallion—an unusual motif for Bennington stoneware—adorns this jug. The horse is perhaps the "beautiful bay horse" that the *Bennington Banner* reported Park purchasing the previous October, "so that 'Cal' now has as fine a team as any one in town, and will be able to cut quite a dash at the Capital this fall." The jug very likely was used to hold ale, wine, or some other sort of liquor, an ironic use, it would seem, in light of the Norton family's active involvement in the state's temperance movement.

Park was closely tied to both of Bennington's pottery families, which probably explains why he was the recipient of these jugs. Not only had he been a partner in business with Christopher Webber Fenton, founder of the United States Pottery Company (1847–1858), but he married Fenton's daughter Fanny, a Norton descendent.

The Norton Pottery (1785–1894), operated by five generations of the Norton family over a 109-year period, made utilitarian redware and stoneware. The pottery was founded by Captain John Norton (1758–1828), originally of Goshen, Connecticut, who was a farmer, a distiller, a keeper of lime kilns, and a dry goods merchant. As early as 1785, Norton began making redware; by 1804, he was making stoneware pots and pans. The pottery developed a widespread reputation as a result of its strong and well-decorated stoneware, the integrity of the Nortons, and the stability of the firm. General stores in Connecticut, New Hampshire, Massachusetts, eastern New York, and southern Vermont all sold Norton stoneware.

However, the pottery had strong competition. West Troy and Fort Edward, New York, both located just a short distance from Bennington, were also major centers for stoneware production. In addition, large stoneware potteries were established in Fairfax and Burlington, Vermont, in the 1840s and 1850s by E. L. Farrar and A. S. Stearns, Nichols & Alford, and O. L. & A. K. Ballard. Other smaller stoneware potteries were founded in Dorset and St. Johnsbury, the latter by relations of Christopher Webber Fenton.   CZ

36 *Platform Scale*

E. & T. Fairbanks Co.
St. Johnsbury, 1903
Iron, steel, hardwood
H: 45 inches   W: 21 inches   D: 38 inches
The Fairbanks Museum and Planetarium,
St. Johnsbury

Many Vermonters created ingenious devices to solve everyday problems, but only a handful translated their necessary inventions into an industry of international repute. In 1830 Thaddeus Fairbanks, looking with his brother Erastus for an accurate scale that would simplify the weighing of hemp, invented the world's first platform scale and transformed the ancient science of weights and measures.[1] The Fairbanks platform scale, quickly put into production by the E. & T. Fairbanks Co., soon became an essential tool of international trade. Preferred by druggists and gold miners, post offices and freight lines, the scales from St. Johnsbury provided quick, accurate weights for commodities in an ever-widening economic network. Before he died in 1886, Thaddeus and his achievement had been recognized by governments around the world.

This portable platform scale with wheels appeared in the 1903 catalogue at a time when rail lines linked most American cities to main transcontinental lines. Wholesale grocers, hardware dealers, and feed and coal merchants in cities across the country all had a use for one of Fairbanks's hundreds of standard models to weigh incoming freight or to parcel out goods for lo-cal distribution. Freight cars themselves were weighed on Fairbanks equipment, as were the canal boats of an earlier era, using a "weighlock" which hefted the entire barge with an overhead lever system.

Fairbanks scales weighed the wealth of the nation, spurring the trade upon which the growth of western cities and eastern ports depended and giving the Fairbanks brothers the wealth to transform their own small corner of the world. Between 1830 and 1900, decades during which the competing Howe Scale Co. was working its own transformation in Rutland, St. Johnsbury grew from a hamlet of fewer than 2000 people to the sixth most populous town in Vermont. The company quite literally built much of the town, constructing workers' housing, gasworks, a water system, the St. Johnsbury Academy, the Athenaeum, and essential other businesses.[2] Employees may have grumbled about having to buy from company stores, but the cultural amenities bestowed on St. Johnsbury made them the envy of their peers. Today, the Fairbanks Museum and Planetarium, another one of the Fairbanks brothers' gifts to the community, hosts a permanent exhibit of Fairbanks scales to explain the roots of the town and the business that built it.   VMW

1. *Fairbanks Standard, 150 Years* (St. Johnsbury, Vt.: Fairbanks Weighing Division, 1980).

2. J. Kevin Graffagnino, *Vermont in the Victorian Age: Continuity and Change in the Green Mountain State, 1850–1900* (Rutland, Vt.: Vermont Heritage Press and the Shelburne Museum, 1985), pp. 95–97.

37 *Chapel Organ*

Jacob Estey Organ Company
Brattleboro, 1884
Walnut
H: 86 inches W: 54 inches D: 23 inches
Old Stone House Museum, Brownington

Vermont boosters in the late nineteenth century saw in the Estey Organ Company positive proof of their belief that Yankee ingenuity and hard work reaped just rewards. Indeed, Jacob Estey's story reads like the Horatio Alger novels so popular at the time: A poor farmer's boy flees ill treatment from his foster family, learns a trade, and builds several businesses before taking over a failing instrument factory[1] which grows into one of Vermont's most successful manufacturing firms.[2] However, a critical element distinguishes Alger's and Estey's stories. Alger's heroes depended on lucky breaks from wealthy benefactors; Jacob Estey's lucky break was timing, buttressed by workmanship and marketing.

Jacob Estey took over the melodeon manufacturing firm of E. B. Carpenter & Co. in Brattleboro in 1853.[3] By 1860, he had increased the firm's output from six organs per month to 600 per year[4] and renamed it the Jacob Estey Organ

Company. His business rode the tide of social change we call the Victorian era, when men were supposed to "go out" and make money and women were expected to create a safe haven at home. A reed organ provided the perfect tool for the wife and mother who aspired to create a tranquil, protected domestic environment for her family. The accomplishment of music, once the domain of the well-to-do, became affordable even to a farm woman who needed to save $75 in egg money to realize her dream of an organ in the parlor.[5] Vivid color advertisements illustrated the refinement that an Estey Organ could bring to any home (cat. 37.1).

An Estey organ's elaborately carved cabinetry and decorative shelves for ornament displays catered to Victorian sensibilities, but Estey did not neglect the inner workings. His company kept pace with new patents, and in 1860 it hired an experienced machinist, Levi Fuller, to supervise iron and brass work.[6] Estey rebuilt the factory after fires in 1857 and 1864. Following the flood of 1867, he relocated the company to higher ground, constructed a complex of eight three-story factory buildings, and developed a whole new subdivision of Brattleboro known as Esteyville.

Estey organs also brought change to church music. The Johnson Baptist Church purchased this chapel organ at the height of the organs' popularity in the 1880s.[7] The mellow chords of the reed organ were able to support the harmonies of hymn-singing, which now replaced the lilting cadences of the psalms and fuguing tunes that had previously dominated the music of worship.[8] But the Baptist congregation ebbed away in the years before the First World War,[9] and the church became a Masonic Temple by the 1930s.[10] The organ made its way to the Old Stone House Museum by way of a leader of the Eastern Star.

VMW

Cat. 37.1 Estey Organ Co. [advertisement]. Lithograph. *c.* 1880. Courtesy, Special Collections, University of Vermont.

1. Henry Burnham, *Brattleboro, Windham County, Vermont: Early History* (Brattleboro, Vt.: D. Leonard, 1880), pp. 142–144.
2. John N. Houpis, *Brattleboro: Selected Historical Vignettes* (Brattleboro, Vt.: Brattleboro Publishing Co., 1973), pp. 20–22.

3. Background chronology, Estey Organ Company papers, Special Collections, University of Vermont.

4. John Houpis and Milton J. Nadworny, "The Perfect Melodeon: The Origins of the Estey Organ Company, 1846–1866," *Business History Review*, 33, No. 1 (Spring 1959), p. 54.

5. For an in-depth discussion of the social role of parlor organs, see "When the Music Stops" in Ken Ames, *Alleged Truths, Authentic Fictions: Culture in Victorian America* (Philadelphia: Temple University Press, 1991).

6. Fuller became son-in-law and partner within six years.

7. Organ popularity began to decline about the time of Estey's death in 1890. The company adjusted to a changing market by manufacturing pianos and pipe organs for churches. Company papers primarily document business in the twentieth century.

8. Anthony G. Barrand, Larry Gordon, and Carole Moody Crompton, *Northern Harmony: Plain Tunes, Fuging Tunes and Anthems From the New England Singing School Tradition* (Plainfield, Vt.: Northern Harmony Publishing Co., 1990).

9. Minute book of the Baptist Church, Johnson, Special Collections, University of Vermont.

10. Workers of the Federal Writers' Project, *Vermont: A Guide to the Green Mountain State* (Boston: Houghton Mifflin Co., 1937), p. 345.

38 *Star of Bethlehem Quilt*

Marie Marin
St. Pie, Quebec, Canada, 1860–1880s
Pieced and quilted wool
H: 73 inches W: 71½ inches

Shelburne Museum

The Star of Bethlehem was a popular quilting pattern in both the United States and Canada. In the states this often-used central-star pattern, made entirely of diamond-shaped pieces, was generally worked in printed or solid-color cottons. American quiltmakers made the transition from woolen to cotton fabrics in the early 1800s, when New England textile mills began producing and distributing large quantities of bright, patterned fabrics. In the Canadian provinces, however, the tradition of woolen pieced quilts continued for a much longer period, and it is not unusual to find pieced quilts composed of hand- and factory-woven wool fabrics.

Marie Marin lived in St. Pie, Quebec, a small town near Montreal and Sherbrooke, before she immigrated in 1899 to Barre, Vermont, to live with her son and daughter-in-law. She died there in 1902. A letter from her family—the previous owners of the quilt—relates that Mrs. Marin wove much of the cloth used by her family of fourteen children. Many of the textiles in this quilt appear to be handwoven and were probably produced by the quilter.

Although the French in the 1730s had established the first white settlement in Vermont in Hocquart, now known as Addison, few remained after the French and English conflict. They began to immigrate to the state in increasing numbers during the early nineteenth century following years of poor harvests, slow economy, and discrimination. Many of the earliest French Canadian immigrants settled in the developing communities of the Champlain Valley, where industrial growth was strong. By 1832, Burlington's French

Canadian population exceeded 500. Others and later immigrant families bought land and built farms just south of the Canadian border in Franklin, Orleans, and Essex counties, where Vermonters of French Canadian extraction represent today a significant portion of the population. Thousands were attracted to textile, glass, and lumber industries in Chittenden County; to the iron industry and stone and slate quarries in Rutland County; and to the granite quarries and paper and agricultural industries in Washington County.

The French legacy has been largely overlooked in Vermont although French continues to be spoken in the state's northern border communities. Nevertheless, the French immigrants' part in the state's cultural legacy is apparent in place names, such as Mallets Bay—named for Captain Mallette, who settled the area in the 1740s—and Isle La Motte, where the French established the Fort St. Anne trading post in 1666. Geographers have also detected evidence of French influence in the way land was divided in Addison County towns that lie along Lake Champlain's eastern shore. More subtle French-Canadian influence can be seen in furniture, textiles, and architectural forms that survive in communities such as St. Albans and Winooski, where large French-Canadian populations settled. Skilled French-Canadian craftsmen and craftswomen integrated their own design and construction traditions with those found in their new homeland.   CYO

REFERENCES

Guyette, Elise A. *Vermont: A Cultural Patchwork* (Peterborough, N.H.: Cobblestone Publishing, Inc., 1986).

McKendry, Ruth. *Quilts and Other Bed Coverings in the Canadian Tradition* (Toronto: Nostrand Reinhold Ltd., 1986).

Meeks, Harold A. *Time and Change in Vermont: A Human Geography* (Chester, Ct.: Globe Pequot Press, 1986).

Orlofsky, Myron and Patsy. *Quilts in America* (New York: McGraw-Hill Book Co., 1974).

39 *Bicycle Sign*

Amideé T. Thibault (1865–1961)
St. Albans, 1895
Wood and high-wheeled Columbia bicycle
H: 84 inches W: 66 inches
Museum of American Folk Art, New York

When Amideé Thibault immigrated to Vermont in the latter nineteenth century from his family's home in North Stanbridge, Quebec, he followed a route that many Canadians of French extraction had trod before. His choice of St. Albans as a place to settle and raise his family reinforced the already strong connections between French Canada and this shire town, which was originally part of the seignorie La Duvalle.[1]

From childhood, Amideé Thibault aspired to greater things than following his father to the family brickyard business. When it became clear that his father would neither support nor release his son for further education, Thibault left home for Montreal to pursue night school and to work at odd jobs. Over the next few years he was occasionally driven home to North Stanbridge by lack of funds, but he also visited Vermont frequently and acquired a variety of skills, including iron-working. After Thibault's marriage, his father-in-law added further to the young man's skills by teaching him sign painting and the complement of skills that he needed to run a successful carriage and bicycle repair business.

Thibault was a man well trained for his times. The United States in 1895 had 300 bicycle manufacturers, and the sport of bicycling had taken the country by storm. In St. Albans, Thibault put all of his skills to use. He opened a shop specializing in sign painting and bicycle and carriage repairs. To attract customers to his business at 29 Catherine Street, he carved this rider for an old high-wheeled bicycle (which was probably all the more eye-catching because the bicycle design was already out of date) and perched the arrangement on his roof. Below the sign, in the precise letter forms of a practiced sign painter, he advertised "Repairs done carefully and promptly" (cat. 39.1).

Cat. 39.1 Amideé Thibault's Bicycle Carriage Repair Shop. *c.* 1900. Courtesy, Museum of American Folk Art.

After carriages gave way to automobiles, Thibault was forced to find another line of business. He took advantage of St. Albans's position as the headquarters for the Vermont Central Railroad to establish a relationship with freight workers, and through them he acquired furniture damaged in transit. He repaired and refinished tables, and reupholstered chairs for sale in his shop.[2] He dabbled in decorating cars, as he had once decorated carriages, and enjoyed a reputation among local farmers for his weathervanes. His creative flair as a carver, combined with a solid jack-of-all-trades mechanical skill, allowed Amideé Thibault to make a good living from the mix of manufacturing and railroad folks in Vermont's sixth-largest city.   VMW

1. Jane C. Beck, *Always in Season: Folk Art and Traditional Culture in Vermont* (Montpelier, Vt.: Vermont Council on the Arts, 1982), p. 137.
2. Agnes Thibault, "My Memories of the Most Lovable and Unforgettable Man in All the World—My Dad," unpublished reminiscence (1971).

40 *Catamount*

c. 1891
Wood, gilded
H: 64 inches   H: 22 inches
Collection of Ken Arthur

No symbol is more deeply engraved in the pantheon of Vermont mythology than the catamount. Its legendary status originates with the stories told of the Green Mountain Boys' efforts to secure control of this territory. They made the catamount the emblem of their struggle when they mounted a specimen atop the sign at "Landlord Faye's" in Bennington. This tavern served as headquarters for their meetings and mock trials, such as the one in which they hoisted Doctor Adams of Arlington up on the signpost and exposed him beneath the snarling catamount[1] whose bared teeth, facing New York, became Vermont's own symbol of defiance.

The stuffed catamount at Faye's Tavern disappeared long before the place burned in 1871, but memories of it were revived with the centennial celebration of Vermont's statehood in 1891. In honor of the event, a bronze catamount monument was dedicated on Monument Ave. in Bennington to mark the site of the old "Catamount Tavern" (cat. 40.1). In his dedication speech in June 1897, F. B. Jennings declared that the panther no longer sneered at New York but at any assailant of freedom and independence.[2]

This handsome replica of the bronze monument may well have been commissioned by some aspiring landlord who hoped to capitalize on its historical associations and symbolism, but its excellent condition suggests that it did not hang outside in the weather for any length of time. The carver clearly knew his trade, for the cat looks more lifelike than most carousel menagerie figures. Its gilded finish was a favorite treatment at the turn of the century for tableaux on circus wagons.[3]

Like the proliferation of bicentennial memorabilia in 1976, this popular treatment of a powerful historical symbol demonstrates the role of imagery in stimulating the popular imagination. The effectiveness of that imagery is apparent in the University of Vermont's choice of the catamount as its mascot and in the hopes obviously pinned on its marketing by a brewer of new Vermont ales.

VMW

Cat. 40.1 Catamount Tavern. 1869. Stereopticon view. Courtesy, Images from the Past, Bennington.

1. "Affidavit in Support of the Petition of Rev. Benjamin Hough, March 7, 1775," *The Documentary History of the State of New York*, vol. 4 (Albany: Charles Van Benthuysen, Public Printer, 1851), p. 541.

2. F. B. Jennings, "Address Delivered at the Dedication of Catamount Monument at Bennington, June 23, 1897."

3. Frederick Fried, *Artists in Wood: American Carvers of Cigar Store Indians, Show Figures, and Circus Wagons* (New York: Bramhall House, 1970), pp. 85–113.

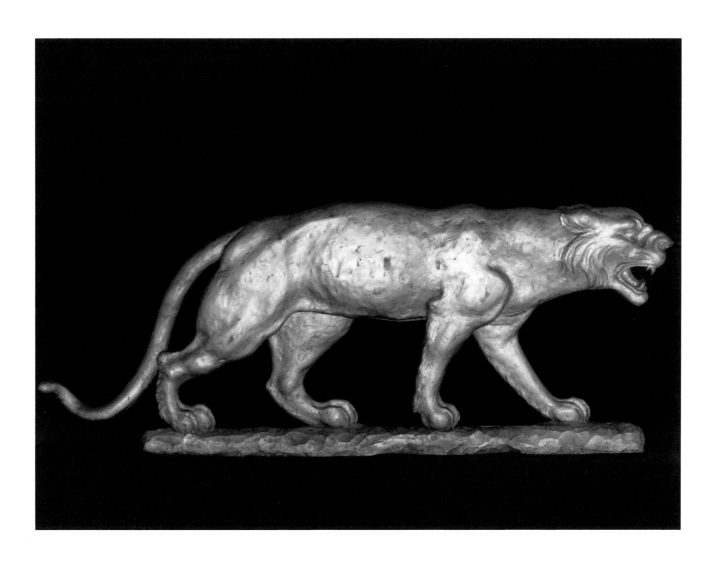

41 *Alexander Crowell and the Barnard panther*

1881

Stereopticon view

Photograph, Special Collections,
University of Vermont
Reproduced as a photomural in the exhibition

The death of the Barnard panther created a sensation throughout the state and turned Alexander Crowell into a celebrity for the winter of 1881. Curious residents bought copies of the photograph and pamphlets describing Crowell's feat and paid ten cents apiece for the thrill of seeing the "King of the American Forest," which measured seven feet long and weighed 182 lbs. after considerable blood loss. Broadsides announced the touring schedule of the catamount, which was "splendidly mounted" in a "perfect life-like representation of him as he appeared when roaming our forests."[1]

The killing of the "Barnard Monster" inflated the legendary stature of the catamount in Vermont folklore. The event took place on Thanksgiving, a nearly sacred holiday in New England. The hunter was a Civil War veteran, a member of Company E, First Vermont Cavalry. The victim was the same creature which had become a symbol of the Green Mountain State more than a hundred years earlier. The double-edged meaning was not lost on Victorian Vermonters, for the triumph of man over nature also signalled the demise of the rugged, wilderness environment which had shaped Vermonters' sense of identity for six generations. Concern for that loss had been growing since 1853, when Zadock Thompson lamented that "the animal is now exceedingly scarce and there may never be another obtained, within the state, for any of our museums."[2]

The catamount's legendary status did not die with the "Barnard Monster," however. Debate continues today over whether catamounts live in the Green Mountains. Believers assemble sighting information through their own informal network, but officials remain skeptical since amateurs have difficulty producing reliable proof of the catamounts' presence here in Vermont. Similar creatures can be found in the Canadian and western wilderness but under different names.   V M W

1. J. Kevin Graffagnino, *Vermont in the Victorian Age: Continuity and Change in the Green Mountain State, 1850–1900* (Rutland, Vt.: Vermont Heritage Press and the Shelburne Museum, 1985), pp. 82–85.
2. Zadock Thompson, *Appendix to the History of Vermont, Natural, Civil & Statistical* (Burlington, Vt.: Published by the Author; Stacy and Jameson, Printers, 1853), p. 12. At the end of its tour, the "Barnard Monster" came to rest and still resides in the collection of the Vermont Historical Society.

42 *Route Seven*

Rowland E. Robinson (1833–1900)
Ferrisburgh, *c.* 1878
Oil on canvas
H: 8 inches W: 10 inches

Rokeby (Ancestral Estate of Rowland Evans Robinson), Ferrisburgh

> But now comes an afternoon with a breathless chill in it . . . Then roofs and woods and fence tops and grassless ground begin slowly to whiten, and boughs and twigs are traced with a faint white outline against a gray background, and the dull yellow of the fields grows paler under the falling snow . . . [1]
>
> Rowland Robinson
> "Danvis Farm Life"

Few Vermonters of the nineteenth century were as influential in perpetuating a romantic vision of the state and its inhabitants as writer and artist Rowland E. Robinson. A third-generation Vermonter, he was born to a family that emigrated from Rhode Island to Ferrisburgh in the late 1700s and established a family homestead that endured until the middle of the twentieth century, when it became a museum and one of the state's historical treasures. Rokeby today is a precious archive of artifacts and records that document one family's life in Vermont through four active generations.

Robinson was a prolific writer of articles examining New England life, its customs, and its culture for *Forest and Stream, Atlantic Monthly*, and *Youth's Companion*, among other magazines. He was also a historian and novelist, whose prose helped keep alive stories of the Green Mountain State's early heroes and whose fictional characters, such as "Uncle Lisha," spread far and wide the image of the state's decent, hard-working inhabitants. His vocabulary was rose-tinged, but at the same time he was a sharp observer of details that gave his descriptions authenticity and power. *Vermont: A Guide to the Green Mountain State*, published in 1937, called Robinson

> probably Vermont's most representative and loved writer, and the outstanding Vermont literary figure of the nineteenth century. No other writer in the State has ever translated so accurately and warmly the personality of Vermont people and Vermont

landscapes, and in so doing Robinson pictured a unique little corner of American civilization that has now vanished from even the remotest backwoods sections. [2]

Like many Vermonters of his generation, Robinson left Vermont as a young man to pursue better opportunities elsewhere. In New York, as a journeyman illustrator, he published cartoons and illustrations of all sorts in *Moore's Rural New Yorker, Harper's*, and the *Atlantic Monthly*. These experiences helped him create a realistic visual landscape and a sense of movement in his work, since he was often required to work quickly and boldly to meet production deadlines. [3] When he became plagued by eye problems, he retreated to the family homestead in Ferrisburgh and turned increasingly to writing. Nonetheless, he continued to paint until he lost his eyesight completely, eight years before his death.

In at least fifty paintings, most no larger than this one, he captured the same moods and details he sought to convey in his writing. *Route Seven* is both a solitary and a warmly familiar view of a place that was part of his daily life experience. The painting's original title, if indeed it ever had one, has long since been lost; *Route Seven*, named for the road that passes in front of Robinson's home, reflects contemporary nomenclature for the state's twentieth-century highway system.

Most of Robinson's best canvases were painted over a ten-year period between 1867 and 1877, a time of economic difficulty for many Vermonters. Paul Eschholz, professor of English at the University of Vermont, has observed that "during hard times Vermonters have turned to the landscape in an effort to define or find meaning in their existence, to establish a firmly rooted sense of place." [4] It is that retreat to the land to which Robinson clung in his artistic activities.

Robinson painted and described his world as he hoped it would remain. He looked to the reassuring isolation of an earlier Vermont—before the encroachment of railroads, of industry, of tourism, of foreign immigrants—and sketched a portrait of a state that was changing irrevocably. Both inside and out of Vermont, thousands of readers,

discomforted by the alarming changes and quick-
ening pace of life in the latter nineteenth century,
were happy to believe once again in the way of life
Robinson recreated for their imaginations.   KEP

1. Rowland Evans Robinson, "Danvis Farm Life" in
Silver Fields and Other Sketches of a Farmer-Sportsman
(Boston and New York: Houghton Mifflin Company,
1921), p. 45.
2. Workers of the Federal Writers' Project of the
Works Progress Administration, *Vermont: A Guide to the
Green Mountain State* (Boston: Houghton Mifflin Co.,
1937), p. 283.
3. H. Wayne Morgan, *New Muses: Art in American
Culture, 1865–1920* (Norman, Okla.: University of
Oklahoma Press, 1978), p. 25.
4. Paul Eschholz, "The Land of a Thousand Hills:
Literary Images of the Vermont Landscape, 1865–
1945," in *Vermont Landscape Images: 1776–1976*, William
C. Lipke and Philip N. Grimes, eds. (Burlington, Vt.:
Robert Hull Fleming Museum, 1976).

43 Rod and Reel

C. F. Orvis Company
Manchester, 1885 (rod) and 1886 (reel)
Lancewood (rod) and steel (reel)
L: 36 inches, each of three pieces (rod);
    D: 2 inches (reel)

American Museum of Fly Fishing, Manchester

The path that the Battenkill River carves through southern Vermont determined a cluster of related enterprises: the location of the Rutland Railroad line, the growth of Manchester as a tourist resort, and the success of the C. F. Orvis Company, manufacturers of fishing tackle. This accident of geography prompted Franklin Orvis to establish Equinox House in 1853 and gave his brother, Charles, the opportunity to fall in love with fly-fishing as a youth. Tourism and tackle thus developed as kindred enterprises in Manchester.[1]

At first, Orvis made fishing rods for his own enjoyment as a fisherman and for the patrons of his brother's hotel. An increasingly urban, middle-class American population was beginning to travel to country locations for summer rest and recreation, providing Orvis with a steadily growing market. With a myriad of exotic woods available from distant places, Orvis experimented until he was satisfied that Cuban lancewood and split Chinese bamboo produced the best rods. Happy customers advertised the wares (cat. 43.1), including the great promoter, Ned Buntline, whose novels made Buffalo Bill a household name. Buntline proclaimed the Orvis reel his favorite, "not as a puff, but as a *truth* that I'll stand by and fish by as long as I and that rod last."[2]

Orvis also worked on reel design until he was satisfied enough to apply for a patent in 1874. The nickel-coated brass reel had perforated sides that allowed air to circulate and dry the line while making the mechanism very lightweight. The reel earned a commendation award at the Centennial Exposition in Philadelphia and remained a standard item for more than forty years.

Charles Orvis entered business just as recreational hunting and fishing became national popular pastimes. While catering to this new middle-

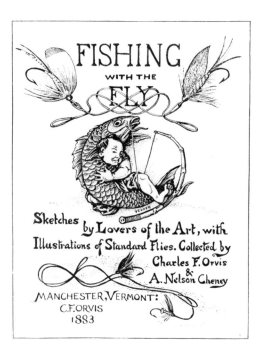

Cat. 43.1 Title page. C. F. Orvis, *Fishing with the Fly* (1883). Courtesy, American Museum of Fly Fishing.

class tourist activity, he took an active role in Vermont's fledgling conservation efforts by fighting against the over-fishing and silting up of the Battenkill, and by contributing to a growing consciousness of the fragility of the state's wildlife. In 1857, just a year after Orvis opened his business, the Vermont Legislature authorized a report on the feasibility of restocking the depleted fish population of Vermont's streams.[3] George Perkins Marsh's findings during this investigation provided some of the data he incorporated into his monumental contribution to the conservation movement, *Man and Nature*, published in 1864. Marsh's book recognized the destructive impact that human activity had on the ways of nature at a time when most people still believed that the earth's resources had no limit.[4]   VMW

1. Austin Hogan and Paul Schullery, *The Orvis Story* (Manchester, Vt.: The Orvis Company, Inc., 1980).
2. Hogan and Schullery, *The Orvis Story*, p. 19.
3. J. Kevin Graffagnino, *Vermont in the Victorian Age: Continuity and Change in the Green Mountain State, 1850–1900* (Rutland, Vt.: Vermont Heritage Press and the Shelburne Museum, 1985), p. 84.
4. George Perkins Marsh, *Man and Nature* (New York: Charles Scribners, 1864).

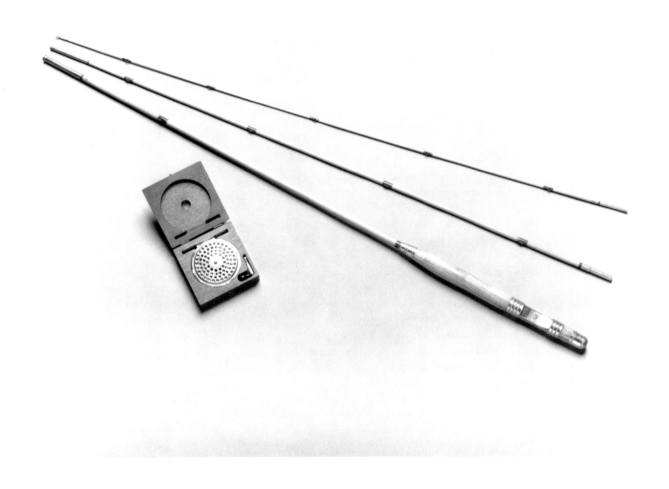

44 *Quillwork Trinket Box*

Abenaki (?), Mid-nineteenth century
Birchbark sides, bound with s-twist spruce
    root; hemlock (?) bottom, vegetable-dyed
    porcupine quills arranged in a herringbone
    pattern. Some rodent damage to
    quillwork. Missing lid.
H: 3⅝ inches D: 5⅞ inches

Abenaki Cultural Center, Swanton

This trinket box fragment, which has a long history in Cambridge, Vermont, is of a style associated with the Micmac people of northern Maine and the Canadian Maritimes. However, this fragment is included in this exhibition to pose an important scholarly question: If this box has been in northern Vermont for a significant length of time, as the oral history of it implies, then how did it get to Vermont?

One hypothesis is that the box was made somewhere in the vicinity of Cambridge, Vermont. A second hypothesis is that the box was part of a native trade network through which it came to Vermont from somewhere nearby or far away. A third hypothesis is that the box was brought to Vermont as a souvenir or as an antique.

No research has been done concerning these containers except among the Micmac, leaving open the possibility in the first hypothesis that the style was more widespread than art historians have heretofore believed. However, the only way to test these three hypotheses is to search out every bark and quillwork container that has a documentable Vermont provenance in an attempt to define temporal, stylistic, and geographical variations in Native American containers of New England–eastern Canadian nations. Since we do not know what a Vermont quilled-bark container looks like—due to art historians' denial of a native Vermont artistic tradition—we may find that it looks like this, or maybe not.

Vermont historians are beginning to document the Abenaki presence in Vermont over the past 10,000 years and to put to rest the long-held myth that the state was never a homeland for native peoples. Deriving from this documentation is an awareness that the Western Abenaki, over the course of all those centuries, must have made an abundance of objects which have almost certainly been misattributed to the Iroquois or Eastern Abenaki. We can begin to see, therefore, what rich possibilities for further discovery are represented by this fragment of a trinket box.   FMW

45 *Thimble Cover, Notions Basket, and Pincushion*

Abenaki, late nineteenth century
H: (circular basket) 3 inches
   H: (thimble cover) 1³/₁₆ inches
H: (rectangular basket) 1¼ inches
   H: (cushion) 1⅜ inches
Plaited, pounded ash splints, sweetgrass
   basketry, silk ribbon hanger with bone ring
Found in Fairfax

Abenaki Cultural Center, Swanton

The way this basket was made, or its technological style, was popular from the Eastern Abenaki of the coast of Maine; through the Central and Western Abenaki of New Hampshire, southern Quebec, and Vermont; to the Mohawk of Akwesasne Reservation of northern New York.

It is unclear whether plaited baskets such as this one were made in New England before the Europeans arrived, but by the early 1800s, wide-splint utilitarian baskets were a staple item in the trade between the Abenakis and the Euroamericans. The outsides of some of these early baskets were decorated with paint.

During the late nineteenth and early twentieth centuries, however, Abenaki basketmakers shifted from producing utilitarian baskets to making so-called "fancy baskets" with sweetgrass, or "cow-wiss," secondary splints that were warped or twisted to achieve distinctive basket surfaces. These new baskets were designed for the tourist trade that was growing up around scenic attractions and spas throughout New England. Many Native American families traveled to Atlantic City or other distant tourist spots to ply their wares.

The undyed ash splints in this basket ensemble (commercial dyes were used to color splints in the first part of the twentieth century) and the bone hanging ring (a celluloid ring would have been substituted in the late Victorian Period) suggest that this basket was made very early in the evolution of the fancy basket. People still living in the Lamoille River Valley remember native people selling baskets such as this from horse-drawn carriages in the early part of this century. Much oral history remains to be done in this region to uncover the history of these itinerant merchants and their wares.   FMW

46 *Beaded Reticule*

Abenaki (?), Found in Tunbridge, *c.* 1880
  with *c.* 1940 beading
Various colored and seed and bugle beads
  appliqué stitched to a cotton (?) bag
H: 6¼ inches W: 6¼ inches

Abenaki Cultural Center, Swanton

The attribution of these popular bags is confusing. They are definitely eastern Native American. The Material Heritage of Native Vermont Project, a research program of the Abenaki Nation at Missisquoi, has uncovered several of these bags in local collections, both public and private. All have a Vermont provenance documented by long oral histories, but this is the only one recovered by the Abenaki Nation. This Vermont bag has remained in use until recently. Loops of iridescent beads sewn with nylon thread unavailable until the mid-twentieth century imply either that the bag received such hard use over the years that it needed to be rebeaded or that some kind of ceremonial reconfiguring occurred in the recent past.

This bag is a Native American version of the reticule, a woman's small, decorated bag with a thin shoulder strap. In the Euroamerican reticule, one side of the bag is decorated while the side that lies against the body is left plain. The pouch is accessed through the top, which is covered by a single, large pendant flap that partly covers the front and is integral to the overall design. The concept of the reticule was transferred to Native American artisans but not its distinctive operation or design. Notice on this bag that both sides are decorated. Notice, also, that this bag has two flaps, unlike the Euroamerican version, and that the bag is entered through an open slit in the top, not from under the protective closure flap.

These differences raise intriguing questions. Could it be that Euroamerican elite women who carried reticules were so socially distant from their Native American sisters that no Native American woman ever saw a reticule opened? The social implications of this conjecture may say much about the relative socioeconomic status of two groups of women who carried different versions of the small beaded bag.   FMW

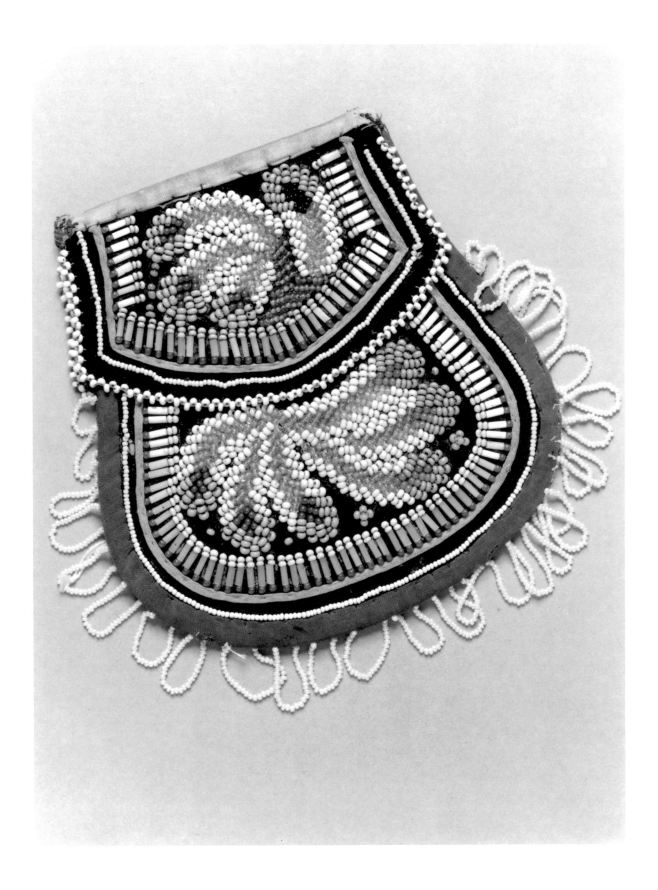

47 *Quilt*

Women's Relief Corps
Calais, 1917
Pieced white cotton with appliquéd red
    crosses
L: 77 inches   W: 76½ inches   D: 23 inches

Calais Historical Society, on extended loan to the
Vermont Historical Society, Montpelier

When the Women's Relief Corps of Calais gathered to stitch together the blocks of its Red Cross quilt in 1917, the quilters raised money twice over. Donors first paid for the privilege of signing their names to blocks that would surround the one that had been sent to the White House for President Woodrow Wilson's signature. Afterwards, a raffle for the quilt itself brought in yet another contribution to the war cause. Across the nation, women followed similar suggestions for Red Cross fund raising.[1]

Generations of needlework tradition come together in this piece, although this is the first known war in which Vermonters sewed quilts in service to the fighting troops. The practice of autographing quilt blocks, however, began as a fad among "available" and newlywed women in New England in the 1840s.[2] Young women stitched patchwork blocks which they signed with a verse, a date, or their names, and then assembled them into friendship quilts for friends or family members. The tradition of charitable sewing was older still, for American women had gathered to sew for the poor or for foreign missions as soon as their own domestic affairs left them any free time at all.[3]

The ladies who nursed, knitted, or sewed in a spirit of service knew that their Red Cross work made them part of the world history that was unfolding far away. Sewing soothed their anxiety for loved ones sent into action. But it also gave them an opportunity to think and talk about their friends and neighbors at the front, and thus connected them to the distant, dramatic events of the Great War.

Vermonters' response to the nation's wars is legendary. Just that year, the Vermont Legislature had appropriated one million dollars for public defense nearly a whole week before the United States government declared its intention to enter the World War then underway. Although not the first state to make such an appropriation, Vermont pledged more than any other state in proportion to its population. A half century earlier, Vermonters' contributions during the Civil War had reached mythic proportions when the state Legislature appropriated a million dollars in support of the war. More than a fifth of the male population had enlisted in the Union Army. Fervor for Union and abolition had also burned brightly among Vermont's sisterhood of sewing circles, as members of relief associations produced blankets, sheets, bandages, and other materials needed by the fighting men.[4]   VMW

1. Nancy Rowley, "Red Cross Quilts for the Great War," *Uncoverings #3* (American Quilt Study Group, 1982).

2. Linda Otto Lipsett, *Remember Me: Women and Their Friendship Quilts* (San Francisco: The Quilt Digest Press, 1986), p. 16.

3. Frances Trollope, *Domestic Manners of the Americans* (1832; reprint ed., edited by Donald Smalley, New York: Alfred A. Knopf, 1949), p. 282.

4. J. Kevin Graffagnino, *Vermont in the Victorian Age: Continuity and Change in the Green Mountain State, 1850–1900* (Rutland, Vt.: Vermont Heritage Press and the Shelburne Museum, 1985).

48 *Edward Marcotte, Backroping Boy,*
Chace Cotton Mill

Lewis W. Hine (1874–1940)
Burlington, Vermont, 1909

Photograph, The Robert Hull Fleming
Museum, University of Vermont
Reproduced as a photomural in the exhibition

Forty-six photographs of Vermont working children were taken by Lewis Hine between 1909–
1916 for the National Child Labor Committee.
Founded in 1904 "to eradicate the old evil of child
labor,"[1] the NCLC engaged Hine as a photographer in 1906. The Vermont photographs represent less than 1 percent of the total number of
photographs taken for the committee over a six-
year period by the photographer on his travels
throughout the North and South. Ronald J. Hill
observed that Hine's photographs from this project "take us far beyond the well-known images of
a single figure isolated against a machine in a
working environment"[2] as typified in this image.
Hine also photographed groups of boys and girls,
many of them displaying an unmistakable cama-
raderie which, in spirit, seems counter to the purpose of the visual evidence Hine was gathering for
the committee. Although mills—both cotton and
woolen—comprise about three-fourths of the
workplaces Hine photographed in Vermont, the
marble and lumber industries are also represented,
as are "newsies" (news boys and girls), and children working on the farm.

One critic has noted that "the child labor condition in Vermont was not severe," because of
its "low population density" and its mandatory
schooling law, just one of ten such state laws in the
nation requiring year-long attendance.[3] Nonetheless, the practice of employing Vermont children
for long hours under less-than-ideal conditions
in factories, mills, and quarries was particularly
loathsome in a state whose predominant industry
was agriculture. However, agriculture itself presented an ironic twist to the plight of overworked
and exploited children. On the farm, where children as young as those in the mills often worked
equally long hours, their work was viewed as an
acceptable contribution to the family toil in which
everyone was expected to play his or her part.

W CL

1. Stanley Mallach, "Child Labor Reform and Lewis
Hine," in *Photography and Reform: Lewis Hine and the
National Child Labor Committee* (Milwaukee: Milwaukee
Art Museum, 1984), p. 13.
2. Ronald J. Hill, "The Documentary Strategies of
Lewis W. Hine," in *Lewis W. Hine: Child Labor Photography* (Washington, D. C.: Lunn Gallery International,
1980), p. 1.
3. K. B. [Kim Borsavage], Catalogue entry on Lewis
W. Hine in *Recent Gifts and Acquisitions: 1976–1980* (Burlington, Vt.: Robert Hull Fleming Museum, 1980),
p. 25.

49 *Thirty Snowflake Prints*

Wilson Alwyn Bentley (1865–1931)
Jericho, *c.* 1890
Microphotographs mounted on backing
 board
H: 24 inches L: 30 inches
Jericho Historical Society

W. A. Bentley fit the stereotype of a reticent Vermonter. Alfred Lawton, a station agent in North Hero, remembered him as "not overly given to conversation"[1] until the talk turned to snowflakes. On that subject, Bentley could wax eloquent, even lyrical, as he described his wonder at the "unexampled freedom of motion" of ice crystal formation.[2]

Bentley became fascinated with ice crystals when his mother, a schoolteacher, lent him her microscope with which to view them in detail. Frustrated by his inability to draw the crystalline shapes, Bentley began experimenting with a bellows camera mounted in an unheated room at the back of his family's farmhouse in Jericho, Vermont. By the time he was twenty, he had succeeded in capturing his first "snow beauty" on film. He went on to perfect a process of capturing snowflakes without injuring their delicate points and photographing them before they melted or evaporated.

In his pursuit of the pure science of observation and hypothesis, Bentley opened a new path of exploration that became the discipline of atmospheric studies. Having discovered the "charm of mystery, of the unknown," Bentley assembled meteorological information from thrice-daily weather observations until he could explain that low, warm clouds produce branching forms of snowflakes while high, cold clouds produce solid, tabular hexagons. He also observed that the latter form can acquire branches if the crystal happens to fall through a lower, warmer layer of clouds.[3]

Bentley marveled at the perfect symmetry and myriad forms of snowflakes, while the world marveled at his persistent dedication to their study. A solitary, dedicated worker, Bentley nevertheless believed in sharing his discoveries. He published his findings in magazines and produced lantern slides for classroom use. On his lecture circuit, he became known as "The Snowflake Man," although he also spoke about frost and dew.[4] In the late 1920s, the American Meteorological Society raised funds to help Bentley catalogue his collection of nearly 5,000 microphotographs, nearly half of which were published in *Snow Crystals* in 1931.[5]

VMW

1. Letter from Alfred J. Lawton to Blair Williams, Jericho Historical Society, n.d.

2. W. A. Bentley, "Snow Beauties," reprinted from *Technical World* in *History of Jericho* (Burlington, Vt.: Free Press Printing Co., 1916), p. 320.

3. Bentley, "Snow Beauties," p. 322.

4. Duncan C. Blanchard, "Wilson Bentley: Pioneer in Snowflake Photomicrography," *Photographic Applications in Science, Technology and Medicine*, 8, No. 3 (May 1973), pp. 26–28, 39–41.

5. Reprinted by Dover Publications in 1971.

50 *Village of Stowe, Vermont*

Luigi Lucioni (1900–1988)
Oil on canvas
H: 33½ inches w: 23⅝ inches
Signed and dated, lower left: "Luigi Lucioni,
    1931"

The Minneapolis Institute of Arts. Gift from the
Estate of Mrs. George P. Douglas, 55.23.

Few twentieth century images better summarize
the pastoral qualities many associate with small-
town life than Luigi Lucioni's *Village of Stowe,
Vermont*. Depicted as it is from a distance, the town
is without flaw. In Lucioni's eyes man and nature
live side by side in perfect harmony. After visiting
the state from New York for the first time in 1917,
the Italian-born artist later observed it was "like
seeing the mountainsides of my birthplace. I was
reborn in this majestic setting and I fell in love
with Vermont."[1]

In 1931, Stowe was a town of just over 1650
residents. Then as now the spire of the Community Church, organized in 1920 through a merger
of the Methodist, Congregationalist, and Uni-
versalist-Unitarian Churches, stood as the town's
sentinel.[2] A patchwork of meadows and forests
provides a foil for Mt. Mansfield, which rises ma-
jestically in the distance. The town itself, curiously
devoid of people and animals, exhibits an unreal
stillness and tranquility. Only the buildings, roads,
pastures and meadows—some even in 1931 beginning to be reclaimed by forest—affirm a human
presence.

The clarity and precision that characterize Lucioni's technique are metaphors for his impression
of Vermont. Here his reductive style overwhelms
the real complexity of small-town life: its politics,
its poverty, and its cycle of birth and death. Such
complexity was, in 1931, about to manifest itself
in the form of significant local development. The
ski industry, then in its infancy, had yet to make
Stowe a magnet for those seeking winter sport.
But two years later the first modern ski trail was
cut on Mt. Mansfield, and by 1940 Stowe had the
largest and highest aerial ski lift in the country; the
winter pilgrimage of thousands of visitors had
begun.[3]

In 1932 Lucioni became the youngest artist to
have a painting purchased by the Metropolitan
Museum of Art. With that honor came recognition, and through his connection with the Metropolitan he met Mrs. J. Watson Webb, owner of
the Shelburne Farms estate. Mrs. Webb invited
Lucioni to Shelburne to paint a landscape for her
daughter as a present. For years afterwards he returned to Shelburne to paint.[4] Certainly it is no
coincidence that one of Vermont's greatest patrons
of the arts, a woman who sought to preserve her
vision of the state's past, would find inspiration in
the paintings of an artist consciously nurturing
that same sanitized image.   RHS

1. The Shelburne Museum, *The Shelburne Museum
proudly presents the painting life of Luigi Lucioni* (1968),
n.p.
2. Edwin L. Bigelow, *Stowe, Vermont: ski capital of the
East, 1763–1963* ([Stowe, Vt.] Stowe Historical Society,
1964), p. 75.
3. Bigelow, *Stowe*, pp. 153–154.
4. The *Sunday Rutland Herald* and the *Sunday Times
Argus*, 18 October 1987, p. 8.

51 *Church Supper,* 1933

Paul Sample (1896–1974)
Oil on canvas
H: 40 inches W: 48 inches
Signed lower left: "Paul Sample"

Museum of Fine Arts, Springfield,
Massachusetts. The James Phillip Gray
Collection. 33.07

Since the seventeenth century, community churches have played an integral role in New England town life. Just as the spires of town churches have physically dominated the community, the pull of the church, whatever the denomination, has had a pronounced influence on the daily lives of most residents. Here Paul Sample draws attention to those seasonal events sponsored by the church that have provided a means of social contact for parishioners. The church supper has been a fixture of American life since the end of the nineteenth century and has been another means by which the church has exerted a positive influence on the tenor of community life. In this instance, however, Sample raises the specter of change and outside influence in the person of a stylishly dressed young woman, clearly an urban outsider, who is attending the event. The reaction to her ranges from indifference to curiosity and trepidation.

After his marriage in 1928 to Sylvia Howland, a native of Montpelier, Sample began to spend his summers in Vermont on Willoughby Lake. Although not acknowledged before, it is the lakeside community of Westmore, where the Howland's Graystone cottage was located, that inspired this painting.[1] In the background stands the Westmore church, built in 1894 and only a short walk from where Sample resided, and the school, which stands across the road.

The painting, as described by Sample, is based on church suppers given for summer people and natives in the area. The central figure holding the tray is Mrs. Tatro, who did laundry for Sample and served at the church suppers. Many other townspeople posed for the artist.[2]

Sample was a graduate of Dartmouth College where for many years he taught painting. Further, he was one of a group of painters (among them Luigi Lucioni, Rockwell Kent, and Andrew Wyeth) that in the 1930s chose to depict rural New England life, just as other artists scattered across the country found inspiration in everyday scenes of other parts of America.[3]   RHS

1. Harriet F. Fisher, *Willoughby Lake: Legends and Legacies* (Brownington, Vt.: Orleans County Historical Society, 1988), p. 114.

2. *Courier-Journal* [Louisville, Ky.], 11 February 1940. I wish to thank Paula F. Glick for providing this information.

3. Robert L. McGrath, "Paul Sample, Painter of the American Scene," in *Paul Sample, Painter of the American Scene* (Hanover, N.H.: Hood Museum of Art, Dartmouth College, 1988), p. 38.

52 *Doorway, Merrill Place, Peacham*

Herbert Wheaton Congdon (1876–1965)
c. 1936–1938

Photograph, Special Collections,
University of Vermont
Reproduced as a photomural in the exhibition

In 1936 Herbert Wheaton Congdon was appointed photographer for the Old Buildings Project, a photographic record initiated by the University of Vermont to document buildings erected in the state before 1850.[1] The project was one of several efforts in Vermont to document an indigenous material culture and thus realized recommendations made in 1931 by the Commission on Country Life and published that year in *Rural Vermont*.

Doorway, Merrill Place, Peacham reflects, in its close-cropped attention to the detailed doorway, the formal and sculptural focus of the photographer, who was also a practicing architect. According to Congdon,

> This sole ornament of an utterly plain house gives more evidence of lusty good will in the use of a moulding-plane than studious consideration of design. The swelling frieze and elaborate door-paneling are attractive, but an architect finds the headlight the noteworthy feature of the composition. This has a row of little arches instead of the usual square-headed panes, a very rare treatment in Vermont.[2]

Viewed as a borrowed architectural motif from the past and in the context of the partially disclosed building, the doorway reads as a shard from an earlier period of settlement.

Congdon had a remarkable gift for describing the environmental and social context of the buildings he photographed. Of the Merrill doorway, he remarked upon the quiet road running south into Peacham and the backdrop of mountains and pastures against which it was set. He particularly noted the side road, which branched into Penny Street, "where two old houses face each other across a tiny Green, a suburb of the shilling's worth of Peacham. One of these houses is the Merrill Place."[3]

In addition to *Old Vermont Houses*, Congdon also published *The Covered Bridge*, in 1941, and *Early American Homes for Today*, in 1963. Today, a new generation of students of architecture and historic preservation is indebted to his remarkable visual record of Vermont's architectural heritage.[4]

WCL

1. Herbert Wheaton Congdon, "Introduction," *Old Vermont Houses, 1763–1850* (1940; reprint ed., Dublin, N.H.: William L. Bauhan, 1973). Sponsored by the University of Vermont's Robert Hull Fleming Museum, under the directorship of Henry F. Perkins, the project was largely funded by the James Benjamin Wilbur Library Fund, "established chiefly to preserve Vermontiana." Prior to the publication of *Old Vermont Houses* in 1940, a selection of Congdon's mounted photographs was exhibited throughout the state.

2. Congdon, *Old Vermont Houses*, p. 127.

3. Congdon, *Old Vermont Houses*, p. 127. Everad M. Upjohn of Columbia University reviewed *Old Vermont Houses* for *Art Bulletin*, 22, No. 2 (June 1940), remarking that it was a "popular and charming sketch of the early architecture of [Vermont]." He was referring to the illustrations as "works of art in themselves, quite aside from the buildings they record." p. 109.

4. For a recent assessment of Congdon's work, see J. Kevin Graffagnino, "Herbert Wheaton Congdon and the Architectural Heritage of Vermont," *Vermont History*, 50 (Winter 1982), pp. 5–12.

53 *Abandoned Farmhouse Near Newport, Vermont*

Carl Mydans (1907–   )
1936

Photograph, Library of Congress
Reproduced as a photomural in the exhibition

Abandoned Farmhouse Near Newport, Vermont is one of the most provocative images of Vermont by Farm Security Administration photographers. Taken in the latter years of the Depression, it contrasts sharply with other Vermont F.S.A. photographs, such as those of Woodstock residents by colleague Marion Post Wolcott.[1] Mydans's stark image of a hill farm in Vermont graphically depicts abandonment, even desolation, against a backdrop of clouds and rolling hills.[2] The rusted body of a vintage car—gutted and disintegrating—functions as a visual cipher for the rotting

architectural structures in the middleground, which in turn depict in varying stages the ravages of time. A wagon wheel, symbol of an earlier age of settlement and promise, is propped against the near structure. The field is littered with fragments of wood and metal.

The viewer comprehends instantly the photographer's carefully chosen title, as well as the relationship between Mydans's words and text. The close correlation between words and text, which Mydans felt was integral to his art, led one critic to observe that "Mydans must be described as a photojournalist rather than a documentary photographer."[3]

Like other memorable F.S.A. photographs, *Abandoned Farmhouse* is "a broader statement—frequently a mood, an accent, but more frequently a sketch and not infrequently a story."[4] Mydans's photograph does not simply convey the scene of a depressed economic period or place, it speaks of the relentless human effort expended in farming and of the defeat that inevitably follows when energy and money are depleted.

Quechee—abandoned farm, buyer wanted (cat. 53.1) is a related photograph, taken by Ewing Galloway and published thirty years later in the updated and revised second edition of *Vermont: A Guide to the Green Mountain State* (1966). While there are striking similarities between the two photographs in the depiction of architectural decay and the concept of abandonment, the title and the context of Galloway's image imply that the federal-style structure will be rescued and turned into a "second home." Such a hope—far-fetched in the Depression—was possible in the 1960s, when a booming economy, a significant increase in population, and an altered perception of rural life assured the purchase and renovation of many abandoned Vermont farms.   WCL

Cat. 53.1 Ewing Galloway. *Quechee—abandoned farm, buyer wanted*. From *Vermont: A Guide to the Green Mountain State* (1966).

1. Many of Marion Post Wolcott's F.S.A. photographs of Woodstock, Vermont, were published as illustrations in Charles Edward Crane's *Winter in Vermont* (New York: Alfred A. Knopf, 1941). For a concise statement on the function of the Farm Security Administration photographs, see Roy Emerson Stryker, "The F.S.A. Collection of Photographs," in *Photography in*

Print. ed. Vicki Goldberg (New York: Simon and Schuster, 1981), pp. 349–354.

2. Cultural historian Sheafe Satterthwaite, in an essay entitled, "Puckerbrush, Cellar Holes, Rubble: Observations on Abandonment in Vermont," published in *Vermont Landscape Images.* eds. William C. Lipke and Philip N. Grime (Burlington, Vt.: Robert Hull Fleming Museum, 1976), makes the distinction that vacant buildings able to be rescued from their disrepair are abandoned; abandoned buildings beyond repair are derelict. Using this terminology, Mydans might have more appropriately titled his photograph, "Derelict Farmhouse."

3. Derrick Price, "Carl Mydans," in *Contemporary Photographers.* eds. George Walsh, Colin Nagler, and Michael Held (New York: St. Martin's Press, 1982), p. 547. Mydans was a 1930 graduate of the Boston University School of Journalism and referred to himself as a "photo journalist." He was one of four photographers hired in 1936 to work for the new *Life* magazine, a publication he remained with until 1972.

4. Stryker, "The F.S.A. Collection," p. 353. "The photograph is only the subsidiary, the little brother, of the word," Stryker said.

54 *Freedom of Speech*

Norman Rockwell (1894–1978)
1944
Lithograph
H: 28 inches W: 20 inches
The Norman Rockwell Museum at Stockbridge, Massachusetts

Any questions about whether Americans associated rural northern New England with bedrock democracy were laid to rest in 1943, when Norman Rockwell distributed the poster, *Freedom of Speech*. Derived from a painting of the same title done the same year (now at the Norman Rockwell Museum, Stockbridge, Massachusetts), the poster was a personal and moving expression of Rockwell's reaction to the concept of the "Four Freedoms," as outlined by President Franklin Roosevelt in his annual message to Congress on January 6, 1941. These fundamental principles—freedom of speech, freedom of worship, freedom from want, and freedom from fear—were articulated by Roosevelt to remind Americans of what they stood to lose if the United States, not yet at war, were overrun by the Axis powers.

Moved by the president's warning, Rockwell was inspired to portray his vision of these precious freedoms using "real" people from a "real" place—his own town of Arlington, Vermont. "I'll illustrate the 'Four Freedoms' using my Vermont neighbors as models," he later observed. "I'll express the ideas in simple, everyday scenes . . . and put them in terms everybody can understand."[1]

The finished paintings and the posters that popularized them embody sacred American ideals. *Freedom of Speech* particularly conveys the concept of grass-roots democracy in action as reflected in the tradition of Vermont town meeting. But more than simply associating Vermont with a cherished political tradition, the posters helped evolve a new mythos that centered not on the state's well-known landscape but on its residents, who now became national models of strength and decency.

Years after World War II ended, Rockwell recalled how his experience of an Arlington town meeting had provided the stimulus for illustrating this particular "Freedom":

> Then one night as I was tossing in bed, mulling over the Proclamation and the war, rejecting one idea after another and getting more and more discouraged as the minutes ticked by, all empty and dark, I suddenly remembered how Jim Edgerton had stood up in town meeting and said something that everybody else disagreed with. But they let him have his say. No one shouted him down. My gosh, I thought, that's it. There it is. Freedom of Speech.[2]
>
> WCL / RHS

1. Norman Rockwell (with Thomas Rockwell), *Norman Rockwell: My Adventures as an Illustrator* (New York: Doubleday & Co., 1960), p. 339.
2. Rockwell, *Norman Rockwell*, p. 339. Although Rockwell cites Jim Edgerton as the inspiration for *Freedom of Speech*, he actually used for his model Carl Hess, the owner of a gas station in Arlington. The most complete identification of Arlington residents used by Rockwell in his paintings has been made by Vrest Orton in "Norman Rockwell's Vermont," *Vermont Life*, 1, No. 4 (Summer 1947), pp. 18–25.

55 *"Nose-Dive Annie"—Mrs. J. Negley Cooke of Cleveland at Stowe, Vermont*
Louise Dahl-Wolfe (1895–1985)
1941

Reproduced as a photomural in the exhibition

Skiing was first recognized as an Olympic sport in 1924, but it was not until the third Olympic Winter Games, held in 1932 at Lake Placid, New York, featured Nordic ski events that Americans began to take notice. Before the end of the decade, what had been a European-dominated winter sport became a popular North American pastime. The first rope tow in the nation was installed in Vermont near Woodstock in 1934, and by 1940, the state's first chairlifts had been installed at Stowe. Alpine events such as the downhill and slalom were finally introduced in the fourth Winter Olympics in 1936. Three years later the Mount Mansfield Ski Lift Corporation in Stowe hosted the first national women's downhill and slalom championships.[1] Not surprisingly, Stowe resident Marilyn Shaw, a student of Mt. Mansfield Ski Area's inimitable instructor Sepp Ruschp, became national women's champion in 1940.

The participation of women in Nordic and Alpine events at the Winter Olympics, as well as in world and national championships, dramatically increased public interest in this relatively new winter sport. Overnight, skiing became fashionable. In the East, Stowe was the place to be and the place to be seen.

Skiing and fashion merged in Stowe in the late 1930s. Louise Dahl-Wolfe's feature spread on women and fashion at Stowe, which appeared in the March 1, 1941, issue of *Harper's Bazaar*, included the carefully composed, yet casually ele-gant photograph of "Nose-Dive Annie," Mrs. J. Negley Cooke of Cleveland, Ohio.[2] The adaptation of controlled studio shots to an outdoor setting by the photographer unmistakably established a level of fashion photography hitherto unknown. "It is easy to learn the technique of the camera by oneself," Dahl-Wolfe reflected,

> But by working in design, I learned the principles of good design and composition. Drawing from the nude in life class made me aware of the grace and flow of line . . . [which] . . . was helpful in photographing fashion.[3]

Stowe, skiing, and fashionable elegance became synonymous, and soon national publicity such as this helped to transform Vermont into more than just a summer vacation spot. WCL

1. "The History of Skiing," in *SKI Magazine's Encyclopedia of Skiing*. ed. Robert Scharff (New York: Harper and Row, 1968), pp. 46–49.

2. Charles Edward Crane devoted a chapter in his *Winter in Vermont* to Marilyn Shaw and "Nose-Dive Annie." Crane wrote about Mrs. J. Negley Cooke: "Her husband, who is vice-president of the [Mount Mansfield] lift corporation, is head of the Cummer Products Company of Cleveland and flies from there to Mansfield for week-ends to join his wife, who practically lives on the Nose-Dive. This winter [1941] she, with her two children, rented a made-over barn at Stowe, to apply themselves earnestly to skiing."

3. Louise Dahl-Wolfe, in *Contemporary Photographers*. eds. George Walsh, Colin Nagler, and Michael Held; entry by Pamela Allara (New York: St. Martin's Press, 1982), p. 176. Dahl-Wolfe's first published photograph appeared in the November 1933 issue of *Vanity Fair*. In 1936 she rose to the position of staff photographer of *Harper's Bazaar*, where she remained until 1958. In the course of her career, she published approximately 600 photographs, including the famous March 1943 cover photograph of Lauren Bacall.

56 *Jumping Jack*

c. 1917
H: 13 inches L: 33 inches
Vermont Historical Society, Montpelier

Occasionally at times during the Winter, when the the deep snow falls or the drifts covered the fence tops and the stone walls in the sloping fields and pasture, there came a brief thaw followed by a freeze which soon produced a heavy shiny crust upon the surface of the snow. With a home made "Scooter" consisting of a barrel stave with a stick of birch or maple firewood nailed upright to it and with a narrow piece of board nailed on top of that for a seat, a thrilling and novel pastime was greatly enjoyed by active boys and eagerly seized upon at every opportunity.[1]

> Herbert Ellis
> *Memories of Boyhood at*
> *Springfield, Vermont* (1940)

Yankee ingenuity teamed up with a zest for outdoor winter activities created the jumping jack. The sport in Vermont dates at least from the 1800s and possibly from as early as the 1700s. Although most references to the sport feature its recreational appeal, loggers may once have used jacks to speed their descent from snow-covered mountainsides, and more contemporary ski-lift operators have been known to use them for similar purposes.

A close cousin of sledding and tobogganning, jack jumping "is related to [skiing] the way a unicycle is to [biking]."[2] Intrepid jack downhillers depend on a sure sense of balance to stay erect on the single ski and use their feet to steer.

Presumably the first jumpers were made, like early skis, from barrel staves: "a relatively simple affair, comprised of a runner and a vertically braced post topped off with a flat piece of wood serving as a seat."[3] This jumping jack—a more carefully refined example, with thin metal braces attached to the single ski and seat—is thought to have been made by a blacksmith in Grafton. Many early and late jacks, including those mentioned above that once skimmed down the fields and hills of Springfield, were handmade, if not homemade, affairs and reflected the idiosyncrasies of their makers and the spare wood and metal at hand. However, as recently as fifteen years ago, Vermont could boast of at least one jack jump manufacturer that produced sleek models of oak and ash for serious backwoods devotees determined to save the sport from oblivion.

Several decades ago Pico Peak ski area hosted jack jumping competitions, and more recently Okemo ski area has held annual jack jumping races, but the sport is not widely known. Nevertheless, jack jumping is forerunner of the now popular sport of snow-surfing, which uses a single ski (minus the seat) and a considerably more sophisticated technology to accomplish the same purpose. WCL

1. Herbert Ellis, from *Memories of Boyhood at Springfield, Vermont* (1940), quoted in Sanders Milens, "Jack Jumping," *Vermont Life*, 31, No. 2 (Winter 1976), p. 28.
2. Hanson Carroll, "Jack Jumpers Are Back!" *Vermont Life*, 18, No. 2 (Winter 1963), p. 43.
3. Milens, "Jack Jumping," p. 29.

57 *Rectangular Bark Container*

Northern Vermont, *c.* 1940
Birch bark with basswood lacings
Handle basswood bark fibre braided over
   commercially tanned leather thong
H: 6½ inches W: 5⅝ inches D: 4¾ inches
Abenaki Cultural Center, Swanton

This basket presented a breakthrough in Vermont birch bark container research in that it represents a very late persistence of the craft without showing a degeneracy of the technological style; it can be traced to a Vermont Native American family; and it has a distinctive technological and artistic style.

The central radial design has already been found on one other utilitarian container from the same family of birch-bark workers. The braided basswood/leather handle, the leather strip tie-and-hinge closure system, and the decorative cutting of the bark margins are very personal touches that may be found on other containers as more examples come to light.

Several Western Abenaki families of northern Vermont made utilitarian birch bark "quickbaskets" to hold berries for sale, but this container implies considerably more skill and care in manufacturing than a utilitarian basket required. It is unclear whether this was made for the tourist trade or, as is more likely from the provenance data, whether it was made for use and display by native Vermont families. Although no Abenaki currently carry on the tradition of bark-craft, these containers were made as recently as two generations ago, and there may be people who still remember the manufacturing techniques. Over the next few years, the Abenaki Cultural Center in Swanton will attempt to locate and interview these people.

FMW

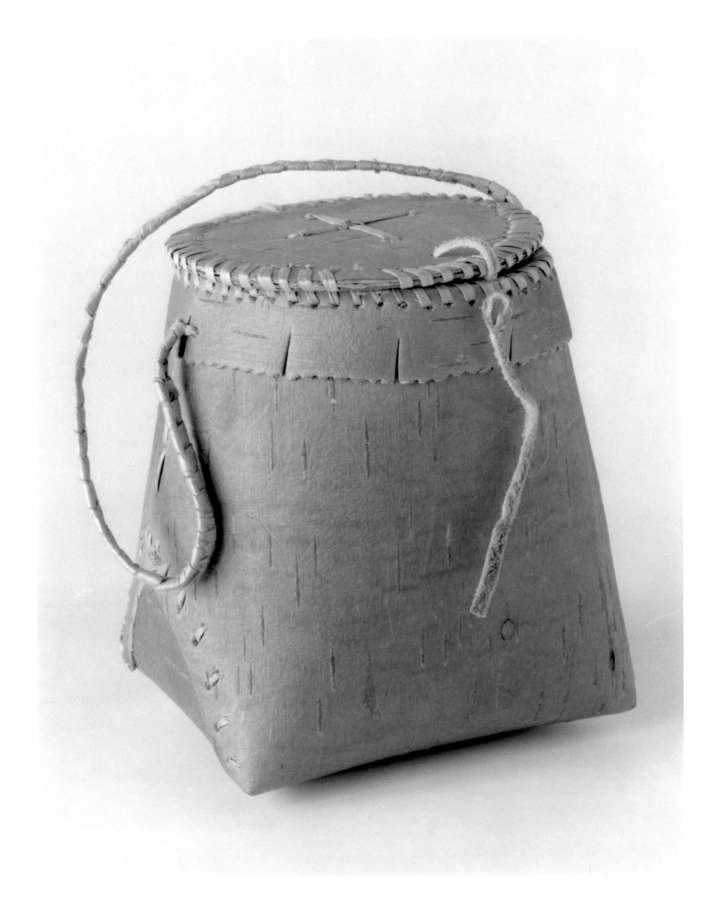

58 *Vermont Life*

Selected Covers: 1946–1990
H: 10½ inches w: 8 inches

Vermont Life Magazine, Montpelier

Cat. 58.1 Cover. Arizona Highways. April 1973.

The first issue of *Vermont Life* appeared in the autumn of 1946. In its early years, *Vermont Life* was aimed at promoting tourism and attracting business and industry to the state. In this regard, the magazine was clearly modeled after *Arizona Highways* (cat. 58.1), one of the first state magazines devoted to examining a single state's life and culture.[1] Both *Arizona Highways* and *Vermont Life* borrowed from the pictorial format and innovative use of color photography initiated by *National Geographic*. The introduction of Kodak Kodachrome transparencies and four-color printing on glossy stock helped to create the now-famous "pictorial spread," where pages of color images are allowed to speak for themselves without benefit of accompanying text.

As *Vermont Life* matured, its function was extended beyond merely marketing the promotional slogan of its early years: "Vermont is a way of life." Today, as in the past, this seasonal publication reaches readers both inside and outside of the state by engaging some of Vermont's best writers and photographers to provide a view of a cross-

section of life in the Green Mountain State.[2] Originally funded in part by the state legislature, *Vermont Life* developed related products, such as calendars and books, which enabled it to become self-supporting. Its first book, *Vermont: A Special World*, has sold more than 60,000 copies and remains one of the most successful books ever published on Vermont.

The quality of the magazine's writing and photography has been the result of enlightened editorial direction, which has always included a board of distinguished writers. Each editor (Earle Newton, Walter Hard, Jr., Brian Vachon, Charles T. Morrissey, Nancy Price Graff, and, currently, Tom Slayton) has depended on the editorial column, "Green Mountain Postboy," on features such as the recent "Vermont Enterprises," and on striking photographs, such as those published in the scenic spreads and "Private View," to express the magazine's philosophy.

Although *Vermont Life* now faces competition from other periodicals that feature the state's life, it continues to assert that Vermont is indeed "a special place." In this small corner of northern New England, remnants of an older way of life still persist and are alive and well, which is cause enough for celebration in light of the state's growing population and increasing urbanization.

W C L

1. Founded in 1921, *Arizona Highways* first appeared in magazine format in 1925. See Tom C. Cooper, *The Best From Arizona Highways* (Phoenix: Department of Transportation, State of Arizona, 1975).

2. "One of the finest and most popular publications issued by any state is *Vermont Life* . . . It is read by most Vermonters, who are proud of it, and there are subscribers in Moscow, Russia, and Moscow, Vermont." *Vermont: A Guide to the Green Mountain State*. ed. Ray Bearse, 2nd ed. (Boston: Houghton Mifflin Co., 1966), p. 120.

59 *Robert Frost*
   Clara Sipprell (1885–1975)
   c. 1962

   Photograph, Special Collections,
   University of Vermont
   Reproduced as a photomural in the exhibition

Clara Sipprell's photographs of Robert Frost at his farm in Ripton, Vermont, depict the Pulitzer Prize-winning poet at the height of his popularity. Frost in the early 1960s was the nation's unofficial poet-laureate, an honor bestowed upon him by President-elect John F. Kennedy, when he invited Frost to participate in the nationally televised presidential inauguration in January 1961. Nearly thirty years later, Sipprell's photographs remain the best-known images of this sometime-Vermont resident and farmer.[1]

A soft-focused background brings the viewer's gaze to the foreground, where Frost, seated on a stone wall, gazes off into the distance. (Another photograph taken by Sipprell the same day depicts Frost standing in profile, hands clasped, looking to his right. The distance of the photographer from her subject and her focus are identical.) In an era of portrait photography characterized by sharp contrast and the artifice of studio settings, Sipprell's conservative mode of vision is appropriate both to the stature of the poet and to the content of his poems. The congruence of photographic and poetic perspectives is especially meaningful because Frost and Sipprell both shared a vision of art grounded in an older, agrarian mythos.

Working within the Pictorial tradition[2] established by turn-of-the century photographers such as Gertrude Kasebier, Sipprell developed a style that remained virtually unchanged throughout her career. She relied on available light and neither enlarged nor retouched her photographs.[3] By the close of the 1960s, however, Sipprell's photographic vision of the world as idyllic and essentially rural seemed anachronistic when contrasted with the dramatic photographs of the earth then being published by NASA. In an instant, rural Vermont became a part of what media-guru Marshall McCluhan would call "the global village." Only recently, in exhibitions such as the one mounted by the Vermont Historical Society in 1989, has the work of Clara Sipprell been reappraised.   WCL

1. Clara Sipprell, *Moment of Light: Photographs of Clara Sipprell* (New York: The John Day Co., 1966), unpaginated.
2. "Women were especially prominent in Pictorialism," Naomi Rosenblum noted in *A World History of Photography* (New York: Abbeville Press, 1989), p. 320.
3. Sipprell spent summers in Thetford, Vermont (see *The Blacksmith Shop*, essay *Fig. 3.3*), and later moved to Manchester, where she photographed neighbors Dorothy Canfield Fisher and Sara Cleghorn. See Jeffrey D. Marshall, *Photographs in the Special Collections Department, Bailey/Howe Library, University of Vermont* (Burlington, Vt.: Bailey/Howe Library, 1990), p. 12; and John F. Smith, "Clara Sipprell," *Vermont Life*, 13, No. 1 (Autumn 1958), pp. 30–31.

60 *Ceramic Plate*

David Smith (1906–1965) and
  Bennington Potters, Inc.
Bennington, May 21, 1964
Stoneware, painted with slip
DIAM: 13½ inches
Incised on obverse: "David Smith May 21";
  and on reverse: "Bennington Potters /
  Bennington Vermont"

Collection of David Gil from Bennington
Potters, Inc.

Decorated by artist David Smith, this dramatic plate was one of a series made at the Bennington Potters, Inc., in 1964. That year, the magazine *Art in America* commissioned a group of painters and sculptors, including Alexander Liberman, Cleve Gray, Seymour Lipton, Helen Frankenthaler, Leonard Baskin, and David Smith to make limited editions of small ceramic objects. Many of these were made in Bennington and were later featured in *Art in America* in an article entitled, "Ceramics by Twelve Artists."

David Smith spent several weeks at the pottery in May 1964, painting plate after plate of a Bennington College student model. Smith was not new to Bennington. He had exhibited work at the college in 1951 and 1959, and was a long-time friend of David Gil, president and creative director of Bennington Potters, Inc.

The plate illustrates not only the collaboration of friends but also David Gil's commitment to creative endeavors. Employing ninety workers today, Bennington Potters' chief products are stoneware kitchenware with a spatter glaze and terra cotta flower pots. Since its inception in 1948, however, the pottery has also made ten to twelve murals; reproductions for the Nelson Rockefeller

Collection, the Museum of Modern Art, the Metropolitan Museum of Art, and The Bennington Museum; and a variety of objects for other manufacturers.

During a time when many large American ceramic companies are marketing products made in the Far East or Mexico, Bennington Potters, Inc., continues to manufacture its own pottery. The firm has introduced more than 915 designs—most of them by David Gil—and has won numerous design awards from the Museum of Modern Art, the Chicago Merchandise Mart, and the Academie Internationale de la Ceramiques in Cannes, France. Gil was also the recipient of the Vermont Small Business "Person of the Year" award in 1974. Today the pottery, which started as a cooperative venture, is a thriving enterprise grossing almost $3 million a year and distributing its "country" wares to big city department stores, such as Macys, Bloomingdales, and Crate & Barrel. As it was in the nineteenth century, the small and unassuming town of Bennington is the home of one of the most significant ceramic industries in New England.   CZ

REFERENCES

Breen, John. "Bennington Potters." *Working People Magazine*, 5 (June/July 1989), pp. 12–15.

Flynn, John. "David Gil and the Bennington Potters." *Pennysaver*, 2 (October 30, 1988), pp. 1–2.

Gray, Cleve. "Ceramics by Twelve Artists." *Art in America*, 6 (December 1964), pp. 27–41.

Hadwen, George E. *The Rock Ribs of Bennington* (Bennington, Vt.: Hadwen, 1977).

Interviews with David Gil, president and creative director, and Rick Swenson, vice president of Bennington Potters, Inc., October 13 and 19; November 22, 1989; and December 13, 1990.

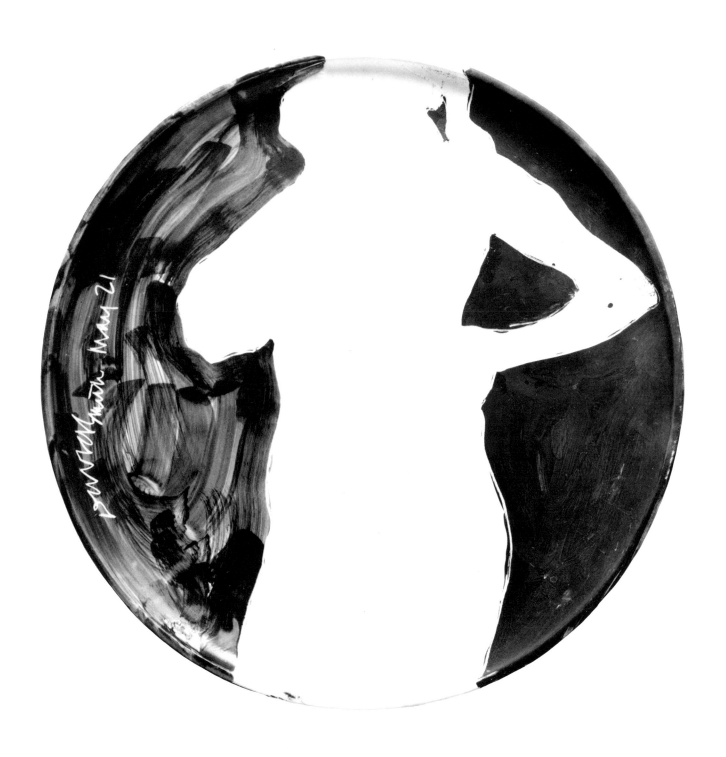

61 *Peace Hand Puppet*

Bread and Puppet Theatre
Glover, *c.* 1972
Painted canvas, fabric, wood, and metal wire
H: 65 inches W: 24 inches D: 14 inches
Bread and Puppet Theatre, Glover

German-born Peter Schumann and the Bread and Puppet Theatre Troupe have resided in Vermont since 1970, when the troupe moved from New York City to Plainfield, Vermont, at the invitation of Goddard College to be the theatre-in-residence. The troupe remained at the Cate farm in Plainfield until 1974, when it moved to its present location in Glover.[1] An internationally acclaimed group of performers first organized by Schumann in the early 1960s, the Bread and Puppet Troupe developed a repertoire shaped by three elements:

> performances with children in workshops held in the slums and parks of New York City; political activism expressed in peace rallies and marches with puppets protesting social injustice and the Vietnam War; and the almost subconscious influences of Schumann's background and education—folklore and folk art, medieval art, and the work of the Dadaists and German Expressionists.[2]

Cat. 61.2 Claire Van Vliet. Cover. *White Horse Butcher.* 1977.

Cat. 61.1 Peace Hand Puppet in parade. 1976. Photograph by Richard Howard. Courtesy, Special Collections. University of Vermont.

"Peace Hand Puppet" exemplifies the political activism of the late 1960s and 1970s. The "Peace Hand Puppet" is worn by a puppeteer who uses wires to manipulate the two figures precariously balanced on top of the two raised fingers, signifying "peace." Below the raised hand is a draped banner painted with stars that conceals the puppeteer within. The overall design is that of a wrapped American flag.

First seen in the Fourth of July parades in which the Bread and Puppet Theatre participated throughout Vermont in the early 1970s, the "Peace Hand" usually appeared either with "Uncle Fatso" (cat. 61.1) or alongside Peter Schumann himself, dressed as "Uncle Sam" and leading his entourage on his eight-foot-high stilts. The Peace Hand's symbolic gesture is a direct reference to Bread and Puppet's protests against the Vietnam War and the growing international stockpiling of nuclear warheads.

Over-sized puppets, costumes, musical instruments, and handmade sourdough rye bread are synonymous with Bread and Puppet.[3] So are posters, banners, and the printed books that Schumann has created, some in collaboration with his troupe, some with his immediate family, and some with artist/bookmaker Claire Van Vliet, a neighbor and founder of the Janus Press. *White Horse Butcher, 1977* (cat. 61.2) is one of several collaborations between Schumann and Van Vliet.[4] Similar to *St Francis Preaches to the Birds*, printed the same year, *White Horse Butcher* was written by Schumann, printed by Van Vliet, and designed collaboratively. Both are bold, dynamic publications filled with vitality and emphasizing an economy of language (both visual and verbal) and an insistent directness that characterize the Bread and Puppet performances and the Domestic Resurrection Circus.[5] The books, posters, and banners share a common stylistic source in the rough and jagged images associated with German Expressionist woodcuts. Schumann and the Bread and Puppet Theatre have been recipients of the distinguished Governor's Award for Excellence in the Arts by the Vermont Council on the Arts.   wcl

1. Madeleine M. Kunin, "The Bread and Puppet Theatre," *Vermont Life*, 31, No. 3 (Spring 1977), pp. 25–29. See also Elke Schumann, "Bread and Puppet Museum," *American Craft Magazine*, 43, No. 3 (June/July 1983), pp. 36–39.

2. Schumann, "Bread and Puppet Museum," p. 38.

3. "The power of bread is obvious," Schumann noted in 1970. "People are hungry . . . Our mind is hungry, and Jesus says: man does not live from bread alone, but from puppet shows as well." Peter Schumann, "The World Has To Be Demonstrated Anew," *Poland*, No. 3 (187) (March 1970). And "We sometimes give you a piece of bread along with the puppet show because our bread and theatre belong together . . . [Theatre] . . . is . . . like bread, more like a necessity." Handout, Bread and Puppet Theatre (October 15, 1977).

4. For a description of the collaborations between Schumann and Van Vliet, see Ruth E. Fine, *The Janus Press, 1975–1980* (Burlington, Vt.: Robert Hull Fleming Museum, 1982).

5. Fine, *The Janus Press*, pp. 14–15. Mary Azarian, an artist from Calais, Vermont, shares a similar expressionist aesthetic with Schumann, although her political and social images are not as well known as her calendars, alphabets, and single woodcut prints.

62 *2-Burner Gas Syrup Finisher*

Leader Evaporator Company
St. Albans, 1990
Stainless steel with brass and wood fittings
H: 18 inches   L: 38 inches   W: 16 inches
Leader Evaporator Company, St. Albans

Native Americans taught early European settlers to Vermont to sugar, and maple syrup has been part of the state's heritage ever since. "Sugaring" derives from maple sugar, the crystalline form of the distilled sap of the sugar maple. However, most sugar maple sap in the state these days is reduced only to the point of syrup, which is graded according to its purity and potency. In Vermont today the maple syrup industry is a $13 million a year business.

The technology of sugaring has changed dramatically in the last half century. In most places, wooden buckets similar to the one President Coolidge presented to Henry Ford for his Americana museum, Greenfield Village, have been replaced by metal buckets with sliding covers. Large operations have generally abandoned buckets entirely, stringing their sugarbushes with black plastic tubing that feeds the sap from hundreds of trees into a central gathering tank. The gathering of sap by horse or oxen, once universal, is now largely obsolete.

The process of boiling the sap has not changed as radically. Sugar sheds with arches and evaporating pans are still plentiful, and in the early spring Vermont's air still carries the fragrance of smoke billowing from hundreds of backwoods sugarshacks. Leader Evaporator is one of the state's largest suppliers of sugaring euqipment. The company's line includes sugaring equipment for both commercial production and backyard enthusiasts, many of whom embody the back-to-the-land philosophy, made popular in the 1960s, that stresses self-sufficiency.

Even the sugar maples themselves are changing. The art of sugaring has been transformed by technology, and scientists at the Vermont Maple Sugar Laboratory are studying ways to improve and simplify production. One of the focuses of their study is an alarming decline in the health of the state's maple trees, thought to be the result of acid rain and global warming. In the past ten years, the maple syrup yield in Vermont—though it remains the largest of any state in the nation—has declined from 545,000 gallons annually to 375,000 gallons, despite an increase in the number of trees being tapped.

Ironically, the packaging containers for syrup have hardly changed at all over the past fifty years. The traditional metal maple syrup can (and frequently its newer plastic cousin) continues to project an image of sugaring that is probably gone forever. Nonetheless, the imagery is potent and not likely to be changed, because it appeals strongly to the human longing to recapture the times in our past that were simpler and less harried than our present.   WCL

63 *Tipi and Canoe*

Abenaki, St. Albans, *c.* 1954
Birch bark
H: 5 ½ inches   L: 4 ¾ inches   W: 3 ⅝ inches
Abenaki Cultural Center, Swanton

I purchased this model tipi from a man at St. Albans Bay, Vermont, who said that he was an Indian who made them. My grandfather, who lived in St. Albans at the time, said that the man was an Abenaki and that there were still quite a few Indians living in Swanton. Over the years, that tipi stayed on my bureau as a memory of my time in Vermont. The fragrance of the sweetgrass trim often came to my nostrils on cool summer nights and reminded me of St. Albans and the old Indian man. When I went away to college, the tipi was left on my bureau, only to be packed away when my parents moved. It ended up in an attic over the carriage house of my parents' new house, where the scanty green porcupine quillwork was nibbled off by mice and the shreds of birch bark representing the woodsmoke from the tipi's smokehole slowly became crumpled and lost. Every time I went into the attic I saw that tipi, and it reminded me of the child who I had been. Now that I know of my Native American heritage and have an obligation to show Vermonters that Abenakis have always been here, this little tipi, my first unknowing link with who I am, stands for the past and the future understanding of the Native American experience in Vermont in this bicentennial year. I am proud to share this bit of me with you.

This small bark model is an anomaly. It has a known provenance from the time of its sale, since I, the author of this description, was there as a child. However, its sweetgrass borders bound with s-twist black cotton thread seem more like Great Lakes region work. Therefore, it raises questions. Was this an item imported by the Native American who sold it to me? Or is the conventional wisdom about sweetgrass borders ill-defined due to a lack of research into Vermont tourist trinket work?   F M W

64 *Samoset*

Gerard Rancourt Tsonakwa (1943–   )
*c.*1985
Maple, horse hair, turkey feathers
H: 20 inches W: 10 inches D: 3 inches
Collection of the artist

This mask represents an important stage in the artistic evolution of the Abenaki Nation—the emergence of a nationally recognized artist who draws inspiration from his natal culture but functions economically and socially within a national and international artistic circle. Heretofore, most Abenaki material culture has been considered either as ethnographica or as rather low-grade "tourist art" by Euroamerican art critics and art historians. If the Abenaki Nation is to be considered seriously by Euroamericans, it must have not only a political presence, which it now has, and a cultural presence, which it is gaining, but a symbolic and artistic presence, which Tsonakwa is helping to affirm.

Tsonakwa is an Abenaki, living in Tucson, whose masks have attracted the attention of serious art critics and collectors. Tsonakwa himself has become a role model for the young people of the Abenaki Nation, who can be reassured by the artist and his masks that it is okay to be different and that this "differentness" can be made explicit through the melding of heritage and art. If the Abenaki know that one among them has "made it," the path exists for anyone with the gift and the courage to walk it.   FMW

65 Ladder-Back Reading Chair

Union Woodworkers
Northfield, 1976
Red oak
H: 43 ¼ inches W: 19⅝ inches D: 19 inches
Union Woodworkers, Northfield

The increasing number of historic buildings in Vermont recently renovated or currently undergoing renovation has created an opportunity for contemporary architects, designers, and furniture makers in the state to experiment with combinations of traditional and modern elements of design and construction.

In 1976 forty ladder-back chairs were commissioned by the University of Vermont Student Association for the newly restored Billings Library (1883–1889), now reborn as the Billings Student Center. Designed by the renowned American architect, H. H. Richardson, the library originally contained furniture designed by Richardson in conjunction with the firm of A. H. Davenport.[1] The original chairs were constructed of oak, stylistically based "on the American vernacular: Windsor chairs imaginatively adapted from an eighteenth-century model."[2] Nearly a century later, Union Woodworkers, of Northfield, Vermont, was contracted to design and build chairs to replace those designed by Richardson and Davenport. The design of the new chairs was to take into consideration both the new function of the building as a student center and the integrity of the original structure. As Union Woodworkers' founders, Mike Goldfinger and John Wall, wrote at the time,

> the new chairs should not imitate the originals and should, instead, take their design from the functional requirements of daily student use in a reading-room setting. . . . The solid-set, ladder-back form was chosen for its strength, comfort, and suitability for the building. All the joinery details were designed for strength.[3]

Woodworking of this calibre is possible in Vermont in part today because of the crafts revival that swept the country in the 1960s and 1970s. "There is no doubt in my mind that a rebirth of

Cat. 65.1 Vermont Castings. "The Defiant." Cast-iron wood stove. *c.* 1976. Courtesy, Vermont Castings.

the ancient art of woodworking is going on in America today," John Kelsey, editor of *Fine Woodworking*, observed in 1979.[4] Here in Vermont, a new generation of designers and woodworkers has emerged, some of them self-taught, some educated in formal crafts courses, and some the products of Foxfire-style apprenticeships to master woodworkers of an earlier generation.

A similar revival took place in woodstove design, following the oil crisis of the early 1970s. Many Vermonters abandoned fuel oil in favor of heating with wood, and Vermont Castings, in Randolph, responded by producing the "Defiant stove" (cat. 65.1) and other similar stoves of varying sizes. Union Woodworkers made the wooden patterns from which the first "Defiant" models were cast.   W C L

1. See Anne Farnham, "H. H. Richardson and A. H. Davenport: Architecture and Furniture as Big Business in America's Gilded Age," in *Tools and Technologies: America's Wooden Age.* eds. Paul B. Kebabian and William C. Lipke (Burlington, Vt.: Robert Hull Fleming Museum, 1979), p. 98.

2. Farnham, "Richard and Davenport," p. 84.

3. Mike Goldfinger and John Wall, in "Furniture for Billings Library at the University of Vermont: Restoration and a Contemporary Response," in *Tools and Technologies: America's Wooden Age*. eds. Paul Kebabian and William C. Lipke (Burlington, Vt.: Robert Hull Fleming Museum, 1979), p. 97.

4. John Kelsey in, "Woodworkers and Woodworking: Current Perspectives," in *Tools and Technologies: America's Wooden Age*. eds. Paul B. Kebabian and William C. Lipke (Burlington, Vt.: Robert Hull Fleming Museum, 1979), p. 98.

66 *Adirondack Chair*

Bruce Beeken and Jeff Parsons
Shelburne, *c.* 1985
White cedar, painted; fabric seat cushion
H: 42 inches W: 34½ inches D: 34 inches
Beeken and Parsons, Shelburne

Bruce Beeken and Jeff Parsons, both graduates of Boston University's Program in Artisanry, are woodworkers from Shelburne, Vermont, specializing in custom furniture. Their firm, Beekens and Parsons, is nationally acclaimed as one of the top in the nation representative of the "second generation of studio furnituremakers."[1] Both Beeken and Parsons exemplify those younger artisans whose work conveys an education based in the colleges rather than apprenticeship; the importance of a vigorous conceptual approach to design and construction; and the small scale of operation distinguished from factories or manufactories.[2]

Inspired by such diverse historical sources as Adirondack guide boats and banjo clocks,[3] Beeken's and Parsons's redesigns of earlier artifacts, often regional in origin, combine the best of traditional and new joining technologies to produce a more permanent piece of furniture. Their Adirondack chair is a case in point.[4] Originally, the Adirondack chair was built for the porches and decks of summer camps in upstate New York, but it quickly achieved a wide popularity elsewhere, too. Its traditional construction employed pine boards nailed together. The result was a short life for what at first appeared to be a durable piece of outdoor furniture. "Owing to joinery that didn't accommodate wood movement," Beeken and Parsons noted, "many Adirondack [chairs] soon worked themselves into kindling." The men were inspired by an exhibit of paintings of Adirondack chairs by Vermont artist Janet Fredericks, and decided to resurrect the turn-of-the-century classic by improving upon "an already appealing design." The chair they produced retains the simple lines of the original while employing shipbuilders' trenails to prevent rust, as well as dry splines and mortise-and-tenon joinery to improve stability. "The north country [has] contributed to our aesthetic sensibilities," they wrote. "By building an improved Adirondack chair, we could reciprocate and enjoy that landscape in comfort."[5]

WCL

1. Edward S. Cooke, Jr., *New American Furniture: The Second Generation of Studio Furnituremakers* (Boston: Museum of Fine Arts, 1989). This catalogue accompanied an exhibition, organized by Cooke, of twenty-five contemporary American furnituremakers. The exhibition was shown at the M.F.A. (December 8, 1989–March 11, 1990) and at the Renwick Gallery of the National Museum of American Art, Smithsonian Institution, Washington, D. C. (April 2–September 3, 1990).

2. Cooke, *New American Furniture*, endnote 3, p. 28. Cooke's definition of "studio furniture" distinguishes this genre from related terms, such as "handmade [which] implies that the craftsperson eschews any machinery in a romantic Ruskinian way," or "art furniture . . . a term with a very historical meaning referring to small-shop custom work in the last quarter of the nineteenth century." p. 28.

3. Cooke, *New American Furniture*, pp. 32–35.

4. Bruce Beeken and Jeff Parsons, "Adirondack Chair: A Fresh Look at an Old Favorite," *Fine Woodworking*, 52 (May/June 1985), pp. 46–49.

5. Beeken and Parsons, "A Fresh Look," p. 46.

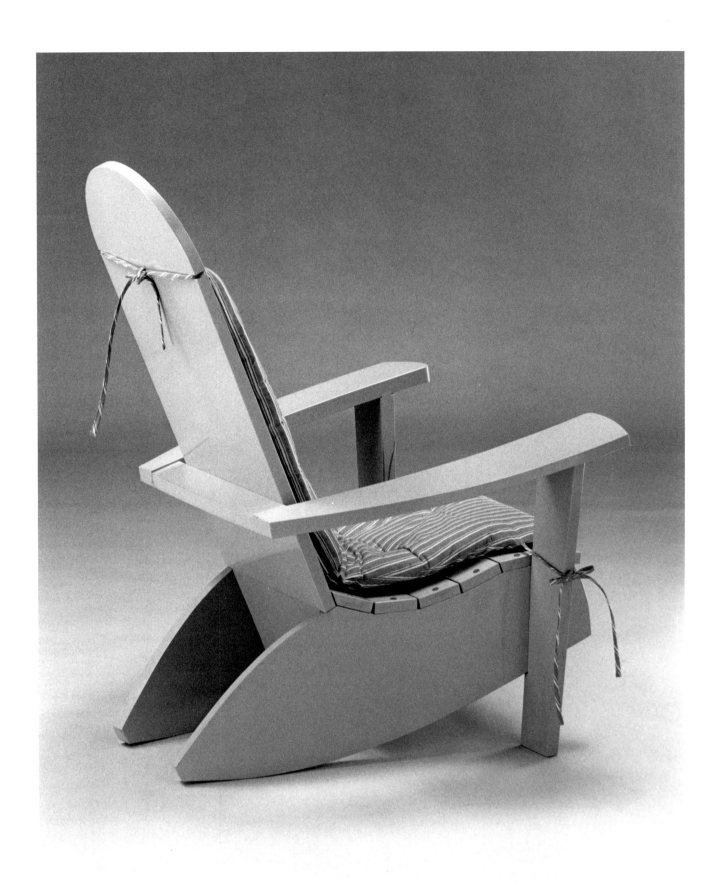

67 *Peace Pop Top*

Learning Materials Workshop
Burlington, 1990
Oak, paint, and paper
H: 4½ inches D: 3½ inches

Private Collection

68 *"1% For Peace"*

1990
Ink on coated paper with adhesive backing
H: 3¾ inches L: 11⅛ inches

Ben & Jerry's Homemade, Inc.,
Waterbury

69 *"Rainforest Crunch" Ice Cream Container*

Ben & Jerry's Homemade, Inc.
Waterbury, 1990
Coated paperboard with colored inks
H: 4⅛ inches   D: 3⅞ inches

Ben & Jerry's Homemade, Inc., Waterbury

The legacy of Vermont's nineteenth-century myth that the state was an agricultural backwater populated by inhabitants who were conservative, homogeneous, and set in their ways, unfairly overshadowed the fervor for national and global issues that has burned brightly in this state for decades, if not centuries. In the 1800s, the urge for reform motivated the state's residents to take active roles in the fights for abolition and temperance. In the twentieth century, continued concern for national and international issues—this time for world affairs and the environment—has again moved Vermonters to translate their perceptions into action.

The *Peace Pop Top* illustrates the practical nature of Vermont's reforms. The Learning Materials Workshop expressed its concern for promoting world peace by creating a child's toy and channeling the proceeds to the national organization "1% for Peace," whose "purpose is to create, promote and fund a positive peace agenda." The local toy company's participation in a growing national association with international aspirations typifies a grass-roots approach to big problems that is in keeping with Vermont's heritage and past experience.

Ben and Jerry's Homemade, Inc., a potent force in the "1% for Peace" movement, has been able, by virtue of its success, to expand its interests further. Recently it introduced Rainforest Crunch ice cream in response to its growing concern for environmental issues, both those close to home and those far away. Vermonters who have teamed up to fight acid rain and rainforest destruction are able to see the state's reputed isolation as a myth. In recognizing Vermont's place in the global community and its inability to escape the problems of the modern world, they uphold a tradition of global awareness in the state that has given birth to everything from the Children's Art Exchange to the Geonomics Institute to church programs to give new homes in Vermont to refugees from Central America and the Far East.   VMW

70 *Champlain Valley*
Sabra Field (1935–   )
South Royalton, 1987
Serigraph on paper, artist proof
H: 11½ inches W: 20 inches
Collection of the artist

71 *"Vermont Classic" VISA Card*
Granite Bank, The Howard Bank, N.A.,
Woodstock National Bank
1990
Plastic
The Howard Bank, N.A., Burlington

72 *Grazing*

Woody Jackson (1948–   )
Middlebury, 1988
Serigraph on paper
H: 22½ inches W: 32 inches
Edition of 200

Holy Cow, Inc., Middlebury

73 *Ice Cream Bag*

Ben & Jerry's Homemade, Inc.
Waterbury, 1990
Paper with colored ink
H: 13½ inches D: 7⅛ inches

Ben & Jerry's Homemade, Inc.,

Commemorative moments like the statehood bicentennial are opportunities to contemplate and re-examine the stories we have agreed on and the objects we have found meaningful in summarizing the nature of our past experience. Most of the objects we choose to analyze form a sort of "canon" that has gained acceptance as the equivalent of the "true cross." But recent history has not yet undergone the canonization process, so our most recent experience must stand on its own, awaiting the judgment of posterity.

Traditionally, artists have fulfilled a role as interpreters of cultural values. Those who achieve popularity succeed because they render images that their patrons find meaningful. Paul Sample depicted the essence of rural Vermont two generations ago (cat. 51), as Thomas Waterman Wood did fifty years earlier (cat. 34.1), and as Jerome Thompson did thirty years before that (cat. 27).

Two contemporary Vermont artists have established their reputations on the basis of their ability to render the redemptive quality of Vermont's landscape in their prints. Both Sabra Field and Woody Jackson work in imagery that speaks eloquently and movingly to Vermonters of a rural landscape whose productivity and aesthetic support the economic and spiritual life of the state. Both these artists have managed to make their artistic vision of the Vermont landscape commercially successful by employing it to promote Vermont's economic future.   VMW

74 *Catamount "Amber" Ale*

Catamount Brewing Company
White River Junction, 1990
H: 7⅝ inches D: 2½ inches

Catamount Brewing Co.,
White River Junction

75 *Grafton Goodjam "Popple Dungeon Cranberry Chutney"*

Grafton Goodjam Company
Grafton, 1990
H: 3¾ inches W: 3¼ inches

Grafton Goodjam Company, Grafton

76 *Cabot "Sharp" Vermont Cheddar Cheese*

Cabot Farmers' Cooperative Creamery
  Company, Inc.
Cabot, 1990
H: 7½ inches W: 3¾ inches D: 3¾ inches

Cabot Farmers' Cooperative Creamery Company,
Inc., Cabot

77 *"Pure Vermont Maple Syrup" One-Gallon Container*

Davies Can Company
Solon, Ohio, 1990
H: 10 inches W: 6½ inches D: 4 inches

Maple Supplies, Barre

78 *The Original Lake Champlain Chocolates*

Champlain Chocolate Company
Burlington, 1990
H: 8 inches W: 8½ inches D: 1¼ inches

Champlain Chocolate Company, Burlington

Marketing Vermont emerged as a legislative priority in the late 1980s,[1] but the impetus had been building since the tourism boom that followed the Second World War. Vermont cheese and syrup boosted the rural economy with tourist dollars, as surviving roadside signage still reminds us. Starting with Vrest Orton's Vermont Country Store in the early 1950s,[2] Vermonters successfully transformed their pastoral myth into a marketable reality.

Ever since Paul Sample's 1944 sugaring scene became the standard Vermont maple syrup can,[3] packaging imagery has drawn on Vermont's romantic, rustic qualities. Cows earned their place in Vermont's iconography as cheese cooperatives revived the traditional dry-curd cheddar cheese, starting a growth spurt that created milk shortages in the entire Northeast. Today, the Sabra Field print that has become the state's official logo for Vermont-made products reinforces the emotional appeal of the state's pastoral landscape.

Vermont's rural mystique imbued its native products with purity and wholesomeness at a time when the American food industry could not respond quickly enough to the popular demand for "health food."[4] But image alone did not guarantee success. Traditional recipes and strict quality controls have allowed Vermont producers to create a vital new food industry in Vermont. Consider Grafton Goodjam, for example, whose success rests not just on the taste and quality of its products, but on its claim that its food is carefully prepared in small batches. This is a message, firmly rooted in the state's image, that speaks directly to consumers in the fast-food age who feel they have too often been victims of mass production and disregard for quality. Cabot Cheese, Champlain Chocolates, and Catamount Ale are similar examples of successful cottage industries that have expanded into specialty markets by shrewdly capitalizing on Vermont, its resources, and its image. Even a small sackful of Vermont products can illustrate the range of Vermont myths still operative today: pastoral purity, traditional values, and a touch of wilderness.

VMW

1. Eloise Hedbor, "What's in a Name?" in "Business Monday," *Burlington Free Press*, 6 August 1990.

2. Vrest Orton, *The Vermont Country Store: Story of a Vermont Institution* (Rutland, Vt.: Academy Books, 1970).

3. Paul Sample, quoted in Earle Newton, *The Vermont Story* (Montpelier, Vt.: Vermont Historical Society, 1949), p. 11.

4. Warren Belasco, *Appetite for Change: How the Counterculture Took On the Food Industry, 1966–1988* (New York: Pantheon, 1990).

Time Line*

Fig. 1 Abenaki Indians tapping maple trees and planting crops. From Moeurs des Sauvages Ameriquains. Courtesy, Special Collections, UVM.

18,000–8000 B.C.
Glacier recedes and land mass rises, lifting region of Vermont above sea level.

1600
Western Abenaki population estimated at about 10,000.

1609
Samuel de Champlain, a Frenchman, explores the lake which now bears his name.

1666
French establish Fort St. Anne, first European settlement in Vermont, on Isle La Motte.

1737
Ethan Allen born, Litchfield, Connecticut.

1749
First New Hampshire Grant—the 23,040-acre town of Bennington—granted to William Williams and associates. As was customary, all white pines large enough for masts are reserved for the Royal Navy.

1759
Rogers' Rangers raid Abenaki settlement at St. Francis, Quebec, killing between 40 and 200.

1763
The Rev. Samuel Peters is said to have christened the region "Verd Mont," though the story has been challenged often.

1764–1783
Vermont is disputed territory, fought over by New Hampshire and New York; Ethan Allen and Green Mountain Boys defend grants made by New Hampshire.

Somewhere, sometime, Indians—Vermont's original settlers—introduce Europeans to the making of maple syrup. Since syrup was best kept and transported in its sugary, crystalline form, the process becomes known as sugaring.

1766
Probable date of Ethan Allen's first visit to the New Hampshire Grants. In 1770 he was named agent to manage legal defense of the New Hampshire land titles against New York.

July 1771
Green Mountain Boys send their first New York sheriff packing.

March 1775
Westminster Massacre—New York sheriff and deputies kill two men among a group trying to keep the court from hearing debtor creditor cases.

July 2, 1777
Constitution of "State of Vermont" adopted, Windsor.

Fig. 2 1785 "Vermontis" copper. Minted by Reuben Harmon, Jr., of Rupert, Vermont. Courtesy, Vermont Historical Society, Montpelier.

---

* Portions of this time line originally appeared in *Vermont Life*, 45, No. 2 (Winter 1990), pp. 3–13. Additional contributions were made by J. Kevin Graffagnino and Nancy Price Graff.

July 7, 1777
American troops, fleeing British soldiers who took Mount Independence in Orwell, fight the Battle of Hubbardton.

August 16, 1777
Battle of Bennington—American forces from New Hampshire and Vermont defeat a force of Hessians, thwarting the British attempt to reach arms stored in Bennington and contributing to the major British defeat at Saratoga in October.

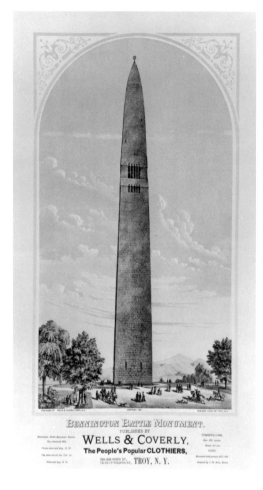

Fig. 3 The Bennington Battle Monument. Height: 306 feet. Cornerstone laid in 1887; monument completed in 1891. Courtesy, Special Collections, University of Vermont.

March 3, 1778
Thomas Chittenden elected first governor of the Republic of Vermont; he serves 18 years as governor of the republic and the state.

March 12, 1778
First Vermont General Assembly convenes, Windsor.

1779
First protection of Vermont's deer herd; hunting prohibited from January 10 to June 10.

October 16, 1780
British and Indians raid Royalton, killing five settlers, including Giles Gibb, said to be the author of the lyrics to "Yankee Doodle."

1783
The Rev. Lemuel Haynes, of Rutland, becomes the first black in America to serve as pastor of a white congregation. Serves 30 years.

1785
First marble quarry in North America begun in Dorset.

1789
Ethan Allen, 52, dies at his home in Burlington's Intervale.

1791
Vermont's population is 85,425. Seventy-five percent of its land is wooded.

March 4, 1791
Vermont becomes fourteenth state of the United States of America.

1791
Ira Allen through a pledge of £4,000 becomes the principal founding father of the University of Vermont. Town of Braintree offers a bounty of six pence for each apple tree planted. Justin Morgan brings his soon-to-be-famous horse to Vermont.

Fig. 4 Anonymous. Ira Allen. Miniature c. 1795. Courtesy, Robert Hull Fleming Museum, University of Vermont.

1798
Dam on the Connecticut River in Turner's Falls, Mass., bars Atlantic salmon and other spawning fish from the river's northern reaches.

1800
Middlebury College founded. Described at the time by Daniel C. Sanders, president of the University of Vermont, as "an institution founded in falsehood and iniquity."

1805
Montpelier chosen as state capital after citizens agree to donate land for a State House and to contribute money for much of its construction. Joseph Smith, prophet and founder of the Church of Latter Day Saints, is born on a farm straddling the Sharon-Royalton line.

1808
First State House completed at a cost of about $10,000.

1814
Thomas MacDonough, wintering over in Vergennes, oversees construction of his flagship "Saratoga" and an entire flotilla, in a record 40 days, before defeating the British in the pivotal Battle of Plattsburgh in the War of 1812. Ira Allen dies, penniless, in Philadelphia and is buried in an unmarked grave.

1814–19
Collegiate instruction for women started at Middlebury by Emma Willard, pioneer educator.

1816
The year without a summer: snow in June, frost in July and August.

1817
Silas Hawes welds together two second-hand saw blades to create the world's first metal carpenters' square. His company, Eagle Square Manufacturing Co. of Shaftsbury, is now the state's oldest organized industry.

1820s
Vermonters begin migrating west to better land.

October 5, 1830
Chester A. Arthur, twenty-first president of the United States, is born in East Fairfield.

1832
Vermont Temperance Society has more than 200 chapters; in the early 1800s, the state had had as many as 200 distilleries.

1834
Thomas Davenport, of Brandon, invents the first electric motor using threads from his wife's wedding dress.

1839
Judge Daniel P. Thompson, of Montpelier, publishes *The Green Mountain Boys: A Historical Tale of the Early Settlement of Vermont.*

1848
Vermont's first railroad begins rolling (between White River Junction and Bethel).

1855
Gold rush in Plymouth.

January 1857
Montpelier residents pack the second State House with snow in an attempt to halt a fire; the blaze destroys the building anyway.

Fig. 5 State House, 1857. Albumen print. Courtesy, Vermont Historical Society, Montpelier. The gutted building after the fire of 1857. The building had been designed by noted architect Ammi Burnham Young (1798–1874), who later became supervising architect in the U.S. Treasury Department.

October 1859
Vermont's new State House (the third and present one) opens.

1860
Lincoln carries every county in Vermont by a wide margin despite the fact that Stephen A. Douglas, his opponent, is a native of Vermont.

1861
Special session of the legislature on April 23 approves sending Vermont troops and $1 million to aid the Union cause in the Civil War.

July 3, 1863
Vermont soldiers help repel Pickett's Charge at Gettysburg, ending Confederate drive into the North.

October 1864
Vermonters distinguish themselves at the Battle of Cedar Creek, Virginia. In Vermont, Confederates raid St. Albans banks after infiltrating the town from Canada.

Fig. 6 Case of Civil War relics from Battle of Gettysburg. Courtesy, Historical Society of Windham County.

1870
Lumber industry booms; 650 lumber mills in the state. Vermont produces more than 3 million pounds of wool, 9 million pounds of maple sugar, 17 million pounds of butter.

1878
Seventeen deer brought from New York state to Bennington and Rutland counties to bolster diminishing herd.

1881
Last known Vermont catamount shot, Barnard.

1883
Copper miners rebel in Vershire and Fairlee.

December 21, 1887
Human hibernation, one of Vermont's great tall tales, reported in the *Montpelier Argus and Patriot*.

March 1888
Blizzard of '88 leaves snow drifts 20 to 30 feet high.

1890
Vermont's population is 332,422. Seventy-five percent of its land is cleared. Deer have nearly vanished from the state.

1864
Vermonter George Perkins Marsh publishes *Man and Nature*, one of the first American calls for environmental conservation.

1865
Deer hunting banned.

May 1870
State Constitutional Convention refuses to extend voting rights to women; the vote is 231–1. Vermont women, who have the right to vote at school meetings, must wait for an amendment to the U.S. Constitution in 1920.

Fig. 8 Barren Hillside, Woodstock, Vermont. c. 1870. Courtesy, Billings Mansion Archives, Woodstock.

1897
Deer hunting again permitted; 103 bucks taken.

October 12, 1899
Thousands attend Dewey Day in Montpelier to honor a native son, Admiral George Dewey, the hero of the Battle of Manila Bay.

Fig. 9 State House decorated for Dewey Day, October 12, 1899. Courtesy, Vermont Historical Society, Montpelier.

1910
First airplane flight in Vermont, St. Johnsbury.

1910
To preserve Camel's Hump as a public park Joseph Battell gives it and the surrounding 1200 acres to the state.

Fig. 10 Rowland E. Robinson. Camel's Hump. c. 1875. Oil on board. Courtesy, Rokeby (Ancestral Estate of Rowland Evans Robinson), Ferrisburgh.

1910–1929
The Long Trail is built through the organizing efforts of James P. Taylor, who founds the Green Mountain Club toward that end.

1916
Barre elects Socialist Robert Gordon as mayor.

1920
Vermont has 435,480 cattle (but only 290,122 cows) and 352,428 people. Edna Beard of Orange becomes first woman elected to the Vermont House; in 1922 she is the first woman elected to the Vermont Senate.

1920–1925
Karl Martin manufactures the automobile "Wasp" in Bennington.

Fig. 11 Karl Martin and the 1924 automobile "Wasp." Courtesy, The Bennington Museum.

1922
Vermont's first radio station (WCAX) opens in Burlington. It has its roots in the "Radio Club" at UVM.

August 3, 1923
Calvin Coolidge sworn in as president, Plymouth Notch.

November 2–5, 1927
Flood takes 84 lives, including that of Vermont's lieutenant governor, S. Hollister Jackson; leaves 9,000 homeless and wreaks $100 million in damage.

Fig. 12 Flood, Scenes at St. Johnsbury, Vt. Nov. 4, 1927. Courtesy, Special Collections, University of Vermont.

December 30, 1933
Vermont's official lowest temperature, -50°, in Bloomfield.

May 8, 1933
National Guard quells violent granite workers' strike in Barre.

Winter 1933–4
The first ski tow in the United States begins operation at Suicide Six ski area, Woodstock.

January 7, 1953
Consuelo Northrup Bailey elected first woman speaker of the Vermont House. In 1954 she is elected the nation's first woman lieutenant governor.

1954
New regulations requiring dairy farms to install bulk tanks drive many marginal hill farms out of farming. WCAX *TV*, Vermont's first television station, begins broadcasting.

1957
Construction begins on Interstate 91 (in Brattleboro). International Business Machines opens Essex Junction plant.

1936
FDR re-elected; Republican candidate Alf Landon carries only Vermont and Maine.

September 21, 1938
Hurricane of '38 smashes into New England. Five die in Vermont; damage estimated at $12 million.

September 1941
Vermont declares war on Germany, prior to U.S. declaration of war.

1946
First issue of *Vermont Life.*

1947
The Shelburne Museum is founded by Mr. and Mrs. J. Watson Webb "to show the craftsmanship and ingenuity of our forefathers."

1958
William H. Meyer becomes first Democrat in 100 years to be elected to Vermont's seat in Congress.

1961
Morgan horse becomes the official state animal.

ETHAN ALLEN.

No. 9. ¾ Full-bodied, 31 inches long $20 00

Copyrighted 1893.

Fig. 16 Ethan Allen. Weathervane. J. W. Fiske Company, Boston, Massachusetts. 1893. Morgan horse foaled in 1849 and considered the fasting trotting stallion in America. Courtesy, Shelburne Museum.

1965

Reapportionment ends the one town—one vote rule. Political power within Vermont begins to shift from rural to urban areas.

1965–1990

The Great In-migration. After a century (1850–1950) during which the state's population grew by only 20 percent, Vermont's population grows by 27 percent between 1970–1989.

1967

Deer herd reaches 200,000.

October 16, 1967

Vermont Educational Television begins broadcasting.

1968

Billboard ban enacted. Vermont's last town poor farm closes, Sheldon.

1970

Act 250 becomes law; April 18th is first Green-Up Day.

1972

Bottle deposit law passed.

September 30, 1972

A band plays as Amtrak's first Vermont train, the Montrealer, rolls into Montpelier.

1975

A small group of Abenaki Indians demands official state recognition of their tribal status. They do not get it, but their claims spur a re-evaluation of Vermont's understanding of its aboriginal past.

Fig. 17 Abenaki License Plate. Courtesy, Abenaki Cultural Center, Swanton.

August 13, 1977

Vermont Public Radio begins broadcasting.

October 29, 1982

Last section of interstate highway in Vermont—Interstate 93 from the New Hampshire border to St. Johnsbury—opens to traffic.

1984

Madeleine Kunin is first woman elected governor of Vermont.

Fig. 18 Governor Kunin unveils Vermont's Bicentennial Stamp, designed by Sabra Field. 1991. Courtesy, The Associated Press.

1986

First Atlantic salmon since 1700s seen in White River, courtesy of a multi-million-dollar restoration program.

November 6, 1990

Bernard Sanders, formerly mayor of Burlington, is elected to the United States Congress as an independent.

Fig. 19 Re-opening of Cornish-Windsor Covered Bridge. December 3, 1989. Courtesy, The Associated Press.

1991

Vermont's population is about 560,000 people, 300,000 dairy cows. Seventy-five percent of its land is wooded. Deer herd at about 80,000. Vermont has approximately one-tenth the number of farms it had in 1945, but it produces nearly twice as much milk, nearly 27 million gallons annually. Almost 100 covered bridges survive.

Selected Bibliography

While a comprehensive history of Vermont is lacking, a wealth of material has been published on the state. This bibliography is primarily intended to provide a brief introduction to secondary source material. Three periodicals essential to anyone interested in studying the state's history are *The Vermonter*, St. Albans, 1895–1939; *Vermont History*, Montpelier, 1930–1991; and *Vermont Life*, Montpelier, 1946–   . Articles in these periodicals which were of particular importance to this project are cited below.

Primary source material on Vermont is scattered across the state. Important collections include Special Collections, Bailey/Howe Library, University of Vermont; Vermont Historical Society, Montpelier; and the Sheldon Museum, Middlebury.

Andres, Glenn M. "Middlebury's Marble Fireplaces." *Vermont History* 55, no. 4 (Fall 1987): 197–211.

Baker, Ronald L. *Folklore in the Writings of Rowland E. Robinson.* Bowling Green, Ohio: Popular Press, 1973.

Bardwell, Kathryn. "The Case for an Aboriginal Origin of Northeastern Indian Woodsplint Basketry." *Man in the Northeast* 31 (Spring 1986): 49–67.

Bassett, T. D. Seymour, ed. *Outsiders Inside Vermont.* Canaan, N.H.: Phoenix Publishing, 1967.

——. *Vermont: A Bibliography of Its History.* Boston: G. K. Hall & Co., 1981.

Beattie, Betsy. "Community-Building in Uncertain Time: The French Canadians of Burlington and Colchester, 1850–1860." *Vermont History* 57, no. 2 (Spring 1989): 84–103.

——. "The Queen City Celebrates Winter: The Burlington Coasting Club and the Burlington Carnival of Winter Sports, 1886–1887." *Vermont History* 52, no. 1 (Winter 1984): 5–16.

Beck, Jane C., ed. *Always in Season: Folk Art and Traditional Culture in Vermont.* Montpelier, Vt.: Vermont Council on the Arts, 1982.

Biddle, Arthur W., and Paul A. Eschholz, eds. *The Literature of Vermont.* Hanover, N.H.: University Press of New England, 1973.

Blow, David J. "The Establishment and Erosion of French-Canadian Culture in Winooski, Vermont, 1867–1900." *Vermont History* 43, no. 1 (Winter 1975): 59–74.

Brasser, Ted J. *A Basketful of Indian Culture Change.* No. 22, Mercury Series. Ottawa: National Museums of Canada, 1975.

Bruhn, Paul, ed. *Historic Preservation in Vermont.* Montpelier, Vt.: The Preservation Trust of Vermont, 1982.

Bryan, Frank. *Yankee Politics in Rural Vermont.* Hanover, N.H.: University Press of New England, 1974.

Calloway, Colin G. *The Western Abenakis of Vermont, 1600–1800.* Norman, Okla., and London: University of Oklahoma Press, 1990.

Clifford, Deborah P. "The Drive for Women's Municipal Suffrage in Vermont, 1883–1917." *Vermont History* 47, no. 3 (Summer 1979): 173–190.

Congdon, Herbert Wheaton. *Old Vermont Houses.* 1940. Reprint. Dublin, N.H.: William L. Bauhan, 1973.

Crane, Charles Edward. *Let Me Show You Vermont.* New York: A. A. Knopf, 1937.

——. *Winter in Vermont.* New York: A. A. Knopf, 1941.

Duffy, John. *Vermont: An Illustrated History.* Northridge, Calif.: Windsor Publications, 1985.

Fisher, Dorothy Canfield. *Vermont Tradition: The Biography of an Outlook on Life.* Boston: Little, Brown, 1953.

Fowle, Richard J. "James Wilson's Globes, An Anniversary Report and Appeal." *Vermont History* 28, no. 4 (October 1960): 245–249.

Graffagnino, J. Kevin. "The Vermont 'Story': Continuity and Change in Vermont Historiography." *Vermont History* 46, no. 2 (Spring 1976): 77–99.

———. *The Shaping of Vermont: From the Wilderness to the Centennial, 1749–1877.* Bennington, Vt.: The Bennington Museum, 1983.

———. *Vermont in the Victorian Age: Continuity and Change in the Green Mountain State, 1850–1900.* Rutland, Vt.: Vermont Heritage Press and Shelburne Museum, 1985.

Hadsel, Christine, ed. *Vermont Museums, Galleries & Historic Buildings.* Montpelier, Vt.: Vermont Museum and Gallery Alliance in cooperation with the Preservation Trust of Vermont, 1988.

Hall, Hiland. *The History of Vermont, from Its Discovery to Its Admission into the Union in 1791.* Albany, N.Y.: Munsell, 1868.

Hastings, Scott, Jr. and Geraldine Ames. *The Vermont Farm Year.* Woodstock, Vt.: Billings Farm & Museum, 1983.

Haviland, William A. and Marjory W. Power. *The Original Vermonters: Native Inhabitants Past and Present.* Hanover, N.H.: The University Press of New England, 1981.

Hayford, James, ed. *Old Stone House Museum Catalogue.* Browington, Vt.: Orleans County Historical Society, 1986.

Hemenway, Abby Marie, ed. *Vermont Historical Gazetteer.* 5 vols. Burlington, Vt.: A. M. Hemenway, 1868–1891.

Hill, Ralph Nading. *Contrary Country: A Chronicle of Vermont.* New York: Rinehart, 1950.

———, Murray Hoyt, and Walter R. Hard, Jr.. *Vermont: A Special World.* Montpelier, Vt.: *Vermont Life* Magazine, 1968.

Hosley, William N., Jr. "Vermont Furniture, 1790–1830." In *New England Furniture, Old-Time New England* 72, no. 259. Boston: Society for the Preservation of New England Antiquities, 1987.

Hubbell, Seth. *A Narrative of the Sufferings of Seth Hubbell & Family.* Bennington, Vt.: Vermont Heritage Press, 1986.

Jacobs, Elbridge. "Iron in Vermont—A Glance at its Story." *Vermont Quarterly* 21 (April 1953): 128–131.

Jennison, Keith W. *Vermont is Where you Find It.* New York: Harcourt, Brace and Company, 1941.

———. *"Yup . . . Nope" & Other Vermont Dialogues.* Photographs by Neil Rappaport. Woodstock, Vt.: Countryman Press, 1976.

Jennison, Peter S. *Roadside History of Vermont.* Missoula, Mon.: Mountain Press, 1989.

Kunin, Madeleine and Marilyn Stout. *The Big Green Book: A Four Season Guide to Vermont.* Barre, Mass.: Barre Publishing, 1976.

Lipke, William C. and Philip N. Grime, eds. *Vermont Landscape Images, 1776–1976.* Burlington, Vt.: Robert Hull Fleming Museum, University of Vermont, 1976.

Ludlum, David. *Social Ferment in Vermont: 1791–1850.* Montpelier, Vt.: The Vermont Historical Society, 1948.

McWilliams, John. "The Faces of Ethan Allen: 1760–1860." *The New England Quarterly* 49 (1976): 257–282.

Mason, Benjamin L. "A 'Simple' Vision" in *An American Sampler: Folk Art from the Shelburne Museum.* Washington, D.C.: National Gallery of Art, 1987: 8–22.

Meeks, Harold. *The Geographic Regions of Vermont: A Study in Maps.* Hanover, N.H.: Dartmouth College, 1975.

———. "Stagnant, Smelly, and Successful: Vermont's Mineral Springs." *Vermont History* 47, no. 1 (Winter 1979): 5–20.

———. *Time and Change in Vermont: A Human Geography.* Chester, Conn.: Globe Pequot Press, 1986.

Miller, Sheldon. *Recollections of Milldale Farm, West Fairlee, Vermont.* Edited by David Donath. Burlington, Vt.: University of Vermont, 1976.

Morrissey, Charles. *Vermont: A Bicentennial History.* New York: W. W. Norton, 1981.

Muller, Nancy. *Paintings and Drawings in the Shelburne Museum.* Shelburne, Vt.: The Shelburne Museum, 1976.

Nutting, Wallace. *Vermont Beautiful.* 1922. Reprint. ed., Garden City, N.Y.: Garden City Publishing Co., 1936.

Orton, Vrest. *And So Goes Vermont: A Picture Book of Vermont As It Is.* Weston, Vt.: The Countryman Press, 1937.

———. *The Vermont Country Store: Story of a Vermont Institution.* Rutland, Vt.: Academy Books, 1970.

Pelletier, Gaby. *Abenaki Basketry.* No. 85. Mercury Series. Ottawa: National Museums of Canada, 1977.

Pendergast, James F. "Native Encounters with Europeans in the Sixteenth Century in the Region Now Known as Vermont." *Vermont History* 58, no. 2 (Spring 1990): 99–124.

Rebek, Andrea. "The Selling of Vermont: From Agriculture to Tourism." *Vermont History* 34, no. 1 (Winter 1976): 14–27.

Robinson, Rowland. *Vermont: A Study of Independence.* 1892. Reprint. Rutland, Vt.: Charles E. Tuttle Co., 1975.

Roomet, Louise. "Vermont as a Resort Area in the Nineteenth Century." *Vermont History* 34, no. 1 (Winter 1976): 1–13.

Samuelson, Myron. *The Story of the Jewish Community of Burlington, Vermont.* Burlington, Vt.: George Little Press, 1976.

Sessions, Gene. "'Years of Struggle': The Irish in the Village of Northfield, 1845–1900." *Vermont History* 55, no. 2 (Spring 1987): 69–96.

Sherman, Michael, ed. *A More Perfect Union: Vermont Becomes a State, 1777–1816.* Montpelier, Vt.: Vermont Historical Society, 1991.

Slayton, Tom. *Finding Vermont.* Montpelier, Vt.: *Vermont Life* Magazine, 1986.

Stameshkin, David. *The Town's College, 1800–1915.* Middlebury, Vt.: Middlebury College, 1985.

Stilwell, Lewis D. *Migration from Vermont.* 1948. Reprint. Montpelier and Rutland, Vt.: Vermont Historical Society and Academy Books, 1983.

Thompson, Judge D. P. *The Green Mountain Boys: A historical tale of the early settlement of Vermont.* Montpelier, Vt.: E. P. Walton and Sons, 1839.

Thompson, Zadock. *History of Vermont: Natural, Civil and Statistical.* Burlington, Vt.: Chauncey Goodrich, 1842.

Van de Water, Frederick. *The Reluctant Republic: Vermont, 1774–1791.* 1941. Reprint. Taftsville, Vt.: The Countryman Press, 1974.

Vermont: A Guide to the Green Mountain State. American Guide Series, Federal Writers Project. Boston: Houghton Mifflin, 1937.

West, Robert E., ed. *Rutland in Retrospect.* Rutland, Vt.: Rutland Historical Society and Academy Books, 1978.

Whitehead, Ruth Holmes. *Elitekey: Micmac Material Culture from 1600 A.D. to the Present.* Halifax: Nova Scotia Museum, 1980.

Wilgus, William. *The Role of Transportation in the Development of Vermont.* Montpelier, Vt.: Vermont Historical Society, 1945.

Williams, Norman, et al. *Vermont Townscape.* New Brunswick, N.J.: Rutgers University Press, 1987.

Wilson, Harold F. *The Hill Country of Northern New England: Its Social and Economic History, 1790–1930.* 1936. Reprint. New York: AMS Press, 1967.

Wright, Catherine and Nancy Means Wright. *Vermonters At Their Craft.* Shelburne, Vt.: The New England Press, 1987.

Photo Credits

Erik Borg, Middlebury, Vermont: figs. 1.4, 1.6, 1.9, 2.4, 2.5, 3.4, 3.5, 3.8; cats. 1, 2, 6, 7, 9, 12, 14, 15, 16, 18, 19, 19.1, 22–25, 28, 30, 32, 33, 36, 37, 40, 42, 43, 43.1, 44–47, 49, 53.1, 55, 56, 57, 58a–f, 58.1, 60, 61, 61.2, 62, 63, 67–78

Ken Burris, Shelburne, Vermont: time line fig. 17

Didier Delmas: cat. 66

Helga Studio, New York, New York: cat. 27

Sherman Howe Associates, Woodstock, Vermont: cats. 13, 17, time line fig. 6

John Hunisak, Middlebury, Vermont: cat. 33.1

Lizzari Photographic, Montpelier, Vermont: fig. 2.7

Tad Merrick, Middlebury, Vermont: cat. 16.1

National Graphic Center, Falls Church, Virginia: fig. 1.1

J. F. Smith, Shelburne, Vermont: time line fig. 10

Williamstown Regional Art Conservation Laboratory, Williamstown, Massachusetts: cats. 21, 54

BOOK DESIGN BY CHRISTOPHER KUNTZE

TYPESET, PRINTED, AND BOUND BY THE STINEHOUR PRESS

IN THE NORTHEAST KINGDOM, LUNENBURG, VERMONT